URBAN INTERSTICES: THE
AND THE POLITICS OF THE

'Left over' or 'in-between' spaces in cities are receiving renewed attention as spaces of possibility, for everything from informal economies and political action to artistic and architectural interventions in the service of public engagement or hipster 'buzz'. This terrific book on urban interstices makes an important contribution to these discussions. The chapters in the book engage with urban interstices not as 'left over' places that simply exist, but as space-times that are constantly in production with complex relationships to events, subjects, laws, technologies, powers, projects and plans. Through engagements with a fascinating variety of places and practices, the authors show us how the possibilities of interstices can be identified and interrogated. Highly recommended.

Kurt Iveson, University of Sydney, Australia

Urban Interstices: The Aesthetics and the Politics of the In-between

Edited by

ANDREA MUBI BRIGHENTI
University of Trento, Italy

LONDON AND NEW YORK

First published 2013 by Ashgate Publishing

2 Park Square, Milton Park, Abingdon, Oxon OX14 4RN
711 Third Avenue, New York, NY 10017, USA

Routledge is an imprint of the Taylor & Francis Group, an informa business

First issued in paper back 2016

British Library Cataloguing in Publication Data
A catalogue record for this book is available from the British Library

The Library of Congress has cataloged the printed edition as follows:
Mubi Brighenti, Andrea.
  Urban interstices: the aesthetics and the politics of the in-between / by Andrea Mubi Brighenti.
    pages cm
  Includes bibliographical references and index.
  ISBN 978-1-4724-1001-6 (hardback)
1. Public spaces—Case studies. 2. City planning—Case studies.
3. Urbanization—Case studies. 4. Sociology, Urban—Case studies. I. Title.
  HT153.M82 2013
  307.1'216—dc23

                                                                    2013011974

ISBN 978-1-4724-1001-6 (hbk)
ISBN 978-1-138-25739-9 (pbk)

Contents

List of Figures

Notes on Contributors

Peter Adey is Professor of Human Geography at Royal Holloway University of London. His work focuses upon the relationship between space, mobility and security with a particular interest in the cultures of air and the governance of emergency. Peter is the author of several books and articles, including *Mobility* (2009); *Aerial Life: spaces, mobilities, affects* (2010) and the forthcoming *Air* (2014).

Nicholas Blomley is Professor at the Department of Geography, Simon Fraser University, Vancouver. He is the author of *Law, Space and the Geographies of Power* and *Unsettling the City: Urban Land and the Politics of Property* (2004).

Iain Borden is Professor of Architecture and Urban Culture at the Bartlett School of Architecture, UCL, where he is also Vice-Dean for Communications for the Faculty of the Built Environment. His wide-ranging research includes explorations of architecture in relation to critical theory, philosophy, film, gender, boundaries, photography, bodies and spatial experiences. Authored and co-edited books include *Drive: Journeys through Film, Cities and Landscapes* (2012), *Bartlett Designs: Speculating With Architecture* (2009), *Skateboarding Space and the City: Architecture and the Body* (2001), *The Unknown City: Contesting Architecture and Social Space* (2001) and *InterSections: Architectural Histories and Critical Theories* (2000).

Andrea Mubi Brighenti teaches Social Theory and Space & Culture at the Department of Sociology, University of Trento, Italy. He researches both empirically and theoretically into space, power and society, with specific concern for the processes of control and resistance. He is the author of *Visibility in Social Theory and Social Research* (2010), *Territori Migranti* [*Migrant Territories. Space and Control of Global Mobility*] (2009) editor of *The Wall and the City* (2009) and co-editor (with Ricardo Campos and Luciano Spinelli) of *Uma Cidade de Imagens* [*Visual City*] (2012). Besides contributions to edited volumes, he has published articles in several international peer-reviewed journals, including *Urban Studies, Theory, Culture & Society, European Journal of Social Theory, Space and Culture, Surveillance and Society, The Journal of Classical Sociology, Distinktion – Scandinavian Journal of Social Theory, The International Journal of Law in Context, Critical Sociology, Convergence – The International Journal of Research into New Media Technologies, Current Sociology, Sortuz, The Canadian Journal of Law and Society/Revue Canadienne de Droit et Société, Thesis Eleven et Law* *and Critique*; in Italian, *Tecnoscienza, Scienza & Politica, Etnografia e Ricerca Qualitativa, Quaderni di Sociologia, Polis, Rassegna Italiana di Sociologia et Sociologia del diritto.* He is the editor of the web journal *lo Squaderno* (www. losquaderno.net),

Kim Dovey is Professor of Architecture and Urban Design in the Faculty of Architecture, Building and Planning. His research on social issues in architecture and urban design has focused on experiences of place and practices of power. These include investigations of housing, shopping malls, corporate towers, urban waterfronts and the politics of public space. Books include *Framing Places: Mediating Power in Built Form* (1999, 2008); *Fluid City: Transforming Melbourne's Urban Waterfront* (2005), and *Becoming Places* (2009). Current research projects include those on urban place identity, creative cities, learning environments and the morphology of squatter settlements. He has worked with government, industry and community groups and has written and broadcast widely in the mass media.

Mattias Kärrholm is Professor of Architectural Theory at the Department of Architecture and Built Environment, Lund University. His research interests include territoriality, actor-network theory, retail architecture, public space, urban form and sustainable urban development. He is the author of the book *Arkitekturens Territorialitet* (*The Territoriality of Architecture*) and has published articles in international peer-reviewed journals such as *Urban Studies, Nordic Journal of Architectural Research, Social & Cultural Geography* and *Space & Culture.*

Ross King is a Professorial Fellow in the Faculty of Architecture Building and Planning at the University of Melbourne, Australia. In recent times his research has focused on the urban conditions and society of East and South-East Asian cities. His most recent book has been *Reading Bangkok* (2011). Present projects relate to Seoul in South Korea and again to Bangkok and Thailand.

Luc Lévesque is an architect and artist, Professor in History and Theory of Architectural and Design Practices at Université Laval (Quebec City); his recent body of research traces the potentialities of an interstitial approach to urban landscape and urbanism. In 2000, he co-founded the collective SYN-, with whom he has produced different works of urban exploration and micro-interventions. As a member of the editorial committee of *Inter, art actuel* (www.inter-lelieu.org), he has edited many issues dealing with architecture, landscape and urban practices. In architecture, he has collaborated with various firms in North America and Europe.

Don Mitchell is an academic geographer at the Maxwell School of Syracuse University. He is a graduate of the San Diego State University (1987), Pennsylvania State University (1989) and received his PhD from Rutgers University in 1992. He is the authors of *The Right to the City: Social Justice and the Fight for Public*

Space (2003), *The Lie of the Land: Migrant Workers and the California Landscape* (1996) and *Cultural Geography: A Critical Introduction* (2000).

Andreas Philippopoulos-Mihalopoulos is Professor of Law & Theory at the University of Westminster, London, and the Director of the Westminster International Law & Theory Centre. His research interests include critical legal theory, autopoiesis, geography, human rights, psychoanalysis, art, phenomenology, linguistics, and their critical instances of confluence. He has edited three anthologies: *Law and the City* (2007), *Law and Ecology* (2007) and *Niklas Luhmann: Radical Theoretical Encounters* (2013), and has published two monographs *Absent Environments* (2007) and *Law, Justice, Society* (2009). He is currently completing a monograph on *Spatial Justice* (Routledge) and an edited collection on *Urban Creative Milieus* (Springer).

Stéphane Tonnelat is a research faculty at the CNRS (Centre National de la Recherche Scientifique), based at the CRH-LAVUE research center, located at the Paris Val-de-Seine School of Architecture. His research focuses mostly on urban public spaces such as spaces of transportation (subway, ferry), parks and gardens and urban wastelands. He is currently leading a research project on the public spaces along the 7 train in New York. This elevated line serves as the backbone of numerous ethnic immigrant communities. The project aims at exploring the effect of this diversity on the subway and conversely how the experience of the subway affects interpersonal relations based on ethnicity, gender, age and so on. More generally, Stephane's interests include urban planning and design, theory of public space, parks and gardens, pluralism and multiculturalism. He is a member of the editorial committee of the journals *Chimères* and *Metropolitiques.eu*.

Introduction

Andrea Mubi Brighenti

This book collects ten contributions from urban scholars pivoted around the notion of 'interstice', or – as we might tentatively call it – in-between space. To our mind, the current interest in this notion is grounded in some general considerations emerging in the field of urban studies at the beginning of an announced *urban century*. For some time now, social scientists, including geographers, economists, sociologists and anthropologists, have been questioning classical models of urban growth, such as for instance the centre/periphery model. It has been argued that both phenomena of urban expansion – such as urban sprawl and the formation of polycentric urban regions – and phenomena related to new forms of land use – including processes as diverse as enclavism, gated communities, new media urbanism, 'splintering' urbanism, capsularized dwelling, slumification, panic-city, squatter evictions and the militarization of urban space – challenge most classic models employed to understand the city.

In particular, a cleavage becomes increasingly evident: it is the current cleavage between two processes that could be termed, respectively, the *urbanization of territory* and the *territorialization of the city*. While urbanized territory corresponds to a territory that is infrastructurally as well as structurally equipped with a wide array of urban devices for communication and control – ranging from street signs to information technologies and the infusion of software into urban spaces and objects – the territorial city seems to evoke a wider, and arguably more complex, aspiration towards a *new urbanity* or a *new civility*.

On the one hand, the process of *urbanization of territory* has been first identified by Michel Foucault (2004/1978) in his studies on the emergence of a modern government of the population – in particular where he examined the 'sciences of police' that appeared in sixteenth- and seventeenth-century Europe, later to be developed into more specialized 'apparatuses of security' and control. On the other hand, the notion of *urbanity* as tied to a specifically *urban* culture has been described in classic works by Jane Jacobs, Erving Goffman and Richard Sennett as a capacity to positively interact with strangers in public. Following the appreciation of 'distance' as a key feature of democratic public space expressed by Hannah Arendt, Sennett (1977: 264) characterized urban civility as an ability that consists of 'treating others as though they were strangers and forging a social bond upon that social distance'. Compared to that classic form of civility – and in measure proportional to the reach of urbanized territoriality – today's new urbanity faces a number of major challenges: the increasing dispersal of public space (see e.g. Amin 2008), and what Sloterdijk (2005: 543) has called the 'asynodic constitution' of contemporary society. At present, the contours of such new urbanity are far from clarified or settled; what is certain is that classic urbanity has been fundamentally reshaped by the spatial, technical and social process of the extensive territorialization of the city.

Into the interstice

In this context, we believe the notion of urban interstice might prove useful. To begin with, to speak of an in-between or interstitial space clearly means to go beyond the centre/periphery dichotomy, the core/margin dichotomy or even the city/suburb pseudo-dichotomy. As King and Dovey (this volume, Chapter 10) argue, 'the metropolis [itself] is always interstitial between the global and the indigenous'. Interstices exist – and come to exist – everywhere in the city and its territory. If so, how do we recognize them? The fact that a certain space is indicated or enacted as a space 'in-between' others presupposes that it is regarded as somehow *minoritarian* vis à vis other spaces that surround or encircle it. The interstice is a 'small space': far from being a merely extensive notion, such smallness inherently signifies a power issue. In other words, 'in-between-ness' refers to the fact of being surrounded by other spaces that are either more institutionalized, and therefore economically and legally powerful, or endowed with a stronger identity, and therefore more recognizable or typical.

Traditionally, interstices have been associated with wastelands and leftover spaces, generated as by-products of urban planning, i.e. as unplanned margins that result *a fortiori*, after a planned action has unfolded on an urban territory (Edensor 2005). Interstices are thus imagined essentially as vacant lots, *terrains vagues* or decaying ruins. While this is certainly the case, we also suggest that such an image does not exhaust the whole extent of the notion of interstitiality. Indeed, an additional complication is due to the fact that in the contemporary city it becomes increasingly difficult to establish a clear and univocal *Gestalt*: what is to count as the foreground shape of the city, and what else as its shapeless – hence, interstitial – background? The complexities generated by the extensive urbanization of territory and the proliferation of criss-crossing plans on the territory carried on by different agencies and actors make it difficult to neatly separate foreground and background phenomena: our very observational point of view is called into question. An enriched observation of the processes of territorial production, stabilization and transformation is required – a veritable territoriology (Brighenti 2010a). As reminded by both Lévesque (this volume, Chapter 2) and King and Dovey (this volume, Chapter 10), rather than a mere gap in the urban fabric, the interstice is in fact an active component. From this perspective, interstitial territorialities can only be appreciated by taking into account the dynamics of power and resistance, of fluidity and boundedness, of mobilities and moorings, of smoothness and striatedness that occur in the contemporary city. It is in a classic passage from Deleuze and Guattari that we can locate the essential coordinates of such a puzzle:

> In contrast to the sea, the city is the striated space par excellence; the sea is a smooth space fundamentally open to striation, and the city is the force of striation that reimparts [*redonnerait*; literally 'would give back'] smooth space, puts it back into operation everywhere, on earth and in the other elements, outside but also inside itself. The smooth spaces arising from the city are not only those of worldwide organization, but also of a counterattack combining the smooth and the holey and turning back against the town: sprawling, temporary, shifting shantytowns of nomads and cave dwellers, scrap metal and fabric, patchwork, to which the striations of money, work, or housing are no longer even relevant. An explosive misery secreted by the city, and corresponding to Thorn's mathematical formula: 'retroactive smoothing.' Condensed force, the potential for counterattack? (Deleuze and Guattari 1987[1980]: 481)

Thus formulated, the issue is clearly a political one: city government represents a force of striation which is resisted and opposed by two fundamentally different forces of smoothness: capitalist large (planetary) organizations, on the one hand, and minority populations (the 'explosive misery') living in urban interstices, on the other. Yet, simultaneously, the issue also looms larger than the – albeit certainly real and dramatic – opposition between social actors with their respective 'material and ideal interests', to use a Weberian category. Rather, what Deleuze and Guattari also illustrate is the functioning and the dynamic production of *material spatial logics*. The city is a force of striation – i.e. of planning, *quadrillage*, urbanization of territory – that by its very functioning constantly reintroduces smoothness in the space thus created: indeterminacy, ambiguity of location, a number folds and underground paths in the urban territory.

While the city colonizes territory through acts of spatial repartition, it also creates within itself a space of distributions and trajectories. Such a process is anything but arcane. In fact, it can be easily observed today. Indeed, the trend towards larger-scale urban planning – for instance through iconic territorial and architectural intervention –inherently produces larger interstices. From an old modernist unsophisticated functionalist viewpoint, interstitiality equates to emptiness. However, emptiness also means possibility – at the very least, some fresh air to breathe that flows through the otherwise asphyxiating landscape of the corporate city. Thus, the interstice could also be observed as an involuntary side-effect of the spatial production of atmospheres (Sloterdijk 2005): whenever a plurality of pressurized, air-conditioned and immunized bubbles are added side by side, a foam is created. The co-isolation and co-fragility which characterize the structure of the foam essentially amounts to the emergence – albeit unwilling – of an under-determination: an urban interstice.

The interstice as urban morphology and urban event

Yet, in our view, the notion of interstice cannot be thoroughly reduced to its morphological characters only. Identifying two general points of view on interstices might help clarifying what is at stake. The first point of view is an essentially *structuralist* one: it regards the interstice as a leftover space, what remains after a single, central planning process, or between two heterogeneous and discontinuous plans. The second point of view is, by contrast, event-oriented or *evental*: from this second perspective, the interstice is to be regarded as the outcome of a composition of interactions and affections among a multiplicity of actors that coexist within a given spatial situation. The second perspective adds, to a realistic – and therefore necessary – consideration of power relations, a genealogical point of view that attends all the minute accidents that eventually constitute the specific atmosphere – understood as both ambience and pressure – of a given place.

Adding *movement* to our understanding of the interstice is what shifts us from the first to the second perspective. The type of urban exploration carried out by Walter Benjamin in the 1930s (Benjamin 1999), as well as the one practised by the Situationists in the 1950s (Situationist International 1958), enacted a type of movement capable of plumbing the uncertain, ill-defined, crepuscular and metamorphic states of urban territories. *Flânerie* and *dérive* are simultaneously aesthetic, cultural and political practices. The spirit of such observers on the move has been inherited by a number of contemporary interstitial explorers, such as for instance Stalker/osservatorio nomade and their urban trekkings across the city of Rome (Careri 2002). When compared to the seemingly stable territories of the urban built environment, *flânerie* and *derive* imply a degree of deterritorialization and the initiation to a more fluid spatiality created by encounters in loose space and their ensuing events.

Overall, our argument is that it is only by taking the evental point of view seriously that we can begin to recognize the simple fact that interstices *cannot be known in advance*: the interstice is not simply a physical place, but very much a phenomenon 'on the ground', a 'happening', a 'combination' or an 'encounter'. This is the reason why studying interstices as mere leftover urban spaces is not enough: interstices result from the actualization of a series of environmental affordances (an expressive potential, a reservoir that is inherent in certain zones) in the context of a phenomenologically relevant encounter (an interactional framework) that unfolds in a given *meaningful spatial materiality* (a specific work on the materials that make the city). Following Mattias Kärrholm (this volume, Chapter 7), interstices 'can be found or produced at any place' and time. They can be usefully conceptualized as a form of 'spatial production through territorial transformation'. Consequently, the task of observing and interpreting in-between spaces requires both historical and territorial reconstruction of such spaces, and an *in situ* exploration through which the researcher can make sense of the events and the encounters (certainly, not always 'good' encounters) that contribute to the creation of an interstice. It is from a similar perspective that in his case study on pier 84 in Manhattan, Tonnelat (this volume, Chapter 8) distinguishes the 'institutional career' of a place from its 'experiential career'; and it is from this perspective that I (this volume, Chapter 9) have carried out an extensive empirical investigation of an Alpine suburb as a peculiar contact zone in the urban fringe.

The in-between-ness of minoritarian spaces refers, as we have remarked above, to the fact that they are surrounded by other more institutionalized spaces. Most importantly, however, the way in which such 'being surrounded' takes place in practice makes interstices more or less liveable, more enclave-like or more threshold-like (on these two notions, see respectively Caldeira (2001) and Stavrides (2011)). As remarked by Lévesque (this volume, Chapter 2) the attempt to make sense of in-between-ness generates 'a polysemous discursive field oscillating between connection and disjunction': the interstice is sometimes a rapture and sometimes an opening up. At first, interstices are places for minority populations ranging from Roma people to hip hop crews, for urban losers and all those who are for many reasons forced to struggle for their right to the city (Mitchell 2003; Marcuse 2009). In this sense, just as it hosts interstitial spaces, the city also hosts interstitial subjects: it is the case of evicted squatters in North American downtowns (Blomley 2004; this volume, Chapter 1) and the inhabitants of tent cities (Mitchell, this volume, Chapter 3). Here interstitiality corresponds to a form of inhabiting that resists 'sanitization', expulsion and deportation. Mitchell cautions us against any easy-going romantic understanding of interstices, showing that, in fact, they can be places of domination as well. It is thus important to stress that the interstice is a descriptive notion rather than one necessarily laden with positive overtones. Tent cities as interstitial spaces of survival are functional to a neoliberal management of public visibilities and invisibilities: they represent a space where the social outcomes of a disastrous economic model can be conveniently hidden. In a different context, the new retail spaces studies by Kärrholm (2012) illustrate how interstices are appropriated and exploited by marketing and advertisement strategies.

The richness of interstitial encounters is not limited either to the brutal clench of power on specific places and subjects, or to the capitalist logic that tends to exploit all visual ecological niches, though. Issues of visibility and invisibility are always ambiguously played out in between the denial of recognition and the possibility of resistance. So, Kim Dovey (2010) has spoken of the invisibility of informal settlements in South-East Asian cities, which can be marginalizing but also protective (see also King and Dovey, this volume, Chapter 10), while Iain Borden (2001) has analysed urban skaters' performative critique of architecture as a fleeting and nightly activity. In-between spaces are invested with desires and imagined (not imaginary) needs, as a conceptualization of urban mobilities that is attentive to affects (Adey 2009) reveals. Driving in the city provides one such affective, as well as imaginative, experience (Borden, this volume, Chapter 6). Interstitiality as *porosity* — literally, 'possibility of ways' — may therefore suggest an approach to the city that stresses the many spatial modes in which a plurality of social differences associate, as well as the ways in which they are allowed to associate or prevented from associating. Rather than being unequivocally 'good' or 'bad', positive or problematic, the space in the middle – as Philippopoulos-Mihalopoulos (this volume, Chapter 4) reminds us – is a space of struggle. Philippopoulos-Mihalopoulos's radical theorization of spatial justice calls for a notion of justice as inherently spatial, moving beyond merely topographic versions of social justice. Because 'space embodies the violence of being lost, of being uncertain about one's direction ... there is no respite from the relentless and simultaneous spatial presence'. Precisely such a recognition could lead us towards a view of spatial justice as 'the movement of taking leave' in order to let the other exist. In this sense, Philippopoulos-Mihalopoulos insists on the affirmative power of the 'middle', the milieu that cannot be reduced to any sort of 'lack'. As Kärrholm writes, '*place making* always starts in the in-between, in the middle of thing, *in medias res*, or *in mitten drinnen* to use a Yiddish expression'. It is therefore not paradoxical after all to discover – in particular thanks to Adey's (this volume, Chapter 5) exploration – that *interstitial* is also the air that envelops us all. The atmosphere has long been confined to a condition of invisibility, but today, as Adey writes, it can no longer 'really be separated from the apparently more solid and persistent story of the city'.

The aesthetic and politics of urban interstices

With this collection of essays, we invite urban scholars to deploy, refine and test the notion of interstice, putting it to work and developing an ability to move back and forth between the aesthetic and the political dimensions of the territorial city. Specifically, we speak of *aesthetics* to address phenomenological, perceptual, embodied and lived space, and we speak of *politics* to attend the ecology of the socio-material connections imbued with power that form today's urban common world (Brighenti 2010b). Thus, we raise a number of questions and explore them at the theoretical, methodological and ethnographic level:

- How do we conceptualize, discover and describe urban interstices vis à vis the macro-phenomena of planning and economic development that shape the city? How is the interstice related to the partitioning and the zoning of the city, and to its current transformations? Where is the interstice localized? How is its legal status shaped and how does its political significance manifest? What is the relation between flows, networks, boundaries, territories and interstices?
- What is the place and function of these interstitial locales in an ordered and 'disciplined' urban environment? And what is, complementarily, their function in a disordered environment evoked by the notions of 'excess', 'danger' and 'threat'? How do these spaces contribute to the construction of the city, the perception and representation of its spaces?

- What happens in urban interstices? What type of phenomena, events and social interaction do these spaces attract? How are they interpreted, represented and managed by the authorities? Which rhythms, speeds and affects characterize interstitial territories? Which different social subjectivities do they breed? Which new aesthetic styles? Which new orientalist observers?
- How do walls, separations, distances, borders, but also legal, administrative, political and media discourses and boundaries concur in the definition of interstitial areas in the city? And what technical, economic, legal, political and governmental significance do these areas assume as a consequence?
- What kind of relation can we find between alternative and underground street performances/practices, on the hand, and the official/mainstream cultural practices and discourses (official art, advertising, political propaganda, military scenarios) on the other?

Interstices have sometimes been described as a failure of urban development, as lack of a 'healthy' public space or even as the prototype of 'anti-public space' (Chevrier 2011), deserts inhabited only by marginalized people and urban outcasts. From this perspective, interstices represent dangerous contact zones where panhandlers, squeegees, street drunkards, drug addicts and homeless people embody at best the otherwise elusive notion of 'public disorder' propounded by broken windows criminology, albeit an echo of early-twentieth-century Chicago School's notion of 'social disorganization' can be heard. However, Luc Lévesque (2008: 145) has observed that the current transformations of public space are inherently transforming public space as a whole into a veritable 'interstitial and fluctuating constellation'. Interestingly, such transformations are linked to the emergence of new architectures *for* social multiplicities as well as new architectures *of* social multiplicities. Urban network topologies (Graham and Marvin 2001) as well as the need for on-going work maintenance of technical infrastructures (Denis and Pontille 2011) reveal the importance of the interstitial in the contemporary urban process. The number of ways in which new associations and dissociations take place increasingly generate interstitial spaces. Thinking and researching through the notion of interstice might thus provide us with an opportunity to re-image contemporary social multiplicities beyond the classic categories of crowd, mass, nation, population, social group and social actor. As Lévesque (this volume, Chapter 2) argues, 'the nature and diversity of the conceptual field related to the interstitial condition rather seems to resist stable and precise visual characterizations'. Yet this should be seen as a promise for research, rather than a fault of the concept. Indeed, it is precisely in this sense that the aesthetic and material dimensions interweave with the political dimension: in a *politics of visibility*.

In conclusion, we think that the notion of interstice, and the related study of urban interstitialities, could shed light on the complex relationships between urbanized territory and the territorial city. It could help us advance in the understanding of a range of crucial phenomena that are accompanying the unstable and shifting relationship between urbanized territory and territorialized city, shaping the forthcoming configurations of urban togetherness – in other words, our common world.

References

Adey, P. 2009. *Mobility*. London: Routledge.

Amin, A. 2008. Collective culture and urban public space. *City*, 12(1), 5–24.

Benjamin, W. 1999. *The Arcades Project*. Cambridge, MA: Belknap Press of Harvard University Press.

Blomley, N. 2004. *Unsettling the City: Urban Land and the Politics of Property*. New York: Routledge.

Borden, I. 2001 *Skateboarding, Space and the City: Architecture and the Body*. New York: Berg.

Brighenti, A.M. 2010a. On territorology. Towards a general science of territory. *Theory, Culture & Society*, 27(1), 52–72.

Brighenti, A.M. 2010b. *Visibility in Social Theory and Social Research*. Basingstoke: Palgrave Macmillan.

Caldeira, T.P.R. 2001. *City of Walls. Crime, Segregation, and Citizenship in São Paulo*. Berkeley, CA: University of California Press.

Careri, F. 2002. *Walkscapes. El Andar Como Practica Estética/Walking as an Aesthetic Practice*. Barcelona: Gustavo Gili.

Chevrier, J-F. 2011. *Des Territoires*. Paris: L'Arachnéen.

Deleuze, G. and Guattari, F. 1987 (1980). *A Thousand Plateaus*. Minneapolis, MN: University of Minnesota Press.

Denis, J. and Pontille, D. 2011. *Nel Mondo della Segnaletica*. Trento: professional dreamers.

Dovey, K. 2010. *Becoming Places. Urbanism/Architecture/Identity/Power*. London: Routledge.

Edensor, T. 2005. The Ghosts of Industrial Ruins: Ordering and Disordering Memory in Excessive Space. *Environment and Planning D*, 23, 829–49.

Foucault, M. 2004/1978. *Sécurité, Territoire, Population: Cours au Collège de France, 1977–1978*. Paris: Gallimard-Seuil.

Graham, S. and Marvin, S. 2001. *Splintering Urbanism, Networked Infrastructures, Technological Mobilities and the Urban Condition*. New York: Routledge.

Kärrholm, M. 2012. *Retailising Space. Architecture, Retail and the Territorialisation of Public Space*. Farnham: Ashgate.

Lévesque, L. 2008. La place publique comme constellation interstitielle: parcours historique et expérimentations, in J. Jébrak and B. Julien (eds) *Les Temps de l'Espace Public: Construction, Transformation et Utilisation*. Québec: Editions Multimondes, pp. 145–69.

Marcuse, P. 2009. From critical urban theory to the right to the city. *City*, 13(2), 185–97.

Mitchell, D. 2003. *The Right to the City: Social Justice and the Fight for Public Space*. New York: Guilford.

Philippopoulos-Mihalopoulos, A. 2010. Spatial justice: law and the geography of withdrawal. *International Journal of Law in Context*, 6(3), 201–16.

Sennett, R. 1977. *The Fall of Public Man*. London: Faber and Faber.

Situationist International 1958. *Situationist International Bulletin*, 2.

Sloterdijk, P. 2005. *Écumes*. Paris: Hachette.

Stavrides, S. 2011. *Towards the City of Thresholds*. Trento: professional dreamers.

Tonnelat, S. 2008. Out of frame: The (in)visible life of urban interstices: a case study in Charenton-le-Pont, Paris, France. *Ethnography*, 9(3), 291–324.

Chapter 1

What Sort of a Legal Space is a City?[1]

Nicholas Blomley

interstice /nˈtːsts/ → noun (usu. interstices) an intervening space, especially a very small one: sunshine filtered through the interstices of the arching trees – ORIGIN late Middle English: from Latin interstitium, from intersistere 'stand between', from inter- 'between' + sistere 'to stand'. (*The Oxford Dictionary of English* (revised edn). Eds Catherine Soanes and Angus Stevenson. Oxford University Press, 2005)

Law, interstices and the city

In August 2006, I met an indigenous man called Dale in the business district of downtown Vancouver. Dale was 46, 'an Aboriginal from the [nearby] Burrard Indian Reserve', as he described himself, living in a rooming house in the inner city. I was glad to see him, as I was looking for interviewees for a research project on panhandling and rights. It had been hard to actually find a panhandler, despite media reports to the contrary. Dale was sitting up against the Anglican cathedral at the intersection of Burrard and Georgia with a sign reading: 'Spare any change, please. Thank you. God bless. I also work part-time.' We spoke for about 45 minutes. He had lived in Toronto, but had returned to the city following the suicide of his brother. HIV positive, he used his earnings to pay for fresh food and milk, and medicinal pot, and for transportation to his part time job as a co-host at a native dancing group.

Socio-legal scholars would insist that law is present not only in formal, bureaucratic moments, but also in everyday urban encounters like this. As such, how was law here? More generally, what sort of legal space was the city in which we talked? Any space, any encounter, should be thought of in terms of a 'standing between-ness', characterized by a rich interstitial form of legal pluralism, it is argued. For Sousa Santos,

> socio-legal life is constituted by different legal spaces operating simultaneously on different scales and from different interpretive standpoints. So much is this so that in phenomenological terms and as a result of interaction and intersection among legal spaces one cannot properly speak of law and legality but rather of interlaw and interlegality. (Santos 1987: 288)

---

1   Thanks to Micheal Vonn, Stacey Bishop and Mariana Valverde.

How was interlaw present in our encounter? It is hard to know where to begin. A distinction could be drawn between what socio-legal scholars term 'law in the books' and 'law in action'. While problematic, this at least alerts us to the existence of formal legal codes that may govern our encounter, as distinct from a set of more informal understandings of the law. For the former, municipal and provincial law governs an offence known as 'aggressive solicitation'. The City of Vancouver also governs the sidewalk through various by-laws (as municipal law is known in Canadian cities). Criminal law may also apply if, for example, someone assaulted Dale. Such law does not need to be invoked for it to be operative. But in deciding how to interact, we both no doubt governed ourselves with reference to more 'informal' understandings of rights, individuality and subjectivity (Blomley 2010). Elsewhere I have noted the existence of a particular legal logic of sidewalk circulation articulated by some observers in justifying the regulation of panhandling (Blomley 2011). Panhandlers themselves, when interviewed, often characterized their behaviour according to legal forms, such as employment. Panhandling, in other words, was a sort of job. Dale saw himself as providing a service – people recognized him and often chatted to him. He had helped to trip up a purse-snatcher on one occasion. As such, the divide between formal and informal law becomes more diffuse: it is in the interstice between the two that the action is.

But getting at this rich, layered interlegal interstiality is hard. For powerful spatial codes appear to order our understandings of law according to notions of the near and the far, the big and the small. That Dale had a bit of a hard time in situating his actions according to a language of rights, despite my prompting, speaks, perhaps, to a view of rights as a concept, above and beyond the local immediacies of 'employment', 'panhandling' and sidewalks. A scalar logic seems to be at play here, whereby rights are construed as 'national', and/or 'constitutional' and thus 'above' everyday, 'local' matters.[2]

Some scholars encourage us to resist such a view. Doreen Massey (1994) asks us to abandon a view of the 'global' (or, in my case, the 'national') as above and beyond, insisting instead that we rather think about particular relations of connection and presence as they are materialized in places. The 'national' and the 'global', then, do not happen somewhere else, but in specific places. It is the

---

2   Others have noted that the way in which we think about the state and law is informed by some powerful spatial metaphors. John Agnew (1994) has noted the perils of what he terms the 'territorial trap' as it applies to conceptions of the state (c.f. Engel 2009). Essentially this entails the presence of some unexamined assumptions about the territorial dimensions of the state, where territory itself is assumed to have a prepolitical objective quality. The effect is to allow us to assume that states are fixed units of sovereign space, to draw distinctions between the inside and the inside of such units (the domestic/ international polarity) and to characterize states as the 'containers' of society. This has a variety of troubling ethical consequences: for example, security is framed according to the security of the territorial state (as opposed to non-territorial concepts, such as ecological security).

particular ways in which the global is localized that produces the differences of place.

John Law (2004) similarly criticizes the way we are encouraged to look 'up' to imagine the whole. Having looked up, we can look down to understand how the part (the city) fits within the whole. Law rejects such a 'romantic' sensibility in place of a 'baroque' geography that 'looks downward', finding complexity and specificity rather than the emergence of some higher order. The 'global', consequently, is not up and outward, but always already present. Complexity, when magnified, leads to more complexity:

> The romantic escape here is appealing. It is tempting to say that 'really' there is a larger coherence of bureaucratic power-plays and social interests, but the baroque sensibility looks down rather than up, and suggests, instead: that the different and countermanding views may not add up to a whole, that the formalism carries a continuing set of differences; that there may be no need to pull it all together; and, indeed, that it is impossible to pull it together and that to try to do so is to miss the point. (Law 2004: 23)

Relational thinking eschews essentialism by insisting that all social entities are to be understood and explained according to their interactions, avoiding a view of internally stable concepts and entities (Murdoch 2006). 'Spaces', such as cities, are not territorial units, but formations of continuously changing composition. Seen in this way, 'cities and regions come with no promise of territorial or systemic integrity, since they are made through the spatiality of flow, juxtaposition, porosity and relational connectivity' (Amin 2002: 34). The attempt here is to move beyond topographic views of space, centred on discernable territories and 'centre-periphery' relations, with power imagined as centralized in discrete locations, moving across space to reach subjects, either far or near, to a topological conception whereby 'the distance between [objects] is less significant than the ways in which they are connected, the nature of their relatedness' (Allen 2011: 285).

Jurisdiction

That such baroque topologies seem a little far-fetched reflects, perhaps, the presence of a powerful legal geography through which we think about law's spaces – in particular, that of the city. One crucial legal device that shapes the way we think of the city as a legal space is jurisdiction. Jurisdiction asks: which law is authoritative? Who speaks the law here? Law is spoken in multiple and sometimes competing registers. I write this while sitting within my suburban municipality. The home in which I live is governed by local municipal building codes. It is situated on fee simple land with underlying title vested in the province. A Canadian citizen, I am protected by 'national' rights codes, criminal law and citizenship protections. The Katzie Indian Band also considers my home to be part of their traditional territory, governed by indigenous law and sovereignty. I am, notionally, a global citizen, protected by international covenants and codes. From one perspective, we can think about these jurisdictional claims as more or less forceful, enrolling more or less resources, people, ideas and things. However, the tendency is to think of jurisdiction less as a network, than as a noun, conceived of as a series of levels or layers, nested in a hierarchy.

Jurisdiction is a legal technicality. Jurisdiction is defined in law as the legal authority to judge or to act (literally, to speak the law) in a given situation or case. Distinctions may arise over certain types of cases or persons: so, for example, the jurisdiction of a criminal court is confined to criminal cases, military law applies only to military personnel and so on. Jurisdiction may also have a geographic dimension, being constrained by particular territorial distinctions. California law does not apply in Oregon, for example. Canadian law does not apply to property disputes in Bolivia. As such, we refer to spaces such as the Vatican, Moscow, or Malaysia as jurisdictions.[3] Disputes may arise between such jurisdictions – Marc Emery, a pot activist in British Columbia is in prison in the USA for distributing marijuana seeds throughout the USA, despite being resident in Canada. The magic that jurisdiction achieves, as Richard Ford (1999) notes, surely depends on a view that law is appropriately contained within such hermetic territories.

My focus is less on such horizontal dimensions to jurisdiction than what we might term vertical tensions (and I will be questioning such spatial metaphors later on). 'Within' (another metaphor) the state, law is said to operate at different scales, each of which can be thought of as a jurisdiction. The Canadian constitution (section 92), for example, divides law-making powers between the federal and provincial governments. Provincial legislatures may only pass laws on matters that are explicitly reserved for them, such as education or charity or 'matters of a merely local or private nature'. Any matters not under the exclusive authority of the provincial legislatures are within the scope of the federal parliament's power, including the postal service, currency, crime and weights and measures. Each of these jurisdictions operates at distinct scales – Canada can enact legislation that applies at the scale of the nation, such as the Canadian Charter of Rights and Freedoms – that apply to all Canadians whether they are in Moose Jaw or Montreal. Provinces are understood as operating at a 'lower' scale.

What sort of jurisdiction is a city, from this perspective? Municipalities, within this frame, are understood as nested within the jurisdictional space of the provinces. Indeed, rather than freestanding legal sites, they are imagined as products (or 'creatures') of the provinces who may bring them into being or dissolve them as they choose. As with the provinces, their powers are of a delegated form: they may only exercise jurisdiction over areas that have been expressly identified by enabling legislation. Municipal law may not conflict with provincial law, and may only be exercised within its defined territory. Legal formulae are in place to

---

3   The fixing of an association between jurisdiction and particular spaces is a consequential (and problematic) one, as we shall see.

determine these jurisdictional boundaries. Canadian courts use 'Dillon's rule' to determine whether a municipality has jurisdiction in a particular case. The rule asserts that there are only three bases for the exercise of a municipality's authority. They are: (a) that the power is expressly conferred by statute; (b) that the power is necessarily or fairly implied by the express power of the enabling statute, and (c) that the power is an indispensable power essential and not merely convenient to the effectuation of the purposes of the municipality (Levi and Valverde 2006).

Jurisdiction, in this sense, seems to be a zero sum game. Either the municipality has jurisdiction, or some other legal order does. Either Dale's panhandling is a 'local' matter, governed by municipal jurisdiction, or it is to be located within a 'national' space, in which federal law applies. Many legal conflicts, of course, necessarily bump up against, challenge or attempt to use such jurisdictional architecture, framing certain phenomena as local, national or international matters, governed by distinct jurisdictions. I sought out Dale in response to the introduction of a series of panhandling regulations passed by both Vancouver and the province. Activist lawyers challenged such legislation by invoking national rights codes, insisting on the essential liberties and expressive rights of the poor. Municipal lawyers countered by characterizing such rights codes as subservient to local legal priorities and needs, such as public order and hygiene. More formal jurisdictional battles may also ensue, as the question of whether such initiatives are *ultra vires* ('without authority') the jurisdictional scope of a municipality. Canadian activist lawyers, for example, seek to characterize such laws as really criminal law in disguise, and as such, an illegitimate encroachment on federal jurisdiction. Municipal lawyers respond by situating the essential purpose (the 'pith and substance') of such laws to fall within a city's provincially defined mandate (for example, that panhandling law should be seen as a form of traffic management). Jurisdictions are conceived as technical devices, sorting mechanisms that can be used to allocate people and objects to particular categories. As Valverde (2009) points out, jurisdiction operates according to a sort of path dependent chain reaction, whereby the answer to one question (where?) answers, seemingly inexorably, a subsequent question.

Unless we're legal technicians, we tend to think about such questions as rather uninteresting. This conception of legal jurisdiction appears obvious, as is law's territorialization (Raustialia 2005). Indeed, there is relatively little reflective literature on the topic, as compared to other legal phenomena, such as sovereignty or rights (though see McVeigh (2007) and Valverde (2009)). They certainly do not seem to be interstitial. There's very little in-between-ness at work here. Rather, matters seem to be sorted according to a cascading, categorical logic. As Valverde (2009: 141) notes, 'legal powers and legal knowledges appear to us as always already distinguished by scale'. Jurisdiction is a *deus ex machina*, a device that appears to resolve the entanglements of law 'as if by magic, and sets up a chain by which (most of the time) deciding who governs where effectively decides how governance will happen' (Valverde 2009: 145). The effect of this is similar to the process noted by Ford (1999): we tend to take it as given that our status, for example, will change as we move from one jurisdiction to another. As such, the work that jurisdiction does is left largely unquestioned. The 'games of scale and jurisdiction work so silently and efficiently', Valverde (2009, 146) argues, that we do not think of asking questions such as: what would happen if, for example, those who have breached the criminal code were governed as if the criminal law were local? What if climate change were imagined as a municipal or regional issue? What if cities seceded from the state? Why can cities not have foreign policy, or national states engage in land use planning?

We do not think of asking such (rather intriguing) questions, I think, because of the powerful presence of a particular and rather odd conception of scalar architecture, hinted at in Ferguson and Gupta's (2005: 106) discussion of 'verticality', which entails a view of the state as an institution 'above' civil society (while the 'grassroots' contrasts with the state as it is 'below'), and 'encompassment', which conceives the state as located within an ever-widening set of circles that begins with the individual or family and ends with the system of states. The two metaphors 'work together to produce a taken-for-granted spatial and scalar image of a state that both sits above and contains its localities, regions and communities'.

Jurisdiction operates according to such a scalar logic. Scale can refer to both size and level: similarly, jurisdictions are assumed to have different reach (the national is 'bigger' than the local), and to work hierarchically (the small local is trumped by the big national). The first point is akin to Ferguson and Gupta's notion of verticality. Critical to modern law and state formation is the production of the idea of a national state, and a national corpus of law, set above and apart from everyday life. The national law-state, then, is a conditional achievement, an effect, that comes into being and is sustained by a variety of practices (cf. Mitchell 2002, Painter 2010). Jurisdiction, structured according to a scalar logic, is both an outcome and a precondition for the national law-state. But, on the second point, what is the relation between the little city and the big state? It is one of 'levels'. Municipal law operates at a different level than national law, making possible its distinctiveness. However, such distinctiveness does not entail otherness: rather, 'lower' levels of the state are integral units in a larger hierarchy. We view jurisdiction through a Russian-doll-like conception of spatial order, in which some levels are higher or lower, or bigger or smaller; and in which one scale nests within another, in an ordered hierarchy. Like a cartographer's use of scale, each component within the hierarchy operates at different analytical levels. Local law is thus a subset of national law. Political geography textbooks routinely invoke such a spatial logic in their accounts of federalism, moving up the steps from little to big, as does neo-Marxist state theory, with its sorting of various social functions to 'levels' of the state apparatus. The modern state, as opposed to its earlier fuzzy and incomplete geographies of reach and presence (c.f. Ogborn 1998), appears ordered and universal. The history of the city is that of its 'municipalization', as it moves from a state within a state to a level in a hierarchy (Isin 1992).

At work here is a view of space as a series of categorical, nested containers. Such a zero-sum form of categorization relies upon a spatial model of meaning, in which law can be ordered into discrete 'areas', surrounded by hard boundaries. This, in turn, draws from a topographical view of space as areal, rather than, say, relational. Moore (2008: 208–9) notes that even scholars who emphasize the socially constructed character of scale still implicitly adhere to a view of them as 'actually existing entities that constitute the spatial context within and among which social action takes place'. As such, we should anticipate that non-academics may well characterize such jurisdictional scales as *a priori*, real phenomena. Each could be thought of as a distinctive platform, operating at different levels. The language we use to describe jurisdiction (above and below, national and local) points to a reified conception of actually-existing scales. What I hope to do here is to trace the emergence of this conception and the work that 'scale' does in making it possible. I then turn to the city as a legal jurisdiction and note the effects of such a scalar logic. In sum, the effect is to militate against an interstitial conception of legal space.

The making of jurisdiction

That this legal geography is a construction or performance, as scale more generally is a social artifact, is significant. For it has not always been with us. Isin (2007) suggests that Roman law imagined rule in terms of a topological relation between Rome and other cities, not a topographic hierarchy between cities and a 'higher' Roman state. In much the way that Isin (2007) points to the history of scalar thought as a technology of government, rooted in the emergence of the Church, the rise of abstract space and colonization, so the hierarchical model of jurisdiction must also have identifiable roots. Space and expertise do not permit such an exploration. However, law itself is both the product and instrument of such a scalar logic. One crucial arena is the attempt by early modern legal writers and practitioners to systematize and 'centralize' English common law. In so doing, as I have suggested elsewhere (Blomley 1994), an important scalar distinction is drawn between what the influential eighteenth century jurist Blackstone termed 'the general map of the law'[4] and lesser or lower scales of legal knowledge and practice. Such a distinction is a modernist one, effacing earlier geographies predicated on competing conceptions of order, distinct legal practices and the localization of justice. Practitioners such as Edward Coke worked hard to subsume and restrain such diversity, and have it conform to what he termed the 'high and honourable building' (quoted in Blomley 1994: 72) that is the common law. The effect, as Diamond (1971: 103) puts it, is that of 'the royal jurisdiction extend[ing]

---

4   Blackstone (1765/1838, Vol. 1: 20) counselled the academic expounder of the law to 'consider his course as a general map of the law, marking out the country, its connections and boundaries, its greater divisions and principal cities; it is not his business to describe minutely the subordinate limits, or to fix the longitude and latitude of every inconsiderable hamlet'.

itself over the whole realm, gradually levelling a maze of local jurisdictions and spreading one coherent system of national law'. To Coke, ultimately, the common law is not a variegated and diverse system of localized practices, but a disembedded and hierarchical structure predicated on uniformity: the law speaks in a unitary voice such that:

> All the Judges and Justices in all the several parts of the realm … with one mouth in all men's cases, pronounce one and the same sentence … [F]or as in nature, we see the infinite distinction of things proceed from some unity, as many flowers from one root, many rivers from one fountain, many arteries in the body of man from one heart, so without question *Lex orta est cum mente divina*, and this admirable unity and consent in such diversity of things proceeds only from God, the Fountain and Founder of all good laws and constitutions. (Coke 1826: §iv)

The city, as a jurisdiction, was not surprisingly deemed a threat to such a unitary, hierarchical geography. The free city was an interstitial legal site, able to exercise to varying degrees distinct forms of jurisdiction, including the power to regulate a local economy and confer citizenship. The result, in modern terms, is a departure from the Russian doll model. Coke worked hard to shift the locus of legal citizenship from the city to the space of the state, holding that all English citizens have the right to dispose of their land and labour as they see fit, not a selective few. Rights are thus remapped as simultaneously universal, being shared by all free Englishmen, wherever they are, and individualized, being lodged within the persons of autonomous legal subjects, 'a drift which makes for a theoretical concentration of right and power in the highest and widest group on the one hand and the individual man on the other, at the cost of all intermediate groups' (Gierke 1958/1990: 87). Foucault noted the irony by which cities, as 'islands beyond the common law', served as 'models for a governmental [and legal] rationality that was to apply to the whole of the territory' (1984: 241).

The workings of jurisdiction

The effect of such moves is to invite a view of 'vertical' jurisdiction operating according to a Russian doll scalar logic. A rich geographic literature alerts us to the prevalence of such a view of scale more generally, and some of its worrisome implications (Collinge 2005, Marston et al. 2005, Moore 2008, Legg 2009). These include a tendency to treat scale as given, rather than subjecting it to investigation, encouraging us to fit that which we see into scalar categories. The complexities of politics, for example, are fit into and explained by scalar categories (is homelessness a local, regional or national issue?), running the risk of unduly narrowing the conversation. As we shall see, the city is treated as inevitably situated in the 'local' categorical box, with all that this smuggles in. As a result, seemingly non-local categories, such as rights, do not fit. The effect is to flatten difference: 'treating scales as the given levels, platforms or arenas of politics profoundly flattens and distorts a variety of sociospatial processes by erasing spatial difference and granularity and oversimplifying the complex, and multiple, spatial positionality of social actors and events' (Moore 2008: 212). That which is designated 'local', for example, is assumed to have certain distinctive characteristics, set apart from other scales. The 'local' is here, while the global is nowhere and everywhere at the same time.

However, to question such a scalar logic does not allow us to abandon it, as some have proposed (Marston et al. 2005) for it operates with powerful performative force to organize legal practice. Moore (2008) urges us, instead, to take scale as an organizing epistemology, and to trace its effects, and the way it is put to work. Rather than treating it as a thing in the world, our task should become that of tracing the ways in which scale solidifies and is made 'real', and under what conditions, and making sense of the work such solidifications do. Similarly, for Ferguson and Gupta (2005: 108), 'The point is not that this picture of the 'up there' state is false ... but that it is constructed; the task is not to denounce a false ideology, but to draw attention to the social and imaginative processes through which state verticality is made effective and authoritative'. Rather than seeing the state (or law) as embedded in pre-existing scalar hierarchies, then, we are asked to see the ways in which such scalar imaginaries are themselves produced, and to see what work such scalar logics serve. One crucial effect of technologies such as jurisdiction (in combination, of course, with 'sovereignty', the 'rule of law' etc.) is to create a distinction between phenomena, similar to Mitchell's (2002: 58) account of colonial property law in Egypt, whereby some processes 'seemed particular and some general: some appeared fixed, singular, anchored to a specific place and moment, like objects, while others appeared mobile, general, present everywhere at once, universal, unquestionably true in every place, and therefore abstract'. Similarly, jurisdiction's scalar arrangements help constitute law as a thing, a concrete reality (akin to Coke's 'high and honourable building'), with all that this makes possible. Rights, in particular, are imagined as circulating at the scale of the nation/state (indeed, in Canada, they have been a tool in the very constitution of the nation). Jurisdictional scale, therefore, is performative, producing the effect of law. Such hierarchies, then, are not incidental, but fundamental to law.

But such scalar logics also shape the way in which we tend to think about law and its interstices in the city. First, as noted, scalar thinking has a hard time with granularity and difference given that scalar thinking supposes that 'lower' jurisdictions are contained within higher ones, such that law as a whole, like some Cokean composite of the parts, speaks with one voice. This is to ignore, however, the possibility that different 'levels' may in fact speak law very differently. But such multivocality is obscured by the prevailing model. Mariana Valverde (2009) points out that different legal knowledges are operative at particular sites, in particular, that of the city. The city is not simply a smaller version of state-level government. Rather, municipal law draws from 'police' powers, which she characterizes as operating not at the scale of the local, but at that of the 'urban' as a legal field. Police powers are distinctive, reliant upon discretion, flexibility and a prudential form of temporality. Urban police powers frequently govern broadly defined grab-bags of phenomena without the felt need to define the purposes of regulation (other than through open-textured and ill-defined wrongs, such as 'nuisance'). Rarely focused on individuals, police law concerns itself with the arrangements of objects (whether bodies or things) and spaces (Blomley 2012).[5]

This takes us to a second implication. In much the same way that the global is posited as complex, while the local is simple and quotidian, so local law can easily appear uninteresting. Municipal law may be of very broad reach, yet its very location (as 'lower', 'local') makes this hard to discern. It is seen as parochial, particular and antediluvian. City ordinances that make it illegal to ride a horse up the court-house steps (Prescott, Arizona), or the requirement that London taxi cabs carry a bale of hay and a sack of oats, are easy targets. Yet we are danger in missing the reach of municipal law: '[e]ven in highly constitutionalized regimes, it has remained possible for municipalities to micro-manage space, time, and activities through police regulations that infringe both on constitutional rights and private property in often extreme ways' (Vaverde 2009: 150). While liberalism fears the encroachments of the state, it seems less worried about those of the municipality. Thus if a national government proposed a statute forbidding public gatherings or sporting events, a revolution would occur. Yet municipalities routinely enact sweeping by-laws directed at open-ended (and ill-defined) offences such as loitering and obstruction, requiring permits for protests or requiring residents and homeowners to remove snow from the city's sidewalks. A 'higher-level' statute compelling aesthetic commonality would cause an uproar, despite city laws compelling homeowners to maintain their front gardens to community standards (and then empowering city authorities to enter onto a non-complying property, effect a makeover and then bill the owner). Scale corrals politics, it seems. A province-wide statute in British Columbia regulating panhandling was created with predictable horror by civil libertarians and anti-poverty activists as an obvious manifestation of 'big' logics, such as neoliberalism, or 'American-

---

5   Section 64 of the Community Charter, the enabling legislation for BC municipalities, stipulates that municipalities have the authority to regulate the following 'nuisances, disturbances and other objectionable situations': (a) nuisances [!]; (b) noise, vibration, odour, dust, illumination or any other matter that is liable to disturb the quiet, peace, rest, enjoyment, comfort or convenience of individuals or the public; (c) the emission of smoke, dust, gas, sparks, ash, soot, cinders, fumes or other effluvia that is liable to foul or contaminate the atmosphere; (d) refuse, garbage or other material that is noxious, offensive or unwholesome; (e) the use of waste disposal and recycling services; (f) the accumulation of water on property; (g) unsanitary conditions on property; (h) drains, cesspools, septic tanks and outhouses; (i) trees, weeds or other growths that council considers should be removed, cut down or trimmed; (j) the carrying on of a noxious or offensive business activity; (k) graffiti and unsightly conditions on property; (l) indecency and profane, blasphemous or grossly insulting language.

style zero-tolerance-policing'. When I asked the Vancouver police, they told me that they much preferred using existing city police power by-laws governing the constitutional black holes of 'loitering' and 'obstruction' as they were far more flexible and powerful. Yet such 'local' by-laws are all too easily dismissed by observers as generally unimportant.

The flip-side of the above alerts us to another crucial consideration, obscured because of the prevalence of vertical scalar logics of law. Urban regulation tends to be antithetical to rights claims. This, in part, is because police powers are incommensurable to rights, given the status of the 'person' in the former (Valverde 2005). However, such incommensurability is hard to trace, given the presumption of a nested and hermetic hierarchy. This does not stop attempts to frame the urban through a rights lens, as evidenced, for example, in the 'right to the city' movement. However, the spatial architecture that jurisdictional scale rests upon helps constitute particular forms of law differently. Some law is local, proximate and familiar. Other law is larger, distant and different. Rights, as a form of 'national' or 'international' law, are thus often framed as interlopers in urban affairs.

We can see this when we trace conflicts in Canadian cities over the municipal regulation of the homeless in which a clear divide is drawn between rights and police powers. The *Federated*[6] and *Adams*[7] cases are broadly similar – both entail attempts by municipalities to regulate poor and/or homeless people who seek to use public space in ways that are deemed objectionable – engaging in aggressive panhandling in Vancouver's streets, and camping out in Victoria's parks, respectively. Both, as we shall see, entail attempts by lawyers to have such regulation struck down as a violation of the rights of the public poor (successfully in *Adams*, unsuccessfully in *Federated*). In this sense, a predictable jurisdictional clash ensues: are the public poor to be governed by municipal law, or national (or even international) rights codes? In *Adams*, in particular, city officials lament what they see as an 'intrusion' into their regulatory domain: as elected officials, they know best how to allocate resources and advance local welfare. In *Federated*, more formal jurisdictional arguments are also made. The by-law is *ultra vires* the City of Vancouver, it is alleged, as it is really a form of criminal law, which is the exclusive domain of the federal government.

Santos's (1987) observation that legal scales translate the same social objects into different legal objects is certainly in evidence in *Adams* and *Federated*, in which the actions of the homeless person are variously constituted as the freedom-loving act of a rights-bearing citizen or an objectionable presence (Blomley 2007, 2011). Different legal rationalities collide here: a rights framing, premised on individual personhood, butts up against a police powers conception premised less on persons than on the arrangement of objects and the maintenance of the public

---

6   Federated Anti-Poverty Groups of BC v Vancouver (City) [2002] BCSC 105.

7   Victoria (City) v Adams [2008] BCSC 1363, Victoria (City) v Adams [2009] BCCA 563.

good. The rights/police conflict is noted by both the trial judge and the appellate judge in *Adams*, who open their opinion by borrowing from the influential US case of *Pottinger v City of Miami*[8] in which the case is described as 'an inevitable conflict between the need of homeless individuals to perform essential, life-sustaining acts in public and the responsibility of the government to maintain orderly, aesthetically pleasing public parks and streets'.

Adams concerns a particular park in Victoria in which homeless people have erected shelters: to compare the different understandings of the park is to reveal the rights/police collision. For Victoria officials, the park is municipal space, held in trust for the public in the advancement of public welfare. They argue that parks are a valuable resources that enhances the quality of life and economic vitality and, strikingly, that homeless people are engaged in the privatization of a public resource: 'It is the City's submission that absent the Bylaws, there will be an inevitable colonization of public spaces with a devastating impact to the economic vitality of adjacent areas' (*Adams*, para. 173). Preventing homeless people from erecting temporary shelters in the park may seem a minor concern. However, in true prudential police form, a slippery slope logic is invoked (*Adams* para. 86–87) in its claim that without regulation, the city risks 'becoming enablers that promote drug abuse, crime, self-destruction, disease, and death'.

For opponents of the by-law, public spaces such as a park are not simply settled and functional spaces that advance circulation or produce public benefits (safety, salubrity and so on). Parks are political spaces in which political identities are constantly in formation, for better or worse. What matters is not the presence of objectionable objects, and their external effects, but the co-presence of people, and the interior life that is thus produced through such encounters. For the BC Civil Liberties Association, the City of Victoria is engaged in a regulation of public space that treats the homeless as beyond the 'public' pale. The homeless had thus become a subclass, excluded from democratic life. This, presumably, is objectionable not only insofar as the homeless is concerned, but also because the production of such a sanitized space militates against productive forms of encounter between them and the non-homeless.

In *Adams*, the by-law is struck down: the homeless person is brought within the fold of citizenship as a site of rights. The park is a space of democracy, the regulation of which is a marker of citizenship. In *Federated*, the by-law is upheld: the panhandler is an object of police, whose actions in public space are governed by codes of circulation, placement and obstruction. He or she is no different than other police objects, whether the lamppost or the hot-dog vendor. In Adams, the park is in a sense a 'national', even 'international' space, governed by universal declarations of rights and citizenship. In *Federated*, the sidewalk is a municipal space, a site not for 'civil rights' but 'civil engineering' (Blomley 2007).

---

8   810 F Supp. 1551, 1554, S.D. Fla 1992.

Adams, then, is a 'victory' for rights. However, *Adams* is unusual.[9] The courts tend routinely to side with municipal police powers arguments, except when egregious rights violations have occurred. This, I believe, has a lot to do with the tendency to use scale to sort and explain legal phenomena, rather than being that which must be explained. Thus, in the *Federated* case, the judge has to decide whether the city of Vancouver has the legal authority to regulate 'aggressive solicitation' (this in the face of the counter argument that this is really criminal/ federal regulation in disguise). The 'magic' of jurisdiction is at work here, as he cites Dillon's rule, and then avers that what is needed is to determine the purpose of the regulation. He notes that the city has the authority to regulate vehicular traffic, and has evidently done so through the regulation of

> the manner and conduct of persons using the street, other than pedestrians, through various by-law provisions and the granting of right-of-ways or easements in terms of hydro or telephone poles. These regulations are found in the various by-laws that govern street vending, busking, sidewalk cafes, and solicitation for charities – all of which are managed through a permit or licencing scheme. (para. 96)

There is no doubt, he confidently asserts, that panhandling can also prove obstructive to pedestrian traffic. As such, the purpose of the panhandling by-law is to control the orderly flow of traffic on the city's sidewalks, and is thus *intra vires* the city's powers.

Cities regulate traffic. The by-law regulates traffic. Therefore, the by-law is an appropriate exercise of the city's legal powers. Absent here, of course, is any examination of why cities regulate traffic (as opposed to, for example, upholding rights). Scale becomes a sorting device, into which bits of law are allocated, rather than that which requires explanation on its own terms. Form determines content, in other words. But legal scale, surely, is something we need to explain, not explain with.

The sorting logic of scale is also evident in the reaction to *Adams*, which was roundly criticized by many observers as an overextension of rights into a domain (city/police) in which it was not welcome. The BC Housing Minister, Rich Coleman, characterized the *Adams* decision as 'head-shaking' and 'ridiculous' (Arab 2009, A 18). A columnist in the *Calgary Herald* lamented the over-extension of rights to urban/community settings (Hannaford, 2008). Robert Sibley (2008) in the *Ottawa Citizen* bemoaned the demise of a 'traditional notion' of public spaces predicated on safety, order and decency: 'It is simply not intelligible to abandon

---

9 Adams was largely upheld on appeal. However, it is interesting to note that a subsequent Victoria by-law prohibiting day-time camping was found to withstand constitutional scrutiny. Essentially, the Pottinger trade-off between the freedom of the (homeless) individual and the police powers responsibilities of the municipality was rebalanced in favour of the latter. See Johnston v Victoria (City) [2010] BCSC 1707.

formal social controls on behaviour – laws against vagrancy, loitering and public drunkenness, for example – for the sake of spurious "rights" that are, in reality, an excuse for private indulgences. That way lies disorder' (A18). Others argued that the decision denied the distinctive jurisdictional character of the city. The Attorney-General, in its submission on appeal, insisted that homelessness was a matter for (presumably city) governments, and was not solved by the 'courts creating a constitutionally entrenched "right"'. The courts ought not to '*extend the reach* of the Canadian Constitution'.[10] The City of Victoria insisted that the matter of homeless people camping in parks was a complex one that was best addressed by the municipality, on the ground, rather than being resolved by the blunt abstractions of rights. In a *reductio ad absurdum*, rights are said to open the door to chaos: where are the limits to be drawn if the by-law is struck down, they ask?[11] The 'questions overwhelm'.[12]

However, there is another important effect of vertical scalar thinking. As well as obscuring the differences between 'scales', we are in danger of ignoring legal diversity *within* the city. The city, in other words, is imagined as a scale, rather than a site: but 'city' and 'municipality' are not coterminous. We can acknowledge the presence of police powers for municipal regulation, while noting the diversity of other legal knowledges within the city. For evidence suggests more overlapping, interstitial dynamics, particularly when we expand our definition of legal actors, the effect of which is to complicate claims for nested, discrete hierarchical jurisdictional scales of legal practice. However, recognizing the diversity of urban legal practices and knowledge formats is hard, given the way the scalar framing of jurisdiction organizes matters for us.

We can begin by complicating the urban/police nexus, and the non-urban nature of rights. While the formal arguments of municipal lawyers do, indeed, invoke a police logic, those of other interested observers frequently run together

---

10   Written submission of the Intervenor the Attorney General of British Columbia, 2008, copy with author, my emphasis.

11   'If the homeless can camp in public places, can anyone? How is the City to differentiate? Are the truly homeless to be issued free passes? What is to prevent a family camping trip stopping at a park near you? What is to stop the overnight grad party or the prostitute's tent? Are all our beaches to be open to addicts who may pass out in the sand where their syringes will fall? Is public land to be allocated and partitioned as so many campsites? Where will businesses go and who will pay taxes when the tourists willing to pay for accommodation are gone? What happens when the public land is all parceled out? If camping is permitted, are foundations and generators and fireplaces far behind? Who will be responsible for safety when danger is courted by such conduct? Who will be liable if unsafe accommodation in a City park results in a fire causing personal injury and property damage? How will the spread of bacterial or viral diseases due to poor sanitation and hygiene be prevented? Are City of Victoria taxpayers to pay for the provision of tents and amenities? What will the City need to spend to protect its parks when they are colonized?' Plaintiff's submissions (2008: 29). Copy with author.

12   Plaintiff's submissions (2008: 29). Copy with author.

police and rights vocabularies. Rather than fixing on the liberal individual as the locus of rights, however, here reference is made to the 'rights of the public'. These rights, again echoing police logic, are not necessarily constitutional rights to expression or security of the person, but rather are triggered by exposure to open-ended problems, such as 'disorder' and 'nuisance' (Blomley 2010b). Take, for example, a response to *Adams* by Roberto Noce (2009), an Edmonton lawyer who acts for several Canadian municipalities, who criticized the *Adams* decision as recognizing only the rights of the homeless, and ignoring those of the 'tax-paying public' who also have a right to the use and enjoyment of public parks, but whose rights are now compromised: 'It would be very intimidating for a person to walk through a park and face large groups of homeless people popping in and out of their tents', obstructing sight lines and engaging in noisy sexual activity, Noce (2009: 7) laments. Proponents of begging regulation in Vancouver, I have noted elsewhere (Blomley 2010), similarly invoked the general rights of the public to walk freely, unimpeded by obstruction.

Similarly, to characterize police power as exclusively an urban legal knowledge is mistaken. As Dubber (2005) notes, the centralization of royal power entailed the expansion of the kingly household to the level of the nation. As such, the sovereign was charged with protecting his realm from external threats and guarding against disobedient members of his household. Nuisance, for Blackstone (1769/1979: 162), is thus an offence against the 'domestic order of the kingdom', being an 'offence against the public order and economical regimen of the state' (ibid. 167). Such offences are not simply 'internal' to the state: foreign policy may also be prosecuted according to a logic of police (Dean 2006, Levi and Hagan 2006).[13]

Further, we can recognize the ways in which rights claims may conflict with urban police powers, yet note that such rights claims are not an imposition from 'above', but rather, invoked within the city by local activist lawyers and civil libertarians. Those lawyers who opposed the Vancouver panhandling by-law, for example, drew from local activist anger and organizing. Interestingly, the lawyers clearly connected with and learnt from other cities – Winnipeg and Toronto, in particular – that were embroiled in similar rights-based challenges. Scalar claims were deployed: the goal was not only to strike down Vancouver's by-law, but to create a precedent that could then apply to other cities who were tempted to follow Vancouver's path. A conscious decision was made by the lawyers also to work with local, provincial and national anti-poverty organizations. Initially, the lawyers had focused on simply using a jurisdictional argument (that the by-law was criminal law, and thus *ultra vires* the city's authority) but the anti-poverty groups had seen this as simply a technical move, wanting instead to use more politically exciting rights arguments.

---

13 Interestingly, Levi and Hagan, in their discussion of Roosevelt's use of police in US international relations, draw from his urban experiences as New York City Police Commissioner, in which he inveighed against the excesses of rights within the city.

The question of homelessness and its regulation was also framed and complicated by jurisdictional scales. In both Vancouver and Victoria, predictably, local politicians complained that they were forced to deal with what was essentially a 'national' issue. Presumably, this means that homelessness is a problem that should be addressed comprehensively by the federal government, a failure of which is then felt unfairly by local politicians. Homelessness – its causes and its management – thus is said to operate, like the economy, at a 'higher', 'bigger' or 'larger' scale than the city, which is much better equipped to deal with traditional issues such as snow removal or land use planning. Victoria politicians, indeed, found some comfort in the *Adams* decision in that it 'turned the spotlight' onto those higher scales. Yet as noted, at the same time, without seeming contradiction, they insisted that the decision was an unwanted encroachment upon municipal legal space. The *Kamloops Daily News* (21 October 2008: A6) in an article entitled 'Homeless decision should be local' labelled *Adams* as 'an unnecessary intrusion into municipal policy-making' given the particular role of the municipality:

> Municipalities, though a creature of the provincial government, are regarded as a level of government all on their own, and have been bestowed with certain authority over the way land is used. That includes the right to ban uses of public space that are contrary to the public good, enforcement against actions that equate to a public nuisance, and some jurisdiction over public health issues.

However, the effect of the decision, worried the paper, was to relocalize the question, given the possibility that tents and sleeping parks may well start appearing in parks everywhere, requiring municipal officials to enact appropriate forms of regulation. But if law is needed, the appropriate vehicle 'is the Community Charter [the enabling legislation for municipal authority], not the B.C. Supreme Court [i.e. Constitutional/rights law]'.

Another consequence of a scalar logic, which posits scale as always already there, is that it makes the 'scalar practices' of legal actors harder to treat as a political move, rather than an expression of the 'magic' of jurisdiction. For in the two cases, the parties worked hard to constitute the urban as either a scale of police or one of rights. So, for example, in *Federated*, the city characterized the sidewalks as serving the 'general welfare' of all inhabitants of the city. That general welfare, it seems, is predicated on the advancement of circulation and flow. Any regulation that governs the behaviour of people like Dale may be discriminatory, but this is justified:

> the By-law provisions – if found to discriminate in the municipal sense – are necessary for the welfare of all inhabitants of the City, in much the same way other 'discriminatory' regimes are provided for specific activities taking place on City streets and sidewalks, such as (a) street vending, (b) limiting the permissible weight of commercial vehicles on City streets, etc. ... As such, the

enactment of the By-law provisions is *intra vires* the City by virtue of the City's implicit power to discriminate in matters grounded in promoting the welfare of the inhabitants of the City. (Written argument of the respondent City of Vancouver: 17)

We should read such manoeuvres as attempts to produce scale, in other words. But given the way law appears as already sorted by jurisdictional scale, such performances are harder to see. Also harder to discern are the gradients built into such scales. Rights claims have to work hard against the inherent tendency to constitute the urban as 'below' rights. From one perspective, such a reconstitution is a form of 'scale-jumping'. But such a claim rests, however, on the notion of upper and lower scales. It is more preferable, surely, to think of lawyerly characterizations, like that of the BC Civil Liberties Association, of Victoria parks as a site of citizenship, as an attempt not so much to move the park 'upwards' into the rarified realm of rights, than a move designed to show the park as always already suffused with rights.

There is also a danger of ignoring how different 'levels' are not discrete and separate, but may in fact interpenetrate and overlap (and thus aren't levels at all, of course, but rhetorical deployments). For such scalar practices need not be antagonistic. Legal actors can work 'across' and through jurisdictional scale in creative and flexible ways. Objects not only move between scales but also can be positioned between them (c.f. Martin 1999). The case of Indian reserves in Canadian cities, like that which Dale identified as his home, is an intriguing one. Indian reserves are a problem for cities as they defy the logic that posits the city as a scale. Owned by the federal government, they are largely outside urban jurisdiction. They occupy the city, in other words, but are governed by a 'higher' jurisdiction. The metaphorical geography of scale runs headlong into a material geography of the here and now. This vertiginious verticality – in which the reserve is inside the city, yet 'above' it – creates not only practical dilemmas when it comes to urban planning and land use (particularly when the residents of reserves decide to develop 'their' land) but also, one must suppose, conceptual dilemmas.[14] Early urban planners in Vancouver, for example, expressed consternation at the presence of spaces in their midst that defied regulation. Yet in so doing, they worked creatively 'between' scales, extending forms of regulation (such as the taxation of non-native reserve residents) and collaborating with the federal government to extinguish reserves (Stanger-Ross 2008).[15] Yet the economic muscle-flexing of some reserves in Vancouver continues to generate municipal anxiety, given that

---

14 This is complicated even further if First Nations lay claim to their own inherent sovereignty as a jurisdiction that falls somewhat outside the scalar architecture of the state.

15 Scale appears fixed and inflexible, yet is capable of creative interstitiality, perhaps. 'Scale may not have the analytical rigour and stability that is demanded of it by scholars but that would point up precisely its effectiveness in transmitting, containing, controlling, regulating and instantiating power relations' (Isin 2007: 217).

they can circumvent municipal zoning, as evidenced by a recent forum on reserves entitled 'Empowered, or too much power?'.

Finally, to finish where we started, the containerized and vertical view of legal space makes it hard to recognize interlegality. Jurisdictional spaces are premised on categorical separation and hierarchy. The 'nomosphere' (Delaney 2010), in which multiple legal voices are at play, is hard to bring into view. A zero-sum categorical logic posits the panhandler as either a rights subject or an obstacle. But Dale told me that he was both (as well as being, of course, more): he talked of the ways in which he felt discriminated against when he was chased out of a mall, and noted, rather vaguely, that he should have the same right as others to use the sidewalk (characterizing his panhandling as not dissimilar to charity drives), while also noting that others have a right to not be harassed. But he was also careful not to panhandle near ATMs, as this would be threatening. He also described his attempts at negotiating the trade-off between visibility and obstructiveness (Brighenti 2007), sitting carefully so that he would not be in the way of pedestrians.

But there are other legalities at play here, beyond the rights/police dyad, that are obscured by a scalar logic. These take us deeper into the richer analytical understanding of urban law that interlegality invites. Why is Dale asking me for change, for example, rather than *vice versa*? To answer such a question requires us, again, to think about law and its interstices, historical entanglements and geographic frictions. For we are both different legal subjects. He is 'Indian', under the terms of the Indian Act, with all its attendant legal subjectivities. His very presence, as a panhandler, is a function of the workings of welfare law, for example. His part time job, he noted, could not pay above a certain amount or he would lose his welfare entitlements. But our relative positions require a richer treatment of the entanglements of law with social, racial and cultural order. The fact that I have change that I may choose to give, or not, or that I am not obliged to humble myself before strangers and suffer their disdain, charity or occasional violence, reflects my privileged legal status as a white male property-owning settler. Indeed, the very fact that we are in a city, carved out of the traditional territories of Dale's ancestors speaks, again, to the workings of law (Blomley 2004). For Santos (1987: 288), 'more important than the identification of the different legal orders is the tracing of the complex and changing relations among them'. To trace such interstitial connections requires an imaginative and conceptual leap, a necessary condition for which is to think around scale, while recognizing its powerful hold.

References

Agnew, J.A. 1994. The territorial trap: the geographical assumptions of international relations theory. *Review of International Political Economy*, 1, 53–80.

Allen, J. 2011. Topological twists: Power's shifting geographies. *Dialogues in Human Geography*, 1(3), 283–98.

Amin, A. 2002. Spatialities of globalization. *Environment and Planning A*, 385–99.

Arab, P. 2008. Put your fears to bed over tent city court decision. *Calgary Herald*, 23 October, A 18.

Blackstone, W. 1765/1838. *Commentaries on the Laws of England*. New York: Dean.

Blomley, N. 1994. *Law, Space, and the Geographies of Power*. New York: Guilford.

Blomley, N. 2004. *Unsettling the City*. New York: Routledge.

Blomley, N. 2007. Civil rights meets civil engineering: Urban public space and traffic logic. *Canadian Journal of Law and Society*, 22(2), 55–72.

Blomley, N. 2010. The right to pass freely: circulation, begging, and the bounded self. *Social and Legal Studies*, 19(3), 331–35.

Blomley, N. 2011. *Rights of Passage*. New York: Routledge.

Blomley, N. 2012. Colored rabbits, dangerous trees, and public sitting: sidewalks, police, and the city. *Urban Geography*, 33(7), 917–35.

Brighenti, A. 2007. Visibility. *Current Sociology*, 55(3), 323–42.

Coke, E. 1826. *The Fifth Part of the Reports of Sir Edward Coke, Knt.* London: Butterworth.

Collinge, C. 2005. The différance between society and space: nested scales and the returns of spatial fetishism. *Environment and Planning D, Society and Space*, 23, 189–206.

Dean, M. 2006. Military intervention as 'police' action?' In: M.D. Dubber and M. Valverde (eds), *The New Police Science: The Police Power in Domestic and International Governance*, Stanford, CA: Stanford University Press, pp. 185–206.

Delaney, D. 2010. *The Spatial, the Legal, and the Pragmatics of World-Making*. New York: Routledge.

Diamond, A.S. 1971. *Primitive Law: Past and Present*. London: Methuen: London.

Engel, D.M. 2009. Landscapes of the law: injury, remedy and social change in Thailand. *Law and Society Review*, 43(1), 61–94.

Ferguson, J. and Gupta, A. 2005. Spatializing states: toward an ethnography of neoliberal governmentality. In: J.X. Inda (ed.), *Anthropologies of Modernity: Foucault, Governmentality, and Life Politics*. Malden, MA: Blackwell, pp. 105–31.

Ford, R.T. 1999 Law's territory (A history of jurisdiction). *Michigan Law Review*, 97(4), 843–930.

Foucault, M. 1984. Space, knowledge and power. In: P Rabinow (ed.) *The Foucault Reader*. New York: Pantheon, 239–55.

Gierke, O. 1958/1990. *Political Theories of the Middle Ages*. Cambridge, UK: Cambridge University Press.

Hannaford, N. 2008. Ruling that leads to shanties cannot be allowed to stand. *Calgary Herald*, 25 October, 26.

Isin, E. 1992. *Cities Without Citizens*. Montreal: Black Rose Books.

Isin, E. 2007. City.State: critique of scalar thought. *Citizenship Studies*, 11(2), 211–28.

Levi, R. and Valverde, M. 2006. Freedom of the city: Canadian cities and the quest for governmental status. *Osgoode Hall Law Journal*, 44, 409–61.

Levi, R. and Hagan, J. 2006. International police. In: M.D. Dubber and M. Valverde (eds), *The New Police Science: The Police Power in Domestic and International Governance*. Stanford, CA: Stanford University Press, 207-247.

Law, J. 2004. And if the global were small and noncoherent? Method, complexity, and the baroque. *Environment and Planning D: Society and Space*, 22, 13–26.

Legg, S. 2009. Of scales, networks and assemblages: the League of Nations apparatus and the scalar sovereignty of the Government of India. *Transactions of the Institute of British Geographers*, 34, 234–53.

McVeigh, S. (ed.) 2007.*Jurisprudence of Jurisdiction*. New York: Routledge.

Marston, S., Jones, J.P. and Woodward, K. 2005. Human geography without scale. *Transactions of the Institute of British Geographers*, 30, 416–32.

Martin, D. 1999. Transcending the fixity of jurisdictional scale. *Political Geography*, 18, 33–38.

Mitchell, T. 2002. *Rule of Experts: Egypt, Techno-Politics, Modernity*. New York: Routledge.

Moore, A. 2008. Rethinking scale as a geographic category: from analysis to practice. *Progress in Human Geography*, 32(2), 203–25.

Murdoch, J. 2006. *Post-Structuralist Geography: A Guide to Relational Space*. London: Sage.

Noce, R. 2009. *Victoria (City) v Adams*, Tents and the city, Digest of Municipal and Planning Law, 4 (2d) May, 3–7.

Ogborn, M. 1998. The capacities of the state: Charles Davenant and the management of the Excise, 1683–1698. *Journal of Historical Geography*, 24(3), 289–312.

Painter, J. 2010. Rethinking territory. *Antipode*, 42(5), 1090–118.

Raustialia, K. 2005. The Geography of Justice. *Fordham Law Review*, 73, 101–55.

Santos, B. de Sousa 1987. Law: a map of misreading. Toward a postmodern conception of law. *Journal of Law and Society*, 14(3), 279–302.

Sibley, R. 2008. Disorder in our public spaces. *The Ottawa Citizen*, 22 October, A 18.

Stanger-Ross, J. 2008. Municipal colonialism in Vancouver: city planning and the conflict over Indian reserves. *Canadian Historical Review*, 89(4), 541–80.

Valverde, M. 2005. Taking 'land use' seriously: toward an ontology of municipal law. *Law Text Culture* 9, 34–59.

Valverde, M. 2009. Jurisdiction and scale: legal 'technicalities' as resources for theory. *Social and Legal Studies*, 18(2), 139–57.

Weber, M. 1966/1925. *Economy and Society: an Outline of Interpretive Sociology*, 3 Vols. New York: Bedminster.

White, J.B. 1990. *Justice as Translation: An Essay in Cultural and Legal Criticism*. Chicago, IL: University of Chicago Press.

Chapter 2

Trajectories of Interstitial Landscapeness: A Conceptual Framework for Territorial Imagination and Action[1]

Luc Lévesque

Perhaps this all started in a wasteland running along the Berlin Wall with images and words from *Der Himmel über Berlin* (*Wings of Desire*) (1987) (Figures 2.1) ... or while crossing the blasted emptiness of a concrete slab in the middle of downtown Brussels ... or in a *terrain vague* or some interval in Montreal, Quebec City, Houston, Tokyo, Rotterdam or elsewhere ... in other words, while exploring cities through their gaps. There was, in these conditions, in these architectural and urban territories, more or less abandoned, accidental and resistant, something that was attractive and stimulating; an intensity that escaped the intentionality of planning; something, paradoxically, from which inspiration could be drawn.

What motivated this interest – shared by many others – for these particular territorial conditions? What was the nature of this fascination? How could it be used? What could it produce? To answer these questions or at least to begin to answer them, we first had to name these conditions and define the starting point from which our reflection was to be structured. We perhaps also had to detach ourselves momentarily from the hard facts of experience and follow another path – that of words – to feed this reflection and parallel field explorations. Two notions progressively emerged to articulate this questioning: the *interstitial* to describe certain situations or conditions; the *landscape* to approach these conditions in an open manner. The merging of these two terms – the landscape (or 'landscapeness') of the interstitial – generated, in turn, its own set of questions, as if interstitiality was opening the theoretical framework of landscape and pushing it towards its limits ...

Landscape, landscapeness and the interstitial

Landscape is approached here as the manifestation of a territorial condition that is constructed by the sensitivity of an individual subject or a community (Roger 1997; Corner 1999). But beyond landscape, it is more the notion of landscapeness

---

[1] Translated from the French by Michel Moussette with the collaboration of the author.

Figure 2.1   *Der Himmel über Berlin* (*Wings of Desire*), **Wim Wenders, 1987 (Reverse Angle Library GmbH and Argos Films S.A.).**

that will here be used in relation to the interstitial. The concept of landscapeness (*paysagéité*) is borrowed from Maurice Ronai (1977) as well as from Deleuze and Guattari (Guattari 1979; Deleuze and Guattari 1980), who give the term a philosophical dimension in correlation to the notion of 'faciality' (*visagéité*).[2]

---

2   In the 'Plateau 7. Year Zero: Faciality' of A Thousand Plateaus, Deleuze and Guattari (1987 [1980]) mostly developed the concepts of 'faciality' and 'face' in correlation to 'landscapeness' (or 'landscapity', as translated by Brian Massumi) and 'landscape': 'All faces envelop an unknown, unexplored landscape; all landscapes are populated by

Ronai associates landscapeness to the development of that which conditions our ways of perceiving and describing the territory: 'the gaze selects, valorises, evaluates, characterizes [...] thus is developed a nebulous landscapeness that would be part of certain spaces and not of others' (Ronai 1977: 132). The notion of landscapeness therefore signals the existence of a construct that mobilizes and directs the attention upon certain aspects or characteristics of the environment. Landscapeness is not landscape; conveying a set of specific preoccupations, it defines the modalities of what should or could eventually become a landscape; it is, to use Ronai's (1977: 80) words, 'landscape's condition of possibility', a potential motive. In light of these considerations, landscapeness could be defined as a process of selection, characterization and valorization of a specific territorial condition. This process generates a landscape potential susceptible to materialize itself in diverse landscape manifestations or expressions. But beyond Ronai's categorization that tends to reduce landscapeness to different 'regimes of aesthetic enjoyment' linked to a more or less passive consumptions of the Spectacular, the landscapeness of the interstitial could engage other trajectories of territorial valorization.

The interstitial relates to the notion of interstice (form the Latin *interstare*: to stand in between), which is usually defined as a 'small empty space' within a substance or between different elements. As such, the term refers to a series of interconnected notions that form a polysemous discursive field oscillating between connection and disjunction. The interstice as a void space within a substance (Lavoiser 1793; Baudrillard 1975) can therefore refer to notions of porosity (Marx 1886 [1863]), permeability (De Certeau 1980), infiltration and passage (Bhabha 1994), interval (Barthes 1970; Virilio 1984; Cache 1995; Zardini 1997), spacing (Gaudin 1992; Tschumi 1993), transition, threshold and border (De Certeau 1980; Remy 1986). Interstices are also often associated with the idea of fault (*faille*) (Foucault 1966), fissure (Chenet-Faugeras 1994), slit, hole, opening, breach or, in this vein, crack, crevice, cavity or cranny (Thrasher 1927).

In addition to its spatial character, the interstice refers to a temporal dimension as an 'interval of time'. Indeed, one the first recorded occurrence of the word in the French language – dating back to 1333 and attributed to Jean de Vignay (Beauvais 1495) – refers to time (*intertisse de temps*) instead of space. The interstice here corresponds to an interlude (Gallet 2002) or a transitory period. Even if it became secondary during the twentieth century, this aspect of the term is important since it would link the interstitial condition to the notions of transition, transformation, process and event.

If the interstice's relation to the margin, the leftover or the residual (Knaebel 1991; Korosec-Serfaty 1991) is often viewed negatively, the term can also take a more positive aspect when connected to opening (Virilio 1976), latitude or room for manoeuvre (Lefebvre 1974; Mons 2003), or possibility for action between certain

---

a loved or dreamed-of face, develop a face to come or already past.' See also Antonioli (2003: 179–206).

spatial limits (Moles and Rohmer 1972; Remy 1986; Koolhaas 1989). Taken on its own, the interstice is moreover generally understood as being in a minority position in relation to what encompasses it, without any predetermined scale. The relation to the encompassing, of the part to the whole, is essential to the notion of interstice. There cannot be an interstice without a differentiated relationship to an exterior since the nature of the interstitial is etymologically to stand or to be between things, in the middle (Deleuze and Guattari 1980), in-between (Lefebvre 1974; De Certeau 1980; Bhabha 1994; Teyssot 2005). Accordingly, depending on the point of view, interstices can be associated, on the one hand, to absence, interruption and interpolation (Gallet 2002), breaks, dislocations and disjunctions (Foucault 1966; Deleuze 1986; Bhabha 1994), gaps (Lefebvre 1974), leaks and escapes (Handke 1987; Massumi 1992; Tonnelat 1999), ruptures and cuts (Deleuze 1985; Tafuri 1987) or, on the other hand, to tissues – drawing on the connective notion of the anatomical 'interstitial tissues' – links and relations (Bourriaud 1998), interactions (Miller 1939), connections and, by extension, hybridity and the meeting of differences (Remy 1986; Bhabha 1994).

This singular situation of oscillation between contradictory significations would tend to relate the interstitial condition to the phenomena of the undecidable (Derrida 1970; Eisenman 1997, 1998), the uncertain, the vague and the blurred (Solà-Morales 1995; Eisenman 1988a, 1988b, 2003) – an association that would be appropriate as much for the functional allocation of space and its temporal variations, as for the perception of form and the general decoding of the environment. As an 'in-between', the interstitial would tend to embody, as much spatially as temporally, a fundamental condition of indeterminacy. Therefore what is designated by the interstitial relates to different categories of actualization of the notion of interstice understood as an open and relative spatio-temporal condition, activated or created in a body, between parts of a body, or in-between bodies.[3]

But how does this conceptual field translate more specifically to urban discourse? Which figures and vectors emerge from it to qualify or give value to an urban interstitial condition?

The Chicago School: in the crevices of the urban mosaic

We probably owe researchers and sociologists of the Chicago School the first theoretical applications on urban territory of the notion of interstice. According

---

3   The term 'open' refers here to indeterminacy (spatial and/or temporal opening) and to the action of opening (by piercing, boring, etc.). The term 'relative' underlines the importance of the relation to a given context: interstices are defined in relation to a referential environment or to elements constituting this environment, whether they are tangible or not. Finally, the notion of 'body' must here be taken in its broadest sense as the principal part of something, characterized by physical or other properties, without any predetermined scale or state.

to their perspective, associated to 'urban ecology' (Joseph and Grafmeyer 1980), the city is a mosaic of differentiated 'natural areas' (McKenzie 1925) that organize themselves in an order resulting from spontaneous and organic tendencies. It is in accordance with this model that Frederick Thrasher (1963 [1927]: 20) presents the interstitial as the 'most significant concept' of his monumental study on Chicago gangs – the interstitial being used here to define the spatial distribution of gangs that infiltrate the spaces between the zones of the urban mosaic, this 'mosaic of little worlds which touch but do not interpenetrate' (Park 1915: 608). Thrasher broadly defines the interstitial as 'pertaining to spaces that intervene between one thing and another'. Referring to the famous concentric zone model developed by Burgess (1925: 55) to describe Chicago, it is mainly in the 'zone of transition' between the more stable urban zones and the periphery that Thrasher (1963 [1927]: 21) situates this interstitial zone conducive to informal practices and the emergence of gangs. The interstice is therefore primarily portrayed as a socially disorganized environment which contrasts with the better organized areas of the rest of the city. At a smaller scale, the regions bordering certain linear infrastructures (along railroad tracks, canals, streams, business streets, etc.) can also be considered as interstitial territories infiltrating well-organized neighbourhoods. Thrasher associates the dynamics of these unstable zones to the destiny of drifting matter: 'In nature foreign matter tends to collect and cake in every crack, crevice, and cranny – interstices. There are also fissures and breaks in the structure of social organization' (Thrasher 1963 [1927]: 20).

The interstitial region described by Thrasher is a result of the urban process of 'competition for space' that can be associated with the naturalistic analogy dear to the Chicago School. According to this view, in the manner of plants, urban populations compete for the most advantageous spaces. Territories are colonized, populations move and follow one another. Therefore, in the period leading up to a predictable commercial and industrial invasion, entire neighbourhoods will, for example, become gradually deserted. These localized transitory zones correspond, according to Thrasher, to a distinct 'interstitial phase of the city's growth', that is to say a specific period in the evolutionary process of the city. This condition, in both space and time, is generally characterized by poverty, environmental deterioration, populations weakened by constant displacements or conversely the inability to move – an unstructured milieu which provides the ideal breeding grounds for youth gangs that constitute 'one manifestation of the economic, moral, and cultural frontier which marks the interstice'. If the interstitial primarily refers here to a space, it is also inseparable from temporality, from certain protagonists (amongst which the youth gangs) and their practices. Thrasher (1963 [1927]: 46) describes the gang as an 'interstitial group' not only because it occupies the interstitial zones of the city, but also because it is primarily a teenager phenomenon, a manifestation of this existential transitory period of readjustments, search and experimentations that occurs between childhood and adulthood.

So, even if Thrasher generally associates the interstitial to social disorganization, delinquency and, ultimately, crime, this study of young people and their practices opens here and there to more constructive dimensions which mitigate the negative aspects. He notes, for example, that through the gang phenomenon, a more constructive form of alternative social organization is in fact activated: 'the spontaneous effort of boys to create a society for themselves where none adequate to their needs exists'. They are expressing in doing so a resistance against the forces of dissimulation and degradation. As noted by Hannerz, Thrasher announces through these observations the subsequent conclusions reached by William Foote Whyte (1983 [1943]) in his important study *Street Corner Society*, 'the slum has a social organisation of its own, rather than merely disorganization' (Hannerz 1980: 39). Similarly, the landscape of the interstitial zone is seen in a more positive light through the observation of the relation of youth to territory. The neglected areas characterizing these zones, often littered with trash and abandoned objects, in fact constitute playgrounds and adventure 'prairies' that are all the more interesting for youth since they are conducive to the exercise of imagination and a romantic 'quest for new experience' (Thrasher 1963 [1927]: 68) (Figure 2.2). This perspective is reflected in the names used to designate the three main territories occupied by gangs in the transition zone. Indeed, if the denominations 'North Side Jungles', 'West Side Wilderness' and 'South Side Badlands' refer to a 'wild' geography consistent with the Chicago School's naturalist referent, they also fully acknowledge the imaginary that animates these young people in their explorations of the city's urban mosaic crevices (Thrasher 1963 [1927]: 6, 85).

Still referring to this naturalization of the urban phenomenon, Maurice Halbwachs (1932) points to another analogy in his commentary on Chicago School research. As emphasized by Grafmeyer and Joseph (1984: 25) Halbwachs indeed offers the 'organicist metaphor' of the *sponge* to visualize the image of the city offered by Chicago School research. Discussing the high rate of 'foreigners' in Chicago's population, he observes how unlike in the ancient cities where people of foreign origin were relegated beyond the city walls, these populations are rather incorporated within voids distributed across the substance of the contemporary city in a sort of inner and reticular margin:

> We must indeed not be too surprised by the proportionally high numbers of foreigners recorded in Chicago [...] In ancient cities and even in certain Middle-Age cities they remained outside, they did not dwell within the walls. Here, they enter and set up, the reason being that the periphery is extremely extensive, that only half the city has been built, that we have confined within it empty spaces, factories, railroad tracks, interstitial zones – places within the city that are not part of the city, that do not yet belong to its flesh and blood: such as those simple organisms, full of holes that, although internal, are bathed in the environment and the exterior liquid. (Halbwachs 1932: 324–25)

Even if it is not further developed by Halbwachs, this reference to the alveolar and porous structure of the sponge indirectly contributes to enriching Thrasher's

Photo by Author

Photo by Author

"PRAIRIES" WHERE GANG BOYS PLAY

The boys call these neglected open spaces, numerous in gangland, "prairies." That they are full of rubbish and discarded objects only makes them more interesting as playgrounds. Below is shown the ball diamonds of the Rinkus gang on property being held for industrial purposes.

Figure 2.2   Images and caption from F.M. Thrasher, *The Gang. A Study of 1313 Gangs in Chicago*. The University of Chicago Press, 1936 [1927].

concept of interstice.[4] According to the perspective opened by Halbwachs, the interstitial is not so much an accidental chasm in the city's mosaic as a structural component that actively participates in the urban dynamic. By describing holes or cavities that are at once internal to the urban 'organism' and bathed in exterior flows, Halbwachs further questions the centre/periphery dialectic that had already been previously challenged by the notion of the city as a mosaic.

This image of the city as a sponge-like body opens a new field of thought around the interstitial by dissociating it from a perspective that tends to reduce it to a spatial symptom of urban pathologies. Carrying on in this regard the work of the Chicago School, Jean Remy and Liliane Voyé (1981) relate interstitial space to the notion of 'secondarity': the secondary spaces to which the interstices correspond would only make sense through the existence of the primarity of power and its drive for control and order against which they are 'a possibility of gap, of a distance, a possibility to do and to be other things and multiple things'. The *terrain vague* is for Remy and Voyé (1981: 71–73) a typical example of an interstitial space that, as an 'undesignated' space, constitutes an opportunity for creative escapes, a counterpoint to pervasive normality.

A similar idea of the interstice as a differential space had already been referred to by Marx on a socio-economic level. In the first chapter of *Das Kapital*, published in 1863 – in English in 1886 – Marx uses the concepts of 'interstices' and 'pores' to describe how 'trading nations' emerged in the ancient world.[5] This specific use of the interstitial figure will be later acknowledged and put to work by Fredric Jameson (1985) when defending, in the context of late capitalism, an alternative and critical position. For Jameson, the interstitial suggests an 'enclave theory' favourable to social transition. He puts forward the utopian possibility of constructing ideological or material enclaves acting as centres of transformation. The 'concrete existence of radically different spaces' in 'the Second and Third Worlds' would be for Jameson what objectively opens the possibility for the development of 'counter-hegemonic values' within the First World itself. The interstitial figure here suggests a mode of social resistance mainly operating in space. Interstitial enclaves would be 'laboratories in which original social relations of the future are being worked out' (Jameson 1985: 72–73).[6] In the wake of Chicago School sociologists, the interstitial condition therefore appears as a

---

4   At another scale, it is also a positive perspective on the 'porous' quality of urban substance that Walter Benjamin and Asja Lacis express in an article on Naples in 1925: 'As porous as this stone is the architecture. Building and action interpenetrate ... In everything they preserve the scope to become a theater of new, unforeseen constellations. The stamp of the definitive is avoided' (Benjamin and Lacis 1978 [1925]).

5   Karl Marx (1886 [1863], book I, tome I): 'Trading nations, properly so called, exist in the ancient world only in its interstices, like the gods of Epicurius in the Intermundia, or like Jews in the pores of Polish society.'

6   A similar use of the interstitial theme is developed by Nicolas Bourriaud (1998) in art and by Kenneth Frampton (1980, 1988) in architecture.

territory for experimentation. In this perspective, beyond the spatial aspects, the interstitial condition also seems to be strongly linked to practices attempting to reinvent the city by inhabiting it differently. So how does this reflect at the level of those who produce urban substance? What about the emergence of a discourse on the interstitial condition among architects and urban planners?

Contemporary architectural discourses: between conjunction and disjunction

No matter how we approach the subject, be it through a preoccupation for the perception of space and form, for the possibilities it offers in respect to spatial practices and occupation, for the exploitation of a biotic potential or for symbolic considerations, the interstitial theme continues to be characterized at a theoretical level by the paradigmatic debate that has thrown modernism, especially in architecture and urbanism, into turmoil during the past 50 years. This debate is part of a critical re-evaluation of modernity's spatial legacy and its humanist ideals. As to the interstitial condition, this translates into radical differences in the approaches to projectual issues. Should the emphasis be on the articulation of transitions and connections or, conversely, on exploring the potentials of the void, the rupture and the accidental? Are these contrasted perspectives compatible? This not only concerns the question of 'urban voids' (created or found), or the conceptualization of the architectural project – it also affects our comprehension, experience and appreciation of the spatio-temporal dynamics of the contemporary city.

In reaction to the Modern Movement's vision of planning, we already see at the end of the 1940s the emergence of a critical sensitivity in, for example, a project like Aldo Van Eyck's playground network that he progressively develops in Amsterdam in the constellation of residual sites that punctuate the post-war landscape of the Dutch metropolis (Tzonis and Lefaivre 1999; Lefaivre and De Roode 2002). The programmatic preference given here to play (Huizinga 1951) extends and supports the colonization of the city by children, giving them an opportunity for experimentation (Van Eyck 1998 [1956]). This project, developed until 1978 with more than 700 playgrounds, presents a major change in attitude compared to the monolithic spatial planning strategies previously favoured by the CIAM[7] and the Athens Charter (Le Corbusier 1957 [1942]). The interstitial condition which had never really been considered in itself by modernist planners as offering projectual and experiential potential becomes, in Van Eyck's project, the starting point for an alternative and empirical approach to planning which focuses on promoting a ludic appropriation of the city.

The ideas of philosopher Martin Buber are some of the most important stepping stones from which Van Eyck develops, from the 1950s onward, the

---

7 The CIAM or Congrès Internationaux d'Architecture Moderne (International Congresses of Modern Architecture), active 1928–59.

theme of the 'in-between'.[8] Buber's (1937 [1922], 2002 [1942]) humanist thought – discovered by Van Eyck while he was studying at ETH Zurich from 1938 to 1942 – is characterized by the importance given to notions of dialogue, meeting and reciprocity. The 'between' (*das Zwischen*) is in the forefront of Buber's thought as a realm of relation, it is 'not a make-shift but a real place and a bearer of interhuman events' (Buber 2002 [1942]). This dialogical conception of the in-between gives Van Eyck the inspiration for the fundamental architectural issue he will associate with this notion: the conceptual extension of the idea of 'doorstep'. Indeed, Van Eyck answers the Smithsons' idea of 'doorstep' – mentioned in 1953 (CIAM 9, Aix-en-Provence) to express the importance of the relation between house and street – by developing *la plus grande réalité du seuil* (the greater reality of the doorstep) (CIAM 10 Dubrovnik, 1956) that acts for his practice as a conceptual, experiential and formal leitmotif.[9] In this perspective, as expressed by Van Eyck (1959: 27) in Otterlo at the last CIAM, 'to establish the "in-between" is to reconcile conflicting polarities', that is, to 're-establish the dual phenomena', by providing a 'place where they can interchange'. Further, by relating in this way the realm of the in-between or intermediary to the notion of place, Van Eyck (1960, 1962b) is essentially referring to a 'space in the image of man'. If the realm of the in-between as a twinning of multiple significations is related to the notion of ambivalence or ambiguity – 'the gratifying sense of uncertainty' (Van Eyck 1963) – it is still the comforting objectives of 'balance' and 'articulation' that in the end motivate Van Eyck's (1960, 1962a, 1963, 2008 [1962]) creation of form. For there is truly in Van Eyck's work a will to give the in-between a tangible 'shape' (Strauven 1998: 354–60). This is notable in the importance given to the 'configuration of intermediary places clearly defined', the configuration of spaces dilating the doorstep line into different shapes to mark and facilitate the 'transitions' by articulating them (Van Eyck 1960, 1962b, 1979). Therefore, even though Tzonis and Lefaivre (1999; Lefaivre and De Roode 2002) are justified in underlining Van Eyck's major contribution to the development of a conception of planning sensitive to the interstitial dimension of the city, it seems however that the Dutch architect never accepted or defended the virtually destabilizing aspect of this concept beyond the empiric demonstration of the projectual potential of urban interstices as a network or constellation of public places.

The planner and researcher Kevin Lynch, through his reflection on open space in the middle of the 1960s, tends to approach in a more clearly positive

---

8   Martin Buber was an Austrian-born Jewish philosopher. Concerning the relation between Jewish tradition and a space of threshold and 'in-between', see the 'thoughts on Jewish space' by French architect Antoine Grumbach (2007).

9   Before the Smithsons, Gutman and Manz, during a preparatory meeting for CIAM 9 in Sigtuna (Sweden), had already in 1952 confirmed Van Eyck's theoretical interest for the notion of in-between by quoting Martin Buber in reference to this subject during their presentation.

way the urban contribution of spaces that have a residual, an ambiguous or an undetermined character. Lynch (1991b [1965]: 397) suggests indeed that open space is 'the negative, extensive, loose, uncommitted complement to the system of committed land uses that make a city region'. Lynch aims to extend the concept of open space to places that are very different from the more or less normalized green spaces to which it is usually associated. This is what makes him defend the importance of unprogrammed spaces open to change, spontaneous manipulations, destruction, ambiguity and the risk of adventure – conditions that are close enough to those that Thrasher (1963 [1927]) associates with the 'wild' and 'interstitial areas' where youth gangs can satisfy their 'quest for new experience', a quest for which, as underlined by Lynch (1991a [1965]: 93), 'a waste lot may be preferable to a rose garden'.

This sensitivity to urban interstitiality is activated at other levels in landscape architecture and environmental design practice. These are the biotic, aesthetic, symbolic and structuring potentials of the 'wild' life gaps which burrow in the city's fabric and arouse projectual imagination. For example, at the metropolitan scale, various urban planning projects aim at organizing into networks urban interstices seen as sources of biodiversity or as new opportunities for public spaces (Décarie 1993; L'Atelier 1999). The interest in urban wilderness constitutes here an important axis for the development of the interstitial theme. If botanists, since the second half of the nineteenth century, have been interested in urban 'vagabond' flora (Lizet 1989, 1999), the theoretical and practical approaches of contemporary landscape designers like Louis-Guillaume Le Roy or Gilles Clément have more recently contributed to establish an ecological aesthetic that values the interstitial condition as an important place for the effervescence of life (Le Roy 1978, 2002; Clément 1985, 1991 1999, 2004). This aesthetic is conveyed in Clément's work through concepts like the 'Garden in Movement' and the 'Third Landscape', that involve a dynamic management of the *friche* (fallow land) and ways of perceiving and intervening that are open to uncertainty and transformation (Clément 1991, 1995, 2004) (Figure 2.3).

The influence of the ruderal model also goes beyond the field of landscape design to appear in urbanism and architecture. It is the case for example of the pioneering work of Lucien Kroll (2001, 2002) – a champion of a participative approach – who, since the 1960s, in various types of projects, has called for a process of appropriation by the inhabitants similar to 'a sort of slow green recolonization like those observed in *terrains vagues*' where 'everything becomes passage, movement, successive advances, continuous mutations' (Kroll 2001: 53–54) (Figures 2.4). On a more iconographic level – from fracture images to vegetation-covered ruins – the ruderal reference (Hladik 2000) has also been present since the 1970s in numerous architectural projects like SITE's 'de-architecture' (Wines 1975, 1987), Hans Hollein's figures of fissure and erosion (Shullin Jewellery Shop 1972–74), Peter Cook's projects designed around the notion of 'disintegration' (Cook 1980) or Lebbeus Woods' (1991) and Coop Himmelblau's (1992) parasitic and fragmented imagery.

Figure 2.3   **Gilles Clément, Garden in Movement, Parc André-Citroën, Paris, 1992 (photo by Luc Lévesque, 2001).**

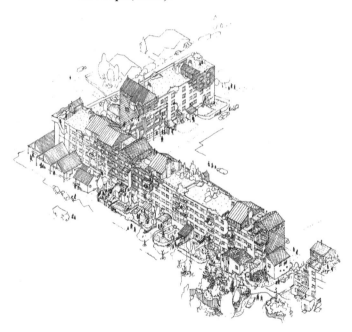

Figure 2.4   **(a) Lucien Kroll, Perseigne Development (ZUP reorganization), Alençon, France, 1978 (drawing by Atelier Lucien Kroll).**

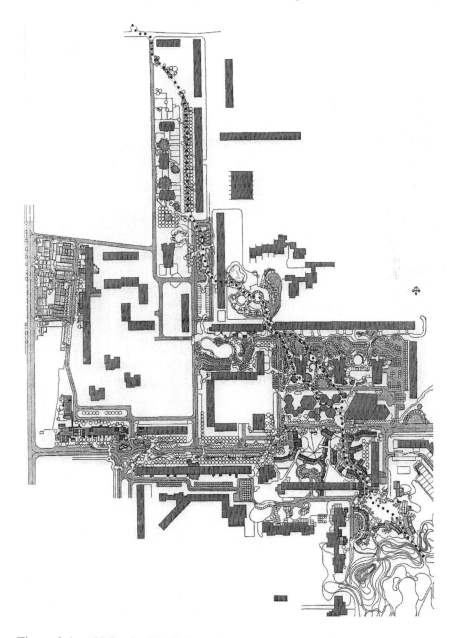

Figure 2.4   (b) Lucien Kroll, Perseigne Development (ZUP reorganization), Alençon, France, 1978 (drawing by Atelier Lucien Kroll).

In the 1970s and 1980s, different positions began to be articulated, diverging from the emphasis given by Van Eyck and *Team 10*[10] to the idea of in-between as a reconciliation of polarities (Van Eyck 1959, 1960, 1962a, 1962b, 2008 [1962]). Such a perspective was developed for example around the architectural journal *Oppositions* published in New York by the IAUS (Institute for Architecture and Urban Studies) and directed by Peter Eisenman (1977). This point of view distances itself from the humanist idealism pursued by *Team 10*, trying instead to come to terms with the problematic aspects of the Modern Movement and of modern society in general. The interstitial condition then tends to express itself as an unresolved residue produced by the exacerbation of differences, an indeterminate zone inseparable from the blurring or transgression of the architectural limit. It appears in the diagrammatic spacing generated by absence or disjunction (Tschumi 1976, 1977; Koolhaas 1985c, 1995d [1985]; Eisenman 1988a, 1988b, 1988c). These approaches look with new eyes and in a more positive way than *Team 10* (Smithson 1968) – or in another vein, than post-modernism (Krier 1978) – at the spatial brutality of the 1950 and 1960s neo-modernist urban developments and, more generally, at the destabilizing and disquieting character of the contemporary world (Eisenman 1988a, 1988b, 1989; Koolhaas 1991a [1985]; Vidler 1992, 2000).

It is in this perspective that the 'void' generated by a method as decried in the West as the *tabula rasa* fascinated Rem Koolhaas (1992a, 1995b) for its planned or indeterminate programmatic potential. The same goes for 'supposedly lost or residual space'–intensely colonized 'friction zones'–next, for example, to congested highway infrastructures of an African metropolis such as Lagos (Koolhaas 2000, 2002).[11] Following a similar interest for openness and indeterminacy, it is not by making a clean sweep of Tourcoing's existing old centre of popular entertainment (1905) that Bernard Tschumi wins the 1991 competition for Le Fresnoy National Studio for the Contemporary Arts, but rather by superimposing a new roof upon the old roofs of the abandoned complex. The proposal offers in this way an in-

---

10   The Team 10 group formed during CIAM 9 (Aix-en-Provence, 1953) and CIAM 10 (Dubrovnik, 1956). The principal members of Team 10 were AldoVan Eyck, Alison and Peter Smithson, Jaap Bakema, Shadrach Woods, Georges Candilis and Giancarlo De Carlo. Many other architects would, as participants, join Team 10 meetings. See Alison Smithson (1968).

11   Reacting to the words of Peter Smithson, who was complaining about the lack of attention given to 'the space between' in architecture and planning – 'Most of the world out there is a nightmare [...] There is no sense of the collective, the space between...' – as reported by Hans Ulrich Obrist, Rem Koolhaas has the following answer: 'I think there is something touching about Smithson and Team 10: they were obsessed with conceptualizing new types and families of connections. And my feeling about their residue, their effect, is both more cynical and more optimistic because I think, to a large extent, things connect in spite of the efforts of the architect [...] In Lagos, connections proliferate in spite of the infrastructure [...] That is typically one of the aspects of the profession that is fighting a rearguard action because it denies all the connections that are already in place already in supposedly lost or residual space' (Koolhaas 2000: 69–70).

between or interstitial space between these two layers as a functionally undefined 'supplement', a conceptual and experiential gain for the project (Fleischer 1993; Tschumi 1993), a theme that will be explicitly pursued and expressed in Tschumi's (2001) subsequent work (Figures 2.5).

For both Tschumi and Koolhaas, the *Parc de la Villette* competition – held in Paris in 1982 and eventually won by Tschumi – was a defining moment in the exploration of programmatic indeterminacy. This strategic opening to process and indeterminacy was here broadly related to the numerous activities that coexist in a city and make it stimulating. The 'Elegy for the Vacant Lot' (Koolhaas 1991b [1985]), where Koolhaas revisits his competition proposal, falls within this perspective. For this competition, the OMA/Koolhaas team[12] put forth a conceptual projection on the La Villette site of the programmatic congestion of a New York skyscraper – the *Downtown Athletic Club* as presented in *Delirious New York* (Koolhaas 1978). Transposed onto La Villette's *terrain vague*, the diagram corresponding to the section of this singular accumulation of programmes only retains from architecture its organizing principle: the bands. Freed from gravitational pull, the skyscraper's 'flipped' floors become, in La Villette, highly permeable boundaries, interstitial friction lines between heterogeneous environments. The project suggests the actualization of a 'congestion without matter' (Koolhaas 1995d [1985]) organized as a hybrid pattern similar to Deleuze and Guattari's (1980: 474) *crazy patchwork* that accounted for potential combinations of 'smooth and striated spaces'. The idea here is to systematically use the clash of differences to catalyse the emergence of unpredictable situations. This shift from an architectural paradigm towards its dematerialization allows among other things – and while never excluding the option of actually building – to open the field of architectural exploration to a fluidity that is in sync with the dynamic characterizing the contemporary urban territory, a state of indeterminacy encapsulated in the conceptual figure of the *terrain vague*.[13] Design and planning can then be understood as a series of tactical actions, inflexions or modulations (Koolhaas 1995f [1994]; Cache 1995; Kwinter 1995, Allen 1995; Corner 1999; Lévesque 1999).

---

12   OMA or The Office for Metropolitan Architecture is the Rotterdam-based architecture firm of Rem Koolhaas founded in 1975 with Elia Zenghelis, Madelon Vriesendorp and Zoe Zenghelis.

13   Later, during one of the ANY international symposiums – Anyplace, Montreal, 1994 – Solà-Morales (1995) notes the appropriateness, at the levels of both theory and project, of the terrain vague as a conceptual and landscape expression of urban interstitiality. Under his initiative, the terrain vague is one of six themes around which a reflection on architecture and the contemporary city is articulated at the 19th Congress of the International Union of Architects (UIA) in Barcelona (Solà-Morales and Costa 1996). In the late 1990s and early 2000s, the interstitial condition further catalysed a diverse set of theoretical and critical proposals (Moralès 1997; Zardini 1997, 1999; Beguin 1997; Leong 1998; Lévesque 1999; Daskalakis et al. 2001; Tonnelat 1999, 2003) in addition to being given a prominent place at Europan, on of the most important competition of ideas on urbanism and architecture open to teams of young designers in Europe (Europan 4-5-6, 1997–99).

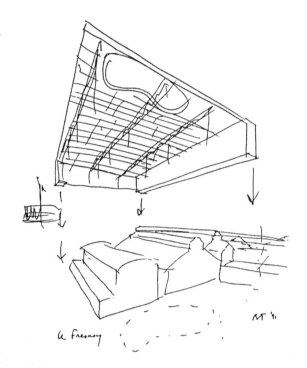

Figure 2.5   (a,b) Bernard Tschumi, Le Fresnoy National Studio for the Contemporary Arts, Tourcoing, France, 1991–1994 (a. drawing by Bernard Tschumi; b. photo by Peter Mauss/ ESTO).

Figure 2.5 **(c,d) Bernard Tschumi, Le Fresnoy National Studio for the Contemporary Arts, Tourcoing, France, 1991–1994 (c. photo by Robert Cesar; d. photo by Luc Lévesque).**

There are also certain specific urban situations that, through the multiple expressions they generated over the years, contributed to define the interstitial condition as a landscape figure and an important urban issue. The case of Berlin is particularly fertile in this regard. Before and after the fall of the Berlin Wall, from the preparation in the 1980s of the International Building Exhibition (*Internationale Bauausstellung* 1984/1987, or IBA[14]) and throughout the 1990s, Berlin was the home to intense debates concerning the future of the central districts torn apart during the Second World War and the East–West political breakdown (Rogier 1996; Huyssen 1997; Robin 2001). Diverging from attempts to repair and 'reconstruct' the pre-war city in a more or less literal or 'critical' way (Krier 1978; Kleihues *et al.* 1987; Stimman 1992), different alternative positions aim, on the contrary, at exploiting the inherent potential of the massive stretches of interstitial territory left by the Wall and the multiple holes interspersed across adjoining neighbourhoods. These alternative positions involve diverse vectors of landscape valorization related to programmatic, mnestic and textual potentials.

Along these lines, Rem Koolhaas (1995e [1993]) is in some ways a precursor when, at the beginning of the 1970s while still a student at the Architectural Association in London, he proposed to document the 'Berlin Wall as Architecture' during a field trip that will prove to be essential for the ulterior development of his thought. As Koolhaas (1991b [1985], 1995e [1993]) will later many times affirm, what is fascinating about the Wall and the 'highly charged emptiness' of the fractured urban territories it goes through, is that the 'void' – the 'absence' of architectural substance – 'can be stronger than presence'. This revelation was developed a few years later in 1977 in the context of his participation in a workshop led by Oswald Mathias Ungers (1978) in Berlin. Resulting from a study of existing conditions, Berlin is approached 'as a city-archipelago' (Ungers *et al.* 1978), a potential set of singular architectural islands 'floating in a post-architectural landscape' made of 'large green interstices' where 'everything is possible'. In these 'interspaces', a sort of 'conceptual Nevadas where the laws of architecture are suspended', the existence would be 'stimulated by a transitory way of life', pure urban intensities devoid of architectural hindrances (Ungers *et al.* 1978; Koolhaas 1991b [1985], 1989). If a similar vision was, as we have seen earlier, proposed at the beginning of the 1980s in La Villette, Koolhaas also during this same period had the opportunity to present a variation specific to Berlin in an IBA competition targeting the Kreuzberg area (Koolhaas *et al.* 1983). In this context, Koolhaas refuses the 'reconstruction' effort advocated by the IBA which 'in the name of history' is trying to reconstruct the pre-war urban fabric, paradoxically erasing the traces – and more importantly the potentials – resulting from the significant post-war turmoil. OMA's proposal for the Kochstrasse/ Friedrichstrasse sector – that will not be selected – tries to capitalize on the spatial variations offered by the 'complex and ambiguous' urban condition of this part

---

14   The IBA architecture exhibition is constituted of projects – most of which result from competitions – built in different target areas in Berlin. First announced for 1984, this exhibit will finally be inaugurated in 1987.

of Kreuzberg next to the Wall. OMA's project, which does not limit itself to one block, in fact puts forth a framework that 'beyond the literalness of the street plan, relates to existing buildings – whether or not they conform the grid – and creates anchors for new insertions' (Koolhaas *et al.* 1983), new insertions that would leave visible the traces of the existing voids. Anticipating a possible future reunification of the two city halves, Koolhaas' proposal also imagines the 'nothingness' of the Eastern part of the Wall zone as 'a narrow linear park encircling West Berlin [...] [that] would preserve a memory of recent phases of the city – the Cold War – without becoming an explicit monument'. Berlin's singular interstitial condition is here considered at once as a historical trace that should not be hidden and a programmatic opportunity to 'cultivate' urban 'emptiness' (Koolhaas 2000: 85).

In the footsteps of Berlin's teachings, an entire series of Koolhaas/OMA projects was subsequently developed as different variations on the potential of an 'emptiness [...] that is not empty' (Koolhaas, 1991b [1985]). In 1987, for example, in the context of an urbanism competition for the extension of the Melun-Sénart *ville nouvelle* (new town) in the south-east suburbs of Paris, Koolhaas establishes a strategy based on an interlinking of strategic voids that constitutes a sort of inversed variation of the 'city as an archipelago' Berlin diagram. In Melun-Sénart, as in Lucio Fontana's slashed paintings – a reference acknowledged by Koolhaas (1991) – the interstices are 'structuring' and at the forefront, giving architectural substance a quasi-residual status. Of diverse configurations, these bands containing voids protect the significant elements of the existing agricultural landscape, historic buildings and ecological resources, trace corridors of controlled intervention along the major circulation axis or still, delimit programmatic zones where collective components can be given priority (Figures 2.6). In doing so, this system of protected 'voids' defines an 'archipelago of residue', residual islands that could have independently and freely been developed, a sort of architectural *friches* left to the unforeseeable movements of urban development. It is a related 'strategy of the void' that was developed by OMA at the architectural scale for their TGB [*Très Grande Bibliothèque*] competition project in Paris (1989): 'a solid block of information' where 'the major public spaces are defined as absence of building, voids carved out of the information solid' (Koolhaas 1995a: 616) (Figures 2.7). If one can see in this scheme the porous figure of the sponge, it is the 'infiltration' potential of a light and liquid urban substance that was explored a few years later in Yokohama (1992), where a 'programmatic lava' invades 'every gap and slit' of a found spatio-temporal condition (Koolhaas 1992b, 1995c). This infiltrating movement can be also seen – similar to Lucio Fontana's *concetto spaziale* of the hole – as a vector that pierces and passes through the architectural mass, a theme that was extensively developed by OMA in examples ranging from the circulatory cuts of the Rotterdam Kunsthal (1992) (Moussette 2003) to the various pedestrian 'trajectories' piercing and 'snaking through' programmes contained in platonic volumes, from the Bangkok Hyperbuilding (1996) to the Chicago IIT Campus Center (2003) or, to return to Berlin, the Netherlands Embassy (2004), where a 'continuous promenade is excavated out of a cube of generic office floors' and 'meanders through the building' (Koolhaas 1999).

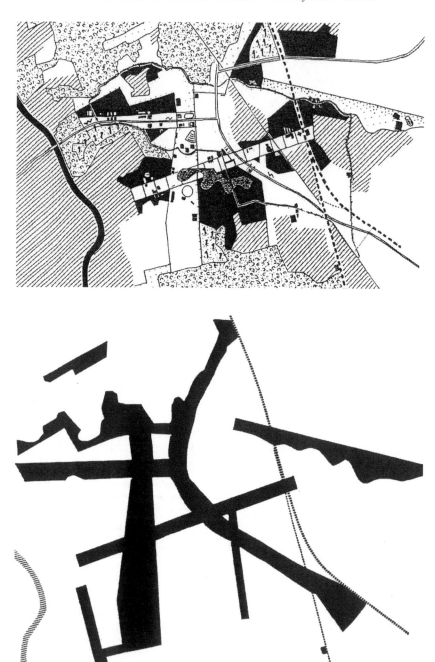

Figure 2.6   (a,b)   Rem   Koolhaas/OMA,   Ville   Nouvelle   Melun-Sénart
(masterplan), Melun, France, 1987. Plan of phase 2 and system
of linear voids (drawings © OMA).

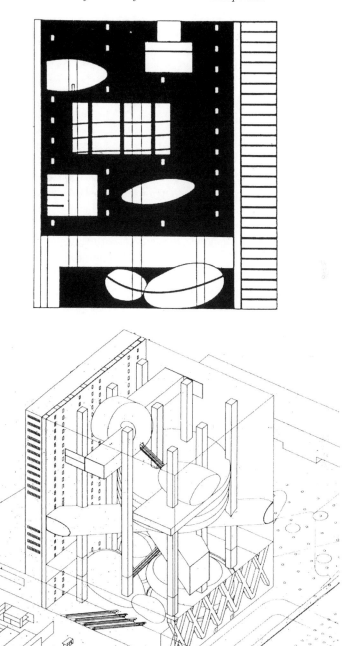

Figure 2.7 (a,b) Rem Koolhaas/OMA, TGB [Très Grande Bibliothèque], Paris, 1989. Section (wall 5) and axonometric (drawings © OMA).

If Berlin's interstitial condition strongly marked Koolhaas' urban vision, it was also very important for Peter Eisenman. Indeed, for perhaps the first time in such a sustained way, the New York architect's conceptual and abstract approach to form is tested in the context of an urban site steeped in history. This is a central phase in his 1980s series of projects known as the 'Cities of Artificial Excavation' (Bédard *et al.* 1994),[15] a name directly derived from his Berlin proposal for the South Friedrichstadt IBA Competition in Kreuzberg. The project expresses the historical importance of Berlin's interstitial character, its suspension 'in time and space' (Eisenman 1980b). This choice is all the more significant since it is made in the context of a competition where the basic premises – as presented more or less tacitly in the IBA's discourse – seem, as we have seen before, to be encouraging the opposite approach of obliterating the traces of indetermination characteristic of Berlin's history to make place for a literal and unbroken reconstitution of its urban fabric.

The site targeted by the competition is adjacent to the Berlin Wall and the famous crossing point Checkpoint Charlie. Eisenman (1983) notes the singular sedimentation of memories[16] as well as 'the dual condition of severance and connection' presented by the site. Similarly to Koolhaas, the American architect avoids reconstituting an 'ideal' built perimeter, his proposition, as he himself maintains, 'eschews patching up, filling in, restoring – which suffocate memory'. The three remaining buildings that occupy only part of the block next to the Berlin Wall are instead integrated to an 'archaeological earthwork' (Eisenman 1980b), a sort of 'garden' of walls resulting from the overlaying of two reference grids that are offset from each other and under tension: the first, resulting from the orientation of the existing buildings on the site, represents the notion of 'place' and of 'memory'; the other, abstract and neutral, based on the universal transverse Mercator grid, establishes the notions of 'anti-memory', of 'every place' and 'no place' (Figures 2.8). Oscillating in this way between 'memory' and 'anti-memory', and between 'place' and 'no place', Eisenman's proposal does not try to create a comforting and falsely homogeneous stabilization of the indeterminate context characterizing Friedrichstadt and Berlin, but rather, gives it a new consistence by artificially reproducing these active elements and using them as the project's very substance. Introduced by Eisenman during the design process, the idea of 'vibration'[17] gives another indication on the nature of the 'void interstices' that the

---

15   In 1989, the completion of the Wexner Center (Colombus, Ohio) – winning entry of a 1983 competition (Eisenman 1984 [1983]) –marks the conclusion of Eisenman's artificial excavations. The idea of an interstitial trajectory cutting between the joined volumes of the two existing auditoriums is one of this project's most striking features.

16   'Berlin […] the memory of its own interrupted history. The competition site – the intersection of Friedrichstrasse and the Berlin Wall – is the paradigmatic locus of that memory. Certainly it represents the place of the city's most significant and most compacted transformations' (Eisenman 1980b).

17   Hand-written note on a drawing, dated 30 October 1980: 'Vibration along a line on a different grid from the Wall'. Peter D. Eisenman Collection, Canadian Centre for

project's 'grid overlay' aims to generate (Eisenman 1980b). It is not the perception of a static spatial condition that is here sought but rather the perception of an interference field, a blurred zone resulting from the encounter of the different superposed layers. The archaeological narrative offered by Eisenman at the IBA competition is based on an open urban stratification process – a vision that is realized through the both fleeting and stratified figure of the 'palimpsest'. In this perspective, if the configurations of the Berlin 'archaeological earthwork' can be understood as an overlaying of traces containing heterogeneous spatio-temporal conditions, the 'interstices' accompanying this 'dislocation of place' (Eisenman 1982) conceptually become the 'faults' (Lassus 1998 [1989]) through which passages could be activated between the different virtual worlds signalled by these traces. Eisenman's projectual narrative seems here, in some respects, to echo the words of Homer, the old poet of *Der Himmel über Berlin* (1987) (Figure 2.1a) who, walking through the Potsdamer Platz wastelands, evokes the interstices – 'Why doesn't everyone see them...?' – giving access to the 'land of storytelling' and Berlin's hidden geography.[18]

After the amputated completion of Eisenman's project in 1987 – no 'garden of walls', but rather a slightly offset housing building – it is Daniel Libeskind's 1989 winning project at the competition for the Berlin Museum (eventually to become the Jewish Museum Berlin completed in 1999) that carried out the first important architectural reinvention of Berlin's singular interstitial condition (Figures 2.9). Libeskind (2000a [1994]) indeed finds in Berlin's turbulent history a particularly interesting urban condition to imagine project schemes that 'navigate between the Scylla and Charybdis' of historicist nostalgia and *tabula rasa*, as he demonstrated a few years later in the Alexanderplatz Urban Development competition. In fact, his suggestion is to accept Berlin's fractured past and incorporate its memory as a fundamental aspect of the project's spatial experience. This dynamic integration of history therefore modulates the entire Museum project's strategy and one of its most important themes: to restore the presence of absence, to make visible the invisible (Libeskind 1990 [1989]).

Two lines architecturally materialize this conceptual programme: 'a tortuous line continuing indefinitely', and 'a straight line broken into many fragments'. The project that Libeskind (1990 [1989], 2000b) entitles 'Between the Lines' (*Zwischen den Linien*) plays itself out in the interplay of these two lines: a first line that explores Berlin's Jewish history in the space of a winding path, and a second line that contains a void – the abysmal emptiness that represents the

---

Architecture, Montreal, DR1991: 0018: 018. This annotated drawing appeared in the catalogue of the Eisenman CCA exhibit held in 1994 (Bédard et al. 1994: 91).

18 Excerpt of the old poet's words. The movie, by Wim Wenders and co-written with Peter Handke, premiered in 1987, the same year the IBA officially inaugurated its projects in Berlin: 'even Berlin has its hidden passes. And it's only there that my country, the land of storytelling, begins. Why doesn't everyone see from earliest childhood, the passes, portals and crevices, on the ground and above in the sky?'

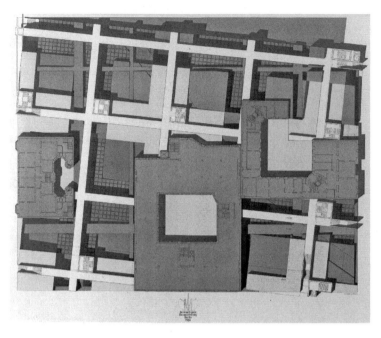

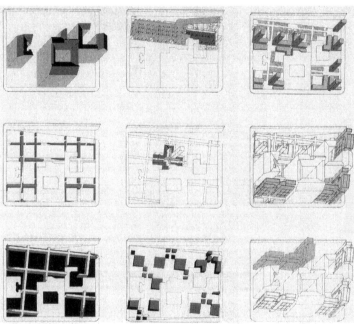

Figure 2.8   **(a,b) Peter Eisenman, City of Artificial Excavation, IBA Berlin 1984, South Friedrichstadt, Berlin, 1980–1981. Site plan and conceptuals diagrams (drawings © Eisenman architects).**

removal of Jewish presence during the Holocaust – and that crosses the first line (Figure 2.9cd). The mysterious presence of this void in the middle of the building makes more present the apparently arbitrary trajectories and traces that criss-cross it, leading one to believe that these signs could in fact bear witness to the almost imperceptible relationships that discretely inhabit the site.

Located in the Kreuzberg area, less than a kilometre away from Check Point Charlie and the Wall, the heterogeneous site is rather typical of disrupted post-war Berlin: a mix of urban traces of the nineteenth and twentieth centuries, open spaces created by wartime destruction, massive examples of 1960s modern urbanism and a few specimens of the 'critical reconstruction' advocated by Kleihues and the IBA in the 1980s (Figures 2.9ab). More specifically, the project wedges itself in between an architectural relic of the Baroque city, the Collegienhaus (1735)[19] – former Berlin Museum and part of the new museum complex – and a 'city in the park' (Rowe and Koetter 1978) modernistic development consisting of 12- to 15-storey tall apartment blocks. The broken-line configuration of the Museum acts as a link between these two urban poles. Beyond the ideal of the modern city or the multiple variations associated with a return to the traditional city, Libeskind (1990 [1989]: 169) is here proposing an architectural expression that seems to arise from the fracture between these two extremes 'exposing the vitality and multidimensionality of Berlin'.

At the end of the twentieth century, Berlin represented the possibilities offered by a mutant urban condition emerging from the upheavals of contemporary history. In an interview with architect Hans Kollhoff, cinematographer Wim Wenders (1988) – who contributed to the 'invention' of Berlin's interstitial condition with *Der Himmel über Berlin* – emphasized the importance, for Berlin's urban life of 'cracks' and 'gaps in the planning.'[20] In 1999, ten years after the fall of the Wall and when the corporate reconstruction of Potsdamer Platz and its surroundings was, despite the triumphant presence of architecture, leaving an after-taste of simulacrum and amnesia (Robin 2001), the construction of the Jewish Museum was one of the rare architectural manifestations that did not deny Berlin's faults, but instead found new ways of leaving them open.[21]

---

19   From outside, the link with the old Collegienhaus is invisible; the new museum doesn't have any exterior public entrance: 'The existing building is tied to the extension underground, preserving the contradictory autonomy of both on the surface, while binding the two together in depth. Under-Over-Ground Museum. Like Berlin and its Jews, the common burden – this insupportable, immeasurable, unshareable burden – is outlined in the exchanges between two architectures and forms which are not reciprocal: cannot be exchanged for each other' (Libeskind 1990 [1989]: 169).

20   In addition, in a conversation held in Montreal in 2001, Wim Wenders explicitly told us that, for him, one of the only post-1989 projects that expresses the importance of the interstitial condition of Berlin was Daniel Libeskind's Jewish Museum.

21   If Libeskind's architecture is sensitive to Berlin's interstitial condition, his approach is very different from that of someone like Rem Koolhaas, for whom Libeskind's answer would still be too dependent on architectural substance : 'For Libeskind, emptiness

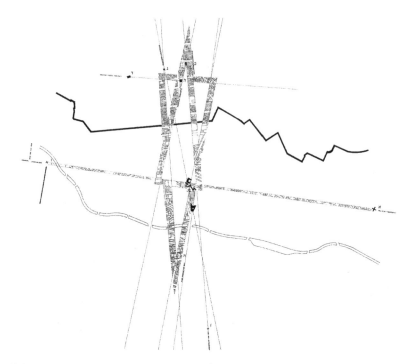

Figure 2.9   (a,b) **Daniel Libeskind, Jewish Museum Berlin, Berlin, 1988–1999. Star Matrix (symbolic siteplan) and aerial view (a. drawing © Studio Daniel Libeskind; b. photo by Guenter Schneider).**

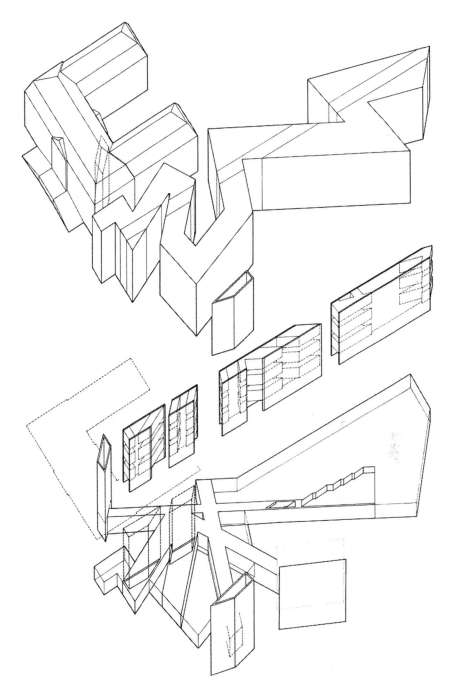

Figure 2.9   (c) Daniel Libeskind, Jewish Museum Berlin, Berlin, 1988–1999.
Axonometric (drawing © Studio Daniel Libeskind).

Figure 2.9   (d) Daniel Libeskind, Jewish Museum Berlin, Berlin, 1988–1999. The Void (photo by Torsten Seidel).

This evocation of the Berlin case closes the panoramic overview of a few practices and conceptual approaches related to the interstitial condition in landscape, architecture and urban planning. The interstitial manifests itself in many diverse ways in urban discourse, especially from the second half of the twentieth century onward. This large body of expressive mediations has contributed, directly and indirectly, to 'invent' this condition as a characteristic landscape of the contemporary city. But what is the nature of such a landscape, what is the nature of the landscapeness mobilizing its construction, its 'invention'?

---

is a loss that can be filled or replaced by architecture. For me, the important thing is not to replace it, but to cultivate it' (Koolhaas 2000: 85).

Figure 2.9 **(e) Daniel Libekind, Jewish Museum Berlin, Berlin, 1989–1999 (photo by Luc Lévesque).**

The landscapeness of the interstitial, a hypothesis

The fleeting and relative nature of the interstitial condition brings us to think of its 'invention' as landscape, less in terms of set emblematic interstitial territories than in terms of a *landscapeness* nurturing in a 'nomadic' way a sensitive culture of the territory. In other words, if the landscapeness of the interstitial can contribute to the invention of some iconic landscape figures – such as for example the *terrain vague* (Solà-Morales 1995) or the *friche* (Clément 1985) – it couldn't however be limited to the physiognomic characteristics of these figures. The nature and diversity of the conceptual field related to the interstitial condition rather seem to resist stable and precise visual characterizations, preventing interstitial landscapes from being reduced to a few typical images.[22] The interstitial condition, dissociated from any exclusive territorial terms, is opened up to different spatial and temporal situations that can be experienced and experimented with.

---

22 In a similar perspective, Pierre Sansot (1989: 239), in his reflections 'for an aesthetic of the ordinary landscapes', refuses to limit the 'interstitial landscape' to fallow lands or friches, instead suggesting to associate it to 'all that allows us to pass from an elsewhere to another elsewhere'.

Diverging from the dominant modes of landscape creation that usually proceed through distanced characterization and contemplation, the landscapeness of the interstitial would operate instead by 'bringing out' virtualities that exceed the dominance of the visual. By 'virtualities' we here refer to a 'realm of potentials' (Massumi 2002) or 'connections', immanent to a given territorial condition, that can engage the past and the present, as well as the future. In this perspective, 'the virtual is not opposed to the real' (Deleuze 1968: 269), it constitutes precisely that part of the real opening the present to new imaginations and unforeseen experience trajectories. In this sense, the landscapeness of the interstitial would be mobilized by the 'indexical'[23] dimension and the 'diagrammatic'[24] potential of the territorial condition – the potential of a field of interrelations – rather than by a visual characterization limited to the explicit aspects of the image. An interstitial landscapeness would tend to inflect the visual and go beyond it. Thus, beyond the iconographic dominance of traditional 'landscape models', the particularity and importance of a landscape 'invention' of the interstitial could be found in the emergence and the development of an 'interstitial approach to landscape' (Lévesque 2009) that valorizes and activates the relational, virtual, processual and often invisible dimensions of the environment.

If, as we have seen, the theoretical, critical and projectual discourses of architecture and other related disciplines can contribute to invent an interstitial landscapeness, or in other words, can contribute to the development of new territorial imaginations of the interstitial condition, it would be wrong to restrict to a particular scale or to a certain discipline the setting into motion of this 'invention'. It is an attitude, an action, a particular way of becoming conscious of our environment, to which would more generally refer the conceptual constellation related to the interstitial. In the banal everyday substratum, in plural

---

23   The indexical refers to the notion of index here defined after Charles S. Peirce (1931 [1901]: 170) as 'a sign, or representation, which refers to its object not so much because of any similarity or analogy with it, nor because it is associated with general characters which that object happens to possess, as because it is in dynamical (including spatial) connection both with the individual object, on the one hand, and with the senses or memory of the person for whom it serves as a sign, on the other hand'. In other words, as formulated by Rosalind Krauss (1977: 59) the index is a 'type of sign which arises as the physical manifestation of a cause, of which traces, imprints, and clues are examples'.

24   The diagrammatic refers to the diagram, itself defined as the actualization or activation of a series of actions aiming at creating interrelations. On this we follow Deleuze and Guattari (1987 [1980]: 177), who associate the diagram with an 'abstract machine [which] does not function to represent, even something real, but rather constructs a real that is yet to come, a new type of reality' (Deleuze and Guattari 1987 [1980]: 142). Deleuze and Guattari borrowed the notion from Peirce – the diagram as a sort of icon representing interrelations – but give it a different role, 'irreducible to the icon' or to representation (Guattari 1979; Deleuze and Guattari 1987 [1980]; Deleuze 1981). Using William James and Gilles Deleuze as a starting point, John Rajchman (1998) relates the diagrammatic that 'mobilizes and connects' to the hypothesis of a 'new pragmatism that invents and experiments'.

social spheres as in the poorest of contexts, an entire field of research is opened up to direct experimentation[25] or simply to attitudes susceptible to create perceptual and existential breaches in the multiple landscapes and environments of the urban contemporary world, intervals of time and space opening onto unforeseen connections, other ways of seeing and experiencing the city (Figures 2.10). What the conceptual field we have briefly covered tends to bring out are the vectors mobilizing the imagination of such possible openings, an interstitial approach to landscape that could only be becoming...

Figure 2.10 (a,b) SYN-, Hypothèses d'amarrages, Montreal, 2001 (photos by Guy L'Heureux).

---

25   See our own empirical urban experimentations – micro-interventions and various urban explorations with atelier SYN-, www.ateliersyn.wordpress.com, www.amarrages. com [accessed: August 2013] (Lévesque 2012). See also Petcou et al. 2007.

Figure 2.10   (c) SYN-, Hypothèses d'amarrages, Montreal, 2001 (photo by Guy L'Heureux).

Figure 2.10   (d) SYN-, Hypothèses d'insertions III, Paris, 2007 (photo by SYN-).

Figure 2.10 (e) SYN-, Hypothèses d'amarrages, Montreal, 2001 (photo by Guy L'Heureux).

Figure 2.10 **(f) SYN-, Hypothèses d'amarrages, Montreal, 2001 (photo by Luc Lévesque/SYN-).**

Figure 2.10   (g,h) SYN-, Hypothèses d'insertions I, Gatineau, 2002 (photos by SYN-).

References

Allen, S. 1995. Dazed and confused. *Assemblage* (27), 47–54.

Antonioli, M. 2003. *Géophilosophie de Deleuze et Guattari*. Paris, Budapest and Torino: L'Harmattan.

Augé, M. 2003. *Le Temps en Ruines*. Paris: Galilée.

Barthes, R. 1970. *L'Empire des Signes*. Geneva: Skira.

Baudrillard, J. 1975. Le crépuscule des signes. *Traverses*, 2, 27–40.

Beauvais, V. de. 1495. *Speculum historiae*. French translation by Jean de Vignay in 1333 as *Miroir Historial*. 7 Volumes. Vol. 2. Paris: Antoine Vérard. Available online at: http://gallica.bnf.fr/.

Bédard, J.-F. (ed.) 1994. *Cities of Artificial Excavation: The Work of Peter Eisenman, 1978–1988*. New York: Rizzoli.

Beguin, F. 1997. Vagues, vides, verts. *Le Visiteur*, 3, 56–69.

Benjamin, W. and Lacis, A. 1978 [1925]. Naples. In: P. Demetz (ed.) *Reflections: Essays, Aphorisms, Autobiographical Writing by Walter Benjamin*. New York: Schocken Books, 163–73.

Bhabha, H.K. 1994. *The Location of Culture*. London: Routledge.

Bourriaud, N. 1998. *Esthétique Relationnelle*. Dijon: Les presses du réel.

Burgess, E.W. 1925. The growth of the city: an introduction to a research project. In: R. E. Park *et al.* (eds) *The City*. Chicago, IL: The University of Chicago Press, pp. 47–62.

Buber, M. 1937 [1922]. *I and Thou*. Edinburgh: T. and T. Clark.

Buber, M. 2002 [1942]. The problem of man. In: *Between Man and Man*. London: Routledge.

Cache, B. 1995. *Earth Moves: the Furnishing of Territories*. Cambridge, MA: MIT Press.

Chapel, E. 2012. Urbanités inattendues: petites fabriques de l'espace public. *Inter*, 111, 56–60.

Chenet-Faugeras, F. 1994. L'invention du paysage urbain. *Romantisme*, 83, 29–36.

Clément, G. 1985. La friche apprivoisée. *Urbanisme*, 209, 92–95.

Clément, G. 1991. Le jardin en mouvement. In: J.-P. Le Dantec (ed.), *Jardins et Paysages*. Paris: Larousse, 573–80.

Clément, G. 1999. L'histoire naturelle des délaissés. In: L'Atelier (ed.) *La Forêt des Délaissés*. Paris: IFA, pp. 16–17.

Clément, G. 2004. *Manifeste du Tiers Paysage*. Paris: Sujet/Objet.

Cook, P. 1980. *A+U (Architecture and Urbanism)*. Peter Cook Special Issue, February.

Coop Himmelblau 1992. La poésie de la désolation. In: *Coop Himmelblau: construire le ciel*. Paris: Centre Georges Pompidou.

Corner, J. 1999. Eidetic operations and new landscapes. In: J. Corner (ed.) *Recovering Landscape. Essays in Contemporary Landscape Architecture*. New York: Princeton Architectural Press, pp. 153–69.

Daskalakis, G., Waldheim, C. and Young, J. (eds) 2001. *Stalking Detroit.* Barcelona: Actar.

Décarie, J., 1993. La réutilisation marginale des emprises ferroviaires à des fins de loisir: le projet de réseau vert de Montréal. *Actes du 5e Congrès de l'Association Québécoise pour le Patrimoine Industriel*, 68–76.

De Certeau, M. 1980. *L'Invention du Quotidien (Arts de faire I).* Paris: Union Générale d'Éditions.

Deleuze, G. 1968. *Différence et Répétition.* Paris: PUF.

Deleuze, G. 1981. *Francis Bacon. Logique de la Sensation.* Paris: Éditions de la Différence.

Deleuze, G. 1985. *Cinéma 2. L'Image Temps.* Paris: Éditions de Minuit.

Deleuze, G. 1986. *Foucault.* Paris: PUF.

Deleuze, G. and Guattari, F. 1987 [1980]. *Mille Plateaux: Capitalisme et Schizophrénie.* Paris: Éditions de Minuit. English edition translated by B. Massumi: *A Thousand Plateaus: Capitalism and Schizophrenia vol. 2.* Minneapolis, MN: University of Minnesota Press.

Derrida, J. 1970. La double séance. *Tel Quel*, 41/42.

Eisenman, P. 1977. Commentary. *Oppositions*, 9, 19–20.

Eisenman, P. 1980a. Interview with H. Klotz and T. Buddenseig. Institute for Architecture and Urban Studies (IAUS) Collection. Montreal: Canadian Centre for Architecture; box 57-009, file D3-4 lot 2 068.

Eisenman, P. 1980b. The City of Artificial Excavation. Peter D. Eisenman Collection. Montreal: Canadian Centre for Architecture; PDE-136-T, unpaginated.

Eisenman, P. 1982. The house of memory: the texts of analogy, introduction to *The Architecture of the City* by A. Rossi. Cambridge, MA: MIT Press, pp. 3–12.

Eisenman, P. 1983. The city of artificial excavation (Koch-/Friedrichstrasse, block 5). *Architectural Design*, 53(1–2), pp. 91–93.

Eisenman, P. 1984 [1983]. Center for the visual arts at Ohio State University. In: P. Arnell and T. Bickford (eds) *A Center for the Visual Arts. The Ohio State University Competition.* New York: Rizzoli, pp. 110–13.

Eisenman, P. 1987. Architecture and the problem of the rhetorical figure. *A+U (Architecture and Urbanism)*, 202, 54–57.

Eisenman, P. 1988a. The authenticity of difference: architecture and the crisis of reality. *Center – Journal for Architecture in America*, 4, 50–57.

Eisenman, P. 1988b. En terror firma: in trails of grotextes. *Pratt Journal of Architecture*, 2, 111–21.

Eisenman, P. 1988c. Architecture as a second language: the texts of between. *Threshold – Journal of the School of Architecture at the University of Illinois*, 4, 71–75.

Eisenman, P. 1989. Blue line text. *Architectural Design,* 58(7–8), 6–9.

Eisenman, P. 1997. Zones of undecidability I: the interstitial figure. In: C. Davidson (ed.) *Anybody.* Cambridge, MA: MIT Press, pp. 240–44.

Eisenman, P. 1998. Zones of undecidability II: the processes of the interstitial. In: C. Davidson (ed.) *Anyhow*. Cambridge, MA: MIT Press, pp. 28–34.

Eisenman, P. 2003. *Blurred Zones: Investigations of the Interstitial – Eisenman architects 1988–1998*. New York: Monacelli Press.

Fleischer, A. 1993 [approximate, undated document]. *Bernard Tschumi: Le Fresnoy. Studio National des Arts Contemporains*. Paris: Massimo Riposati.

Foucault, M. 1966. *Les Mots et les Choses*. Paris: Gallimard.

Frampton, K. 1980. *Modern Architecture: A Critical History*. London: Thames and Hudson.

Frampton, K. 1988. Place-form and cultural identity. In: J. Thackara (ed.) *Design After Modernism: Beyond the Object*. London: Thames and Hudson, pp. 51–66.

Gallet, B. 2002. *Le Boucher du Prince Wen-houei*. Paris: Musica Falsa.

Gaudin, H. 1992. *Seuil et d'Ailleurs*. Paris: Éditions du Demi-Cercle.

Girard, C. 1986. *Architecture et Concepts Nomades: Traité d'Indiscipline*. Bruxelles, Liège: Mardaga.

Grafmeyer, Y. and Joseph, I. 1984. *L'École de Chicago. Naissance de l'Ecologie Urbaine*. Paris: Aubier.

Grosz, E. 2001. *Architecture from the Outside. Essays on Virtual and Real Space*. Cambridge, MA: MIT Press.

Grumbach, A. 2007. *L'Ombre, le Seuil, la Limite: Réflexions sur l'Espace Juif*. Paris: Musée d'Art et d'Histoire du Judaïsme.

Guattari, F. 1979. *L'Inconscient Machinique. Essais de Schizo-Analyse*. Paris: Editions Recherches.

Halbwachs, M. 1932. Chicago, expérience ethnique. In: Y. Grafmeyer and I. Joseph (eds) *L'École de Chicago. Naissance de l'Ecologie Urbaine*. Paris: Aubier, pp. 279–326.

Handke, P. 1987. Interview with H. Gampert. In: *Espaces Intermédiaires* (1992). Paris: Christian Bourgeois.

Hannerz, U. 1980. *Exploring the City: Inquiries Toward an Urban Antropology*. New York: Colombia University Press.

Hardy, J. 1959. The threshold – land of in-between. *Forum*, 8.

Hladik, M. 2000. Figure(s) de la ruine. *L'Architecture d'Aujourd'hui*, 331, 50–57.

Huizinga, J. 1951. *Homo Ludens: Essai sur la Fonction Social du Jeu*. Paris: Gallimard.

Huyssen, A. 1997. The voids of Berlin. *Critical Inquiry*, 24(1), 57–81.

Jameson, F. 1985. Architecture and the critique of ideology. In: J. Ockman (ed.) *Architecture Criticism Ideology*. New York: Princeton Architectural Press.

Kleihues, J.P. *et al.* 1987. International Building Exhibition Berlin 1987. *A+U (Architecture and Urbanism)*, May 1987.

Knaebel, G. 1991. Le rangement du résidu. *Les Annales de la Recherche Urbaine*, 53, 22–31.

Koolhaas, R. 1978. *Delirious New York: a Retroactive Manifesto for Manhattan*. New York: Monacelli Press.

Koolhaas, R. *et al.* 1983. Koch-/Friedrichstrasse, Block 4. *Architectural Design*, 53(1–2), 88–90.

Koolhaas, R. 1989. La grande ville [interview with B. Fortier]. *L'Architecture d'Aujourd'Hui*, 262, 90–93.

Koolhaas, R. 1990. Dessiner entre indétermination et spécificité [conversation with C-A. Boyer]. *L'Architecture d'Aujourd'Hui*, 269, 34–39.

Koolhaas, R. 1991a [1985]. The terrifying beauty of the twentieth century. In: J. Lucan (ed.) *Rem Koolhaas/OMA*. New York: Princeton Architectural Press, pp. 154–55.

Koolhaas, R. 1991b [1985]. Imagining the nothingness. In: J Lucan (ed.) *Rem Koolhaas/OMA*. New York: Princeton Architectural Press, 156–57.

Koolhaas, R. 1992a. Gridding the new. In: C. Davidson (ed.) *Anywhere*. New York: Rizzoli, 152–61.

Koolhaas, R. 1992b. Urban operations. *Columbia Documents of Architecture and Theory*, 3, 25–57.

Koolhaas, R. 1995a. Strategy of the void. In: *S,M,L,XL*. New York: Monacelli Press, pp. 602–62.

Koolhaas, R. 1995b. Tabula rasa revisited. In: *S,M,L,XL*. New York: Monacelli Press, pp. 1091–135.

Koolhaas, R. 1995c. Programmatic lava. In: *S,M,L,XL*. New York: Monacelli Press, pp. 1210–37.

Koolhaas, R. 1995d [1985]. Elegy for a vacant lot. In: *S,M,L,XL*. New York: Monacelli Press, p. 937.

Koolhaas, R. 1995e [1993]. Field trip (A) A memoir (The Berlin Wall as architecture, 1972). In: *S,M,L,XL*. New York: Monacelli Press, pp. 214–32.

Koolhaas, R. 1995f [1994]. What ever happened to urbanism? In: *S,M,L,XL*. New York: Monacelli Press, pp. 960–71.

Koolhaas, R. 1999. Netherlands embassy. In: C. Davidson, *Anytime*. Cambridge, MA: MIT Press.

Koolhaas, R., with Obrist, H.U. 2000. *Rem Koolhaas Hans Ulrich Obrist – The Conversations Series*. Köln: Verlag der Buchhandlung Walter König.

Koolhaas, R. 2002. Africa comes first [interview with L. Spuybroec]. In: A. Mulder *et al. TransUrbanism*. Rotterdam: V2 Publishing/NAI Publishers, pp. 160–93.

Korosec-Serfaty, P. (1991). La ville et ses restes. In: A. Germain (ed.) *L'Aménagement Urbain: Promesses et Défis*. Québec: Institut Québécois de Recherche sur la Culture, pp. 232–67.

Krauss, R. 1977. Notes on the index: Seventies art in America. Part 2. *October*, 4, 58–67.

Krier, L. 1978. La reconstruction de la ville. In: *Rational Architecture: the Reconstruction of the European City*. Brussels: Archives d'Architecture Moderne, pp. 33–42.

Krier, L. 1980. Les Halles: an everlasting void. *Architectural Record*, 9–10, 47.

Kroll, L. 2001. *Tout est Paysage*. Paris: Sens et Tonka.

Kroll, L. 2011. De l'architecture action comme processus vivant. *Inter*, 108, 8–15.

Kwinter, S. 1995. Politics and pastoralism. *Assemblage*, 27, 25–32.

L'Atelier (I. Allégret, J. Attali, P. Bouchain, M. Boulcourt, G. Clément, L. Julienne, R. Paris) 1999. *La Forêt des Délaissés.* Paris: IFA.

Lassus, B. 1998 [1989]. Theory of faults. In: *The Landscape Approach/Bernard Lassus.* Philadelphia, PA: University of Pennsylvania Press, pp. 62–64.

Lavoisier, A.L. 1793. *Traité Elémentaire de Chimie Présenté dans un Ordre Nouveau et d'Après des Découvertes Modernes.* Paris: Cuchet.

Le Corbusier 1957 [1942]. *La Charte d'Athènes.* Paris: Éditions de Minuit.

Lefaivre, L. and De Roode, I. 2002. *Aldo Van Eyck: the Playgrounds and the City.* Rotterdam: NAI Publishers.

Lefebvre, H. 1974. *La Production de l'Espace.* Paris: Éditions anthropos.

Leong, S. T. 1998. Readings of the attenuated landscape. In: M. Bell and S.T. Leong (eds) *Slow Space.* New York: Monacelli Press, pp. 186–219.

Le Roy, L.G. 1978. Le jardin écologique. *Urbanisme*, 168–69, 64–68.

Le Roy, L.G. 2002. *Louis G. Le Roy: Natuur, Cultuur, Fusie = Nature, Culture, Fusion.* Rotterdam: NAI Publishers.

Lévesque, L. 1999. Montréal, l'informe urbanité des terrains vagues. Pour une gestion créatrice du mobilier urbain. *Annales de la Recherche Urbaine*, 85, 47–57.

Lévesque, L. 2002. Interstitial landscapes as ressources. A few thoughts about a tactical approach to urban intervention. In: *Resource Architecture, Main Congress Report and Oulook.* Berlin: Birkhäuser, pp. 112–13.

Lévesque, L. 2005. Entre lieux et non-lieux: vers une approche interstitielle du paysage/Between place and non-place: towards an interstitial approach to landscape. In: S. Babin (ed.) *Lieux et Non-Lieux de l'Art Actuel – Places and Non-Places of Contemporary Art.* Montreal: Esse, pp. 38–63.

Lévesque, L. 2008. La place publique comme constellation interstitielle: parcours historique et expérimentations. In: J. Jébrak and B. Julien (eds) *Les Temps de l'Espace Public: Construction, Transformation et Utilisation.* Montreal and Quebec City: l'Institut du patrimoine de l'UQÀM, Éditions Multimondes.

Lévesque, L. 2009a. Towards an interstitial approach to urban landscape. *Territorio*, 48, 77–82.

Lévesque, L. 2009b. Eisenman, Team 10 et les Smithson: à travers et par delà 'l'espace entre'. *Trames,* 16, 104–15.

Lévesque, L. 2012. Towards hybrid and situational urban spaces: objects and bodies as vectors. In: F. Zanni (ed.) *Urban Hybridization.* Milan: Maggioli, pp. 25–39.

Libeskind, D. 1990 [1989]. Zwischen den linien/Between the lines [architect's report]. In: V. Heise and S. Holstein (eds) *Realisierungswettbewerb. Erweiterung BERLIN MUSEUM mit Abteilung Jüdisches Museum. Voraussetzungen Verfahren Ergebnisse.* Berlin: Senatsverwaltung für Bau- und Wohnungswesen, pp. 169–70.

Libeskind, D. 2000a [1994]. Traces of the unborn. In: *Daniel Libeskind: the Space of Encounter.* New York: Universe.

Libeskind, D. 2000b. *Daniel Libeskind: the Space of Encounter*. New York: Universe.

Lizet, B. 1989. Naturalistes, herbes folles et terrains vagues. *Ethnologie Française*, XIX(3), 253–72.

Lizet, B *et al.* 1999. *Sauvage dans la Ville. De l'Inventaire Naturaliste à l'Ecologie Urbaine*. Paris: Publications Scientifiques du Museum.

Lynch, K. 1991a [1965]. The city as environment. In: T. Banerjee and M. Southworth (eds) *City Sense and City Design. Writings and Projects of Kevin Lynch*. Cambridge, MA: MIT Press, pp. 87–95.

Lynch, K. 1991b [1965]. The openness of open spaces. In: T. Banerjee and M. Southworth (eds) *City Sense and City Design. Writings and Projects of Kevin Lynch*. Cambridge, MA: MIT Press, pp. 396–412.

Mckenzie, R. D. 1925. The ecological approach to the study of human community. In: R.E. Park *et al.* (eds), The City. Chicago, IL: The University of Chicago Press, pp. 63–80.

Marx, K. 1886 [1863]. *Capital. A Critical Analysis of Capitalist Production*. London: Swan Sonnenschein & Co.

Massumi, B. 1992. *A User's Guide to Capitalism and Schizophrenia: Deviations from Deleuze and Guattari*. Cambridge, MA: MIT Press.

Massumi, B. 2002. *Parables for the Virtual: Movements, Affect, Sensation*. Durham, NC: Duke University Press.

Moretti, G. 2012. Habiter la friche: des machines à paysages, *Inter*, 111, 52–55.

Miller, H. 1939. *Tropic of Capricorn*. Paris: Obelisk.

Moles, A. and Rohmer, E. 1972. *Psychologie de l'Espace*. Paris: Casterman.

Mons, A. 2003. De la ville ou l'espace de l'errance. In: P. Baudry and T. Paquot (ed.) *L'Urbain et ses Imaginaires*. Pessac: MSHA, pp. 113–21.

Moralès, J. 1997. Terrain vague, emplacements incertains. *Quaderns*, 214, 164–68.

Moussette, M. 2003. 'Do we need a canopy for rain?': interior/exterior relationships in the Kunsthal. *Architectural Research Quarterly*, 7(3–4). 280–94.

Park, R.E. 1915. The city: suggestions for the investigation of human behaviour in the urban environment. *American Journal of Sociology*, 20(5), 577–612.

Peirce, C.S. 1931 [1901]. In: C. Hartshorne and P. Weiss (eds), *Collected Papers of Charles Sanders Peirce, Volume II, Elements of Logic, Book II*. Cambridge, MA: Harvard University Press.

Petcou, C. and Petrescu, D. 2011. Agir l'espace : notes transversales, observations de terrain et questions concrètes à chacun de nous. *Inter*, 111, 2–7.

Petcou, C., Petrescu, D. and Marchand, N. (eds) 2007. *Urban Act: a Handbook for Alternative Practice*. Paris: AAA and PEPRAV.

Rajchman, J. 1998. A new pragmatism? In: C. Davidson (ed.) *Anyhow*. Cambridge, MA: MIT Press, pp. 212–17.

Remy, J. 1986. La limite et l'interstice: la structuration spatiale comme ressource sociale. In: P. Pellegrin (ed.) *La Théorie de l'Espace Humain. Transformation Globales et Structures Locales*. Geneva: Craal, pp. 219–27.

Remy, J. and Voyé, L. 1981. *Ville, Ordre et Violence: Formes Spatiales et Transactions Sociales*. Paris: PUF.

Robin, R. 2001. *Berlin Chantiers*. Paris: Stock.

Roger, A. 1997. *Court Traité du Paysage*. Paris: Gallimard.

Rogier, F. 1996. Growing pains: from the opening of the Wall to the wrapping of the Reichstag. *Assemblage*, 29, 44–71.

Ronai, M. 1977. Paysages II. *Hérodote*, 7, 71–91.

Rowe, C. and Koetter, F. 1978. *Collage City*. Cambridge, MA: MIT Press.

Sansot, P. 1989. Pour une esthétique des paysages ordinaires. *Ethnologie Française*, XIX(3), 239–43.

Sieverts, T. 2004. *Entre-Ville. Une Lecture de la Zwischenstadt*. Marseille: Editions Parenthèses.

Smithson, A. (Ed.) 1968. *Team 10 Primer*. Cambridge, MA: MIT Press.

Smithson, A. and P. 1974. The space between. *Oppositions*, 4, 76–78.

Solà-Morales, I. de. 1995. Terrain vague. In: C. Davidson (ed.) Anyplace. Cambridge, MA: MIT Press, pp. 118–23.

Solà-Morales, I. de and Costa, I. (eds) 1996. *Present and Futures. Architecture of Cities, Barcelone (UIA Barcelona 96)*. Barcelona: Collegi d'Arquitectes de Catalunya.

Stimman, H. 1992. Reconstruction without destruction. *Telescope*, 7, 80–81.

Strauven, F. 1998. *Aldo Van Eyck. The Shape of Relativity*. Amsterdam: Architecture and Natura Press.

Tafuri, M. 1987. *The Sphere and the Labyrinth: Avant-Gardes and Architecture from Piranesi to the 70s*. Cambridge, MA: MIT Press.

Teyssot, G. 2005. A topology of thresholds. *Home Culture*, 2(1), 89–116.

Thrasher, F. M. 1963 [1927]. *The Gang. A Study of 1313 Gangs in Chicago*. Chicago, IL: The University of Chicago Press.

Tonnelat, S. 1999. Times Square. Superpositions. *Les Annales de la Recherche Urbaine*, 85, 43.

Tonnelat, S. 2003. *Interstices urbains. Paris – New York: Entre Contrôles et Mobilités, Quatre Espaces Résiduels de l'Aménagement*. PhD Thesis, New York, CUNY Graduate School.

Tschumi, B. 1976. Architecture and transgression. *Oppositions*, 7, 65–78.

Tschumi, B. 1977. The Pleasure of architecture. *Architectural Design*, 214–18.

Tschumi, B. 1993. Le Fresnoy/Architecture. In: A. Fleischer (ed.) *Le Fresnoy: Studio National des Arts Contemporains*. Paris: Massimo Riposati.

Tschumi, B. 1999. The architectural project of Le Fresnoy. In: *Tschumi, Le Fresnoy: Architecture in/between*. New York: Monacelli, pp. 9–13 and 33–77.

Tschumi, B. 2001. Deviations from the normative. In: *Bernard Tschumi & Hugh Dutton, Glass Ramps/Glass Wall. Deviations from the Normative*. London: AA Publications.

Tzonis, A. and Lefaivre, L. 1999. *Aldo Van Eyck. Humanist Rebel. Inbetweening in Postwar World*. Rotterdam: 010 Publishers.

Ungers, O.M., Koolhaas, R., Kolhoff, H., Riemann, P., Ovaska, A. 1978. Cities within the city. *Lotus International,* 19, 82–97.

Van Eyck, A. 1959. Is architecture going to reconcile basic values? In: O. Newman and J. Joedicke (eds) *CIAM 59 in Otterlo. Documents of Modern Architecture* (1961). London: Alec Tiranti, pp. 26–35.

Van Eyck, A. 1960. The medecine of reciprocity tentatively illustrated. *Forum,* 6–7, 237–238 and 252.

Van Eyck, A. 1962a. Steps toward a configurative discipline. *Forum,* 3, 81–94.

Van Eyck, A. 1962b. Place and occasion. *Progressive Architecture,* 155–60.

Van Eyck, A. 1963. Wheels for heaven. *Domus,* 426, 2–3.

Van Eyck, A. 1979. The ironbound statement. *Spazio e Società,* 8, 62–63.

Van Eyck, A. 1998 [1956]. When snow falls on cities. In: F. Strauven (ed.) *Aldo Van Eyck. The Shape of Relativity.* Amsterdam: Architecture and Natura Press, p. 169.

Van Eyck, A. 2008 [1962]. The child, the city and the artist – an essay on architecture: the in-between realm. In: V. Ligtelijn and F. Strauven (eds) *Aldo van Eyck Writings,* Vol. 1. Amsterdam: SUN.

Verret, F. 1992. *Le Fresnoy* [movie].

Vidler, A. 1992. *The Architectural Uncanny.* Cambridge, MA: MIT Press.

Vidler, A. 2000. *Warped Space: Art, Architecture, and Anxiety in Modern Culture.* Cambridge, MA: MIT Press.

Virilio, P. 1976. *L'Insécurité du Territoire.* Paris: Stock.

Virilio, P. 1984. *L'Horizon Négatif: Essai de Dromoscopie.* Paris: Galilée.

Wenders, W. and Handke, P., 1987. *Der Himmel über Berlin* (*Wings of Desire*) [movie]. Paris: Argos Films; Berlin: Road Movies; in association with Westdeutscher Rundfunk (Cologne).

Wenders, W. and Kolhoff, H. 1988. The city. A conversation. *Quaderns,* 177, 70–77.

Whyte, W. F. 1983 [1943]. *Street Corner Society. The Social Structure of an Italian Slum.* Chicago, IL: The University of Chicago Press.

Wines, J. 1975. De-architecturization: the iconography of disaster. *Architectural Design,* 426–28.

Wines, J. 1987. *De-architecture.* New York: Rizzoli.

Woods, L. 1991. Terra Nova. In: P. Noever (ed.) *Architecture in Transition between Deconstruction and New Modernism.* Munich: Prestel, 133–51.

Zardini, M. 1997. The prevalence of the landscape. In: E. Bru. and S. Landrove (eds) *Nuevos Territorios. New Territories. Nuevos Paisajes. New Landscapes.* Barcelona: ACTAR, 204–8.

Zardini, M. (ed.) 1999. *Paesaggi Ibridi.* Milan: Skira.

Chapter 3

Tent Cities: Interstitial Spaces of Survival[1]

Don Mitchell

Tent City is less a single location than a nomadic but constant phenomenon,
a shifting blue-tarped shadow to the glass and steel American metropolis. (Ben
Ehrenreich, *The Nation*, 3 June 2009)

Let's start with an example – an example from Camden, New Jersey. The example
is as typical as it is depressing. Maybe the specific deprivations that make up the
context for what I am about to tell you are more extreme than might be found
in some parts of the USA, but as the editors of the exposé from which I draw
this story suggest: 'Camden, New Jersey, stands as a warning of what huge
pockets of America could turn into' (Hedges and Sacco 2010: 15). The editors call
Camden the 'City of Ruins', an appellation that could just as easily be applied to
Detroit, Youngstown, whole swaths of the south side of Chicago or the north side
of Philly, to much of Cleveland, Oakland and St Louis, to not a little LA, and,
though perhaps less strikingly visibly, to pockets of Denver, Seattle, San Diego
and Atlanta. Written by investigative journalist and former war correspondent
Chris Hedges (author of *War is a Force that Gives Us Meaning*, among other
important works), the story of Camden's destruction by the forces of capitalism
makes for sobering reading. Camden's real unemployment rate, Hedges writes, is
likely between 30–40 per cent, median household income is $24,600 (a little more
than half that of the USA as a whole), the high school dropout rate is 70 per cent
and city services are being radically slashed: the police force in a city routinely
described as America's most violent, was about to be cut by half, libraries by two-
thirds, all departments by at least 25 per cent (Hedges and Sacco 2010: 15).[2] If
that is not enough, the political establishment is deeply corrupt (the political boss
runs the place from a suburb, not even bothering to live in the city he dominates).
Though Campbell's Soup has retained its corporate headquarters in the city,
there is virtually no manufacturing in what had once been 'an industrial giant'.
Shipbuilding, electronics, food manufacturing and more have all fled for greener
pastures or distant shores. As Hedges puts it,

---

1   An earlier, slightly different, version of this chapter was published as 'Tent City:
Spaces of Homeless Survival and Organizing in the American City'. In: A. Phillips and
F. Erdemci (eds) Social Housing – Housing the Social: Art, Property and Spatial Justice.
Amsterdam: SKOR and Sternberg Press, 2012, pp. 277–306.

2   It was indeed cut in half at the beginning of December 2010.

> Camden is the poster child of postindustrial decay. It stands as a warning of
> what huge pockets of the United States could turn into as we cement into place
> a permanent underclass of the unemployed, slash state and federal services in
> a desperate bid to cut massive deficits, watch cities and states go bankrupt and
> struggle to adjust to a stark neofeudalism in which the working and middle
> classes are decimated. (Hedges and Sacco 2010: 17)[3]

In the midst of Camden's post-apocalyptic landscape – a landscape torn apart,
destroyed and left for dead in capital's never-ending war against humanity
– dozens of homeless people, perhaps 60 of them, lived in tents and tarpaulin
shelters under an interstate highway on-ramp. They called their encampment
Transitional Park. This was just one redoubt of the city's homeless; there had to
be others. Camden city counted 775 people as officially homeless, but there were
only 220 shelter beds in the whole of the county. The 'mayor' of Transitional
Park, according to Hedges, 'ran the tent city … like a military encampment'
(Hedges and Sacco 2010: 17). The mayor had an assistant – whom he called his
CEO – and together they conducted tent inspections every weekend, held a camp
meeting every week and posted rules banning drugs, fighting, selling food stamps
and prostitutes' bringing their tricks into the camp, as well as requiring trash to
be picked up. Repeat violators were expelled from the camp. A guard detail was
established to keep residents safe at night. Amidst the ruins, this was survival; this
was self-organization. This was the interstices put to use. Transitional Park was
not a commons, and though an alternative to the abject, isolated, disorganized life
of the street, it was not really an alternative to the world that capital and its flight
likes to make. But it was something.

And it was something the city tolerated through the winter of 2010, perhaps
because it seemed to have no other option. But the visibility of that something,
perhaps the potential of the interstices, eventually became too much. With spring's
arrival, therefore, also came the wrecking crews. 'Those tossed out scattered, and
about a half-dozen migrated to live in squalor under the concrete ramps of Route
676, where it runs across the river into Philadelphia' (Hedges and Sacco 2010: 17).
The alternative that was no alternative was now no more – destroyed for no good
reason except that the city leaders thought it a blight on their already thoroughly
blighted landscape. This often is the fate of tent cities, not only in Camden, but
also in Fresno or Phoenix, Sacramento or St Petersburg (FL). As soon as tent cities
spring up, as soon as they get organized well enough to provide a bit of security
for their residents, they're destroyed.

Why?

---

3   A week after Camden slashed its police force and many other services President
Barack Obama reached a 'compromise' with Republicans in Congress, extending a massive
tax-cut to the most wealthy Americans.

Homelessness and interstitial space: a historical geography

Every time we get leadership, they get a bus ticket out of town. (St Petersburg
Ten City Resident Brad Bradford, *St Petersburg Times*, 30 December 30 2006)

In a lengthy though still highly partial (and deeply problematic) account, law
scholar Robert Ellickson (1996) asserted that in the Skid Row of the 1960s, police
had homeless men – bums as he calls them – right where they wanted them. As
long as homeless people stuck to their district, the city provided a space for them.
Aspects of this argument can also be found in Jim Duncan's (1978) influential and
important argument about tramps' classification and use of space. But Duncan
goes a step further, showing how it was precisely the marginal, or what we are
here calling the *interstitial*, spaces of the city, that made it possible for homeless
men to survive. In this struggle for survival, visibility mattered. To the degree that
homeless men were confined to Skid Row, then they could be kept out of sight. To
the degree that their numbers were not huge, their encampments were hidden away
under bridges, in back alleys or behind abandoned buildings, they were tolerated.
Episodic visibility – to panhandle or cadge cigarettes, to visit soup kitchens or take
an occasional day job – was tolerated in non-Skid Row locales just so long as it
became neither large nor more than episodic. The interstices were the spaces of
survival. They were, in Jeremy Waldron's (1991) terms, spaces where homeless
people could *be* (see also Kawash 1998). Even more than the public property that
Waldron felt kept homeless people from the annihilation that would face them if
we truly lived in a 'libertarian paradise' of only private property, the abandoned,
in-between and un-surveilled spaces of the city – whether publically or privately
owned – together with the relatively benign Skid Row provided the very conditions
of possibility for being for 'men without property', to use Duncan's term (see also
Mitchell and Heynen 2009).

Ellickson's and Duncan's accounts of Skid Row are partial because Skid Row
never really was such an abandoned space; it played a vital economic function in
industrial-era America, as did tramping workers (DePastino 2003; Groth 1994;
Kasinitz 1986; Schneider 1996). And neither was Skid Row a particularly benign
location: the police could be impressively violent in their control of tramping
workers, homeless men and alcoholics on the street, and the 'private' violence of
jackrollers and muggers took its steady toll (Anderson 1923, 1940). And now of
course, in city after city – if not in Camden (which in any event never really had a
well-developed Skid Row) – Skid Row has been thoroughly gentrified, brought in
from the margins, from the interstices, and into the heart of the city.

Nonetheless, interstices in cities remain – under bridges, in abandoned lots
still waiting redevelopment, on the grounds of old factories, in the scrub and silt
of the rivers that run through town – and they remain vital for homeless people
and their pursuit of life (Mitchell and Heynen 2009). Sometimes these interstitial
spaces become, for homeless people, absolutely central. They become tent cities –
relatively stable encampments of the desperately poor.

Poor people's encampments have a long and important history in the USA. During America's post-Civil War industrialization, tramps – that is, migratory, casual (predominantly male) workers – 'slept just about anywhere they could', as Cresswell (2001: 41) has put it. Municipal lodging houses, jailhouse floors, Rescue Missions, single room occupancy (SRO) hotels and the 'cage' hotels of Skid Row, bunkhouses provided by employers at the lumber and farm camps and sometimes park benches all formed part of the tramps' archipelago of housing (Kusmer 2002; Hopper 2003; DePastino 2003). But of particular significance was 'the jungle'. Usually tramps' jungles developed in wastelands near the railroad (the primary mode of travel for tramping workers). 'Hobo sociologist' Nels Anderson (1923: 17) described the conditions that made for a good jungle:

> It should be located in a dry and shady place that permits sleeping on the ground. There should be plenty of water for cooking and bathing and wood enough to keep the pot boiling. If there is a general store near by where bread, meat, and vegetables may be had, so much the better. For those who have no money but enough courage to 'bum lumps,' it is well that the jungles be not too far from town, though far enough to escape the attention of the natives and officials. (quoted in Cresswell 2001: 43; see also DePastino 2003)

Jungles might be permanent or temporary, but they existed by a strict code – a culture if you like – of mutuality, even if this mutuality was also organized around a hierarchy (especially in sexual relations): sharing was sine qua non. If one had a decent 'stake', they were expected to look out for their brothers who did not in the knowledge that the tables would soon be turned. According to Anderson (1923), the jungles were frequently multiracial.[4]

Importantly, the jungle was frequently a *political* place, especially after the founding of the Industrial Workers of the World (IWW or 'Wobblies') in 1905. No doubt tramping casual workers who lived off and on in the jungles were a despised class, condemned as 'beggars, mental inferiors, habitual drunks, and lousy workers' (Mitchell 1996: 64; Monkkonen 1984) – a kind of condemnation that has lived down through the ages and more or less defines dominant perceptions of the contemporary homeless (see, perhaps especially, Baum and Burnes 1991). Against such characterizations, however, tramping workers created their own political culture, in which the jungle was central.[5] Seeking to both capitalize on

---

4   On the multi-racial world of tramping more generally, see Higbie 2003: 107–16.

5   As important as the jungle in the archipelago of places that shaped casual labourers' life and politics was the IWW union hall. The IWW was an intellectual as well as a political and union movement. According to Philip Foner (1965: 151), 'The typical hall, especially in the West usually contained dog-eared copies of Marx, Darwin, Spenser, Voltaire, Tom Paine, Jack London and a variety of government documents.' Progressive reformer and academic Carleton Parker (1917: 651–52) wrote of the IWW: 'Presumably they were better acquainted with American social statistics than the academic class.' And another historian

and revolutionize this culture, IWW organizers travelled with the union 'under their hats' as the saying went (Dubofsky 1969, 293), taking the local with them on the road. In the western USA they specifically sought to organize casual labourers in the jungles. Through both formal recruiting for the One Big Union and through less formal agitation, not only in the jungles, but also quite famously on the streets and in the empty lots of the Main Stem (Skid Row), the IWW sought to turn migratory and homeless workers into a revolutionary class – or if not entirely that, than at least a radical one ready to fight for its rights as workers and as outcasts (Dubofsky 1969; Foner 1964, 1981). In doing so the IWW developed a particular renown among migratory workers. Indeed, as one undercover agent in California wrote of the IWW:

> The extent and activity of this organization's workings are almost beyond belief. One sees the notices everywhere. You hear the 'Wobblies' spoken of favorably in 'jungle' conversations. There is widespread knowledge of and interest in its doings that is of far more than passing importance in any consideration of the problems concerned with this organization. (quoted in Woirol 1984)

The jungle was a space of organizing for the IWW; it was a space of worry and danger for the bourgeoisie. Its hiddenness together with the seeming impenetrability of its mores – its very status as an interstice – together with the obvious fact that it was a space of radical organizing, added to its threatening power. To eliminate this power, the state eventually sought – during the First World War – to not only eliminate the IWW, but also to eliminate the jungle, to bring tramping workers into visibility, as it were, and to thereby weaken their subversive potential (Mitchell 1996).

Jungles were only one form of political encampment for tramping workers, hobos and homeless people. In the midst of economic depressions, various 'armies' formed to march on state capitals and Washington, DC, where they often encamped at length, making demands on the state. Coxey's and Kelly's armies of the 1893 depression provided the precedent, but a further Kelly's Army in California in 1913 and the Bonus Marchers of the Great Depression (cleared out of their encampment by the US Army) showed the threatening power that organized, destitute workers and homeless people could sometimes possess, especially if they were successful in controlling both the spaces and places of their radicalism (McMurray 1923; McWilliams 1939: 164–167; Schwantes 1984; Dixon and Allen

---

(quoted in Foner 1965, 151) wrote of Wobblies: 'Entering a hall in the evening one might see several shabbily dressed young men reading from books taken from shelves of the library in the room. Others crouched over a makeshift stove brewing a mulligan stew, its ambitious odor permeating the hall. While they tended supper, they argued some point in economics or religion.' A similar culture permeated the jungles, even if the books may have been far fewer, being typically replaced by a range of newspapers carried in by workers and hobos come to bed down for the night.

2004). Coxey's and Kelly's Armies commandeered trains; they camped en mass in empty lots, city streets and farmers' fields; they marched. They took space and from it they planned and organized their further moves. It is not surprising then, that the 1913 Kelly's Army met such fierce resistance when they camped in Sacramento not far from the statehouse – the resistance of firehouses and horse-charges determined to roust them from their encampment and push them out of the city they had quickly come to dominate.[6] Yet in this instance, it was not only the interstices that mattered, but also the way that organized poor and homeless people managed to transform a centre into the interstices: into a tent city at the heart of the city that had real political effectivity, and thus was a real threat to bourgeois business-as-usual. Together jungles, marches, and the seeming ability of tramping workers to disappear into the margins led to panic-after-tramp-panic, creating something like an era of the 'tramp-scare' lasting from the 1870s into the 1940s (Cresswell 2001: 9; Monkkenen 1984).

Of equal importance to the Bonus Marches as the Great Depression deepened were the innumerable 'Hoovervilles' that sprang up in cities and countryside alike. Squatters built shacks in New York's Central Park, and other Hoovervilles climbed up the banks of the Harlem River (to which they would return in the 1980s). In California, shacktowns filled empty lots in all the major cities; encampments of tents, wooden or cardboard boxes and brush filled the river bottoms and irrigation ditchbanks in the agricultural countryside. These margins too possessed the potential to unleash a new and scary politics, as Steinbeck's Tom Joad – perhaps America's most famous Hooverville denizen – made clear in his famous soliloquy near the end of *The Grapes of Wrath*:

> I'll be ever'where – wherever you look. Wherever there's a fight so hungry people can eat, I'll be there. Wherever they's a cop beatin' up a guy, I'll be there … An' when our folks eat the stuff they raise an' live in the houses they build – why, I'll be there. (Steinbeck 1939: 463)[7]

In the wake of the Second World War, however, such *mass* interstitial living began to evaporate. In some instances – in rural California, for example – tent and shack cities in unincorporated areas gradually were transformed into more settled, if

---

6   'Troops Called Out to Halt Hobo Army', New York Times, 8 March 1914; 'Streams of Water Rout 1,500 Hoboes', New York Times, 10 March 1914.

7   Some of those in California's Hoovervilles had undoubtedly been driven out of the large – several thousand resident – tent city in the 'river bottom' section of Oklahoma City. In the wake of a rare order from a governor ordering the Oklahoma City mayor and police in 1931 to cease arresting unemployed people on charges of vagrancy and sentencing them to either finding a (non-existent) job or leaving the jurisdiction, Oklahoma City police resorted to the much more direct expedient of shutting down the tent city on the grounds of 'insanitary living conditions'. In the wake of this sweep, unemployed families were reportedly 'leaving the city', and no doubt heading west (Pretshold 1931: 361).

still often informally built, settlements (Stein 1974; Gregory 1988; Starr 1996). Labour markets were altered, as much labour was decasualized, and that which wasn't, such as agricultural work in California, was handed over to Mexican 'guest workers', in a federallysponsored plan to drive 'domestic' – that is, citizen and long-term resident – labour out of the fields; armies of undocumented workers were also assiduously recruited, many of them living in brush-encampments in the desert and ravines or squatting in (or under) abandoned farmhouses (Galarza 1977; Mitchell 2012). The face of homelessness in the cities thus changed. Skid Rows became largely the domain of older men, frequently alcoholic (Spradley 1970; Bahr 1970, 1973; McSheehy 1979). Skid Rows were then soon subject to the one-two punch of urban renewal followed by gentrification further radically altering their nature as an outsiders' space (Kasinitz 1986; Groth 1994). With the exception of rural encampments of undocumented workers, tent-city-like encampments seemed to fade from the scene in the post-war, but pre-neoliberal, era; hobo jungles had largely become a thing of the past, now so safe they could, for example, annually be nostalgically recreated in an annual Hobo Convention in Britt, Iowa.

With the Reagan Revolution, tent cities returned. Already declining during the Carter Administration, the public housing budget was cut in half in the first Reagan Budget, and slashed and slashed again in the years that followed (since 1996 there was been absolutely no money budgeted for new public housing, though Section 8 housing vouchers still exist, with a waiting list of tens of thousands in any major jurisdiction: see Ehrenreich (2009)). Disability and mental health support budgets were likewise slashed, and the inevitable effects of unsupported deinstitutionalization quickly made themselves felt in city after city (Dear and Wolch 1987; Wolch and Dear 1996; Hopper 2003). The deep recession of 1982–83, in many ways a culmination of the increasingly severe series of 'post-Keyensian' recessions that marked the 1970s (Harvey 2010), as well as a further deepening of the Great U-Turn of America's industrial and social history (Bluestone and Harrison 1982; Harrison and Bluestone 1988), threw working families out of their homes and sent them either on the road or into the old Skid Row districts in search of work and lodging (Maharidge and Williamson 1996). The new face of homelessness was increasingly dark and increasingly female. The new fact of homelessness expressed itself in the old form: shanty towns and tent cities.

One of the most famous was in Los Angeles' Skid Row: Justiceville. Constructed on an LA sidewalk in 1985, Justiceville was led by the charismatic Ted Hayes, and in some ways reflected the cult of personality that developed around him.[8] This cult had its important effects, bringing significant attention to the plight of homeless people in Skid Row and the city's on-going attempts

---

8   Hayes is a controversial figure. A strong supporter of George W. Bush, he stood for Congress as a Republican against long-serving Los Angeles progressive Democrat Maxine Waters; he later formed the Crispus Attucks brigade, an African American organization that agitates against illegal immigrants.

to uproot their encampments, memorialized in a documentary film and Motown song. For some the cult of personality – and indeed the rather dictatorial manner in which Justiceville was run – encouraged defection even before the LA city government moved to close the tent city down. Not far away, therefore, Love Camp, another encampment of homeless people, this one at least slightly more cooperatively organized, developed (with at least some early support from nearby businesses). For some homeless residents of Love Camp,

> the camp became so supportive that residents attempted to remain on the sidewalk and build quasi-permanent structures (plywood homes) as a personal long-term 'solution' to a more transient homeless existence. The intent was not to rejoin mainstream society, but instead to remain as a member of a homeless street community. (Rowe and Wolch 1990: 200)

Such a move to stability and autonomy, however, is something most cities cannot countenance. As with Camden's Transitional Park a generation later, Love Camp was swept away, its residents dispersed. 'It took so long for us to build that up,' one resident said, 'and took five minutes to tear it down' (quoted in Rowe and Wolch 1990: 200).

Innumerable similar Justicevilles, Love Camps, Dignity Villages and more developed around the country, pushed and shoved around the wastelands of the city, as at times city officials schizophrenically tolerated their presence as the least bad option, and at other times sought to shut them down. They were joined by encampments in riverbeds, under on-ramps, and on disused rail lines. And they grew in number, size, and precariousness as they Reagan era gave way to the Clinton era. Such spaces moved around, but they never disappeared. 'In good times and bad, Tent City comes and goes,' as investigative reporter Ben Ehrenreich (2009) recently wrote; it 'forms and scatters and takes shape again.' Sometimes Tent City takes official shape, with architects' help (Gragg 2002). After Justriceville was chased around Skid Row a few times, for example, Ted Hayes managed to secure a fenced site and a $250,000 grant from the oil company ARCO to erect 20 geodesic domes for homeless people, designed by an acolyte of Buckminster Fuller. Dome Village lasted until 2006, when the owner of the land reclaimed it – part of an anti-Republican campaign according to Hayes (see http://domevillage.tedhayes. us/). Dignity Village in Portland, now 20 years old, calls itself a 'campground for the homeless', and boasts a flashy website, a board of directors and a Facebook presence. Like Dome Village, it is an official non-profit organization and it has garnered a great deal of popular and critical attention (Gragg 2002; http://www. dignityvillage.org). These are (or were) not really interstitial spaces, however, even if they are, in their own ways, important attempts to secure a vital space for homeless people's survival.

They are, also, fenced and carefully policed spaces. And the historical geography of tent city is replete with such attempts and corralling and containing the homeless. As street homelessness continued to grow in Los Angeles in the

1990s, the City made plans to develop a 'drop-in centre' funded in part by a large grant from HUD. A city official described the drop-in centre as a 'fenced-in urban campground where up to 800 people could take a shower and sleep on a lawn' (quoted by Dear and Wolch 1994, in Takahashi 1998: 113). The city planned to purchase a hidden-away vacant lot in Skid Row, put a fence around a large lawn on the site and build a 50-bed shelter that would also house some social services. Homeless people would be bussed to the site from various places around the city and locked up for the night. Homeless advocate and UCLA law professor Gary Blasi called the plan 'a first step on a slippery slope to concentration camps in rural areas for homeless people' (quoted in Takahashi 1998: 114). Eventually the plan for an overnight camping lawn was dropped (though due more to merchant than homeless-advocate opposition) and the drop-in centre itself was long-stalled (Takahashi 1998: 114).

Plans for such fenced encampments are not rare, and they continue to this day. Ontario, California has managed to build one. Its 'Temporary Homeless Services Area' (THSA) is a formalization – and fencing – of a tent city that police had long been directing homeless people to.

> In March [2008], after herding the local homeless population to Tent City, police and code enforcement officers descended on the encampment and required its inhabitants to prove they were residents of Ontario. Those who could not – all but 127 – were evicted. The city bulldozed and graded the field, erected orderly rows of matching green tents, issued ID card to those who remained, fenced the encampment and posted a list of rules: no re-entry after 10 pm, no alcohol, no pets, no minors, no visitors. Now private security guards patrol THSA's perimeters, ejecting anyone who doesn't have permission to be there, including reporters. (Ehrenreich 2009)

As Ben Ehrenreich goes on to detail:

> None of the Tent City residents I interviewed from just outside the fence complained much. They were fed three meals a day and were otherwise left alone. The rules were infantilizing, but the people largely shrugged them off. Still, more than a third of those permitted to stay in the THSA have left for good. No new arrivals have been admitted. Isaac Jackson, coordinator of the county's Office of Homeless Services, credited Ontario with doing a 'great job' of reducing Tent City's population. Neither city nor county officials, though, knew if any of those who have left the Tent City have found a better source of shelter than a tent. It seems unlikely. (Ehrenreich 2009)[9]

---

9   In another official tack, city officials in San Diego, under a court order to provide winter shelter for homeless people, spent the 1990s scrambling each year to locate a disused warehouse of office building in that rapidly gentrifying and redeveloping city; by the dawn of the new century they had thrown in the towel and taken to erecting large 'sprung shelters'

Ehrenreich's in-depth account of struggles over tent cities in contemporary California came in the wake of massive publicity surrounding Sacramento's bulging tent city on the banks of the American river in late 2008. Media glare had been shone on Sacramento by Oprah Winfrey, who saw it as paradigmatic of the new poverty becoming visible in the wake of the burst financial and housing bubbles. Sacramento was the epicentre of foreclosures in 2007, and it remained a deeply effected place in 2008. But as Ehrenreich (2009) makes so clear, the residents of Sacramento's tent city were largely *not* these newly evicted, but ones who had long-since been evicted from the mainstream economy and from standard housing. Tent City, he writes, 'tells the grueling backstory of the current recession – nearly thirty years of cuts in social services to the poor and mentally ill, the decimation of the industrial economy and the cruel underside of the housing boom.' Contemporary tent cities, then, are not evidence of capitalism in crisis, but of contemporary capitalism in full flower (c.f. Harvey 2010). They are what they always have been: deeply troubling interstitial spaces only by dint of which capital's reserve army can survive, whether that survival has radical or revolutionary potential or is merely infantilizing – or, now with a space to *be*, just *is*.

Tent cities: tenuous spaces of survival

> Survival is the biggest time-filler here. Tents must be shored up against wind and rain. The schedule for meals, clothing giveaways and shower times at local agencies must be strictly followed. (Maria La Ganga, *The Irish Times*, 21 March 2009)

> Tent city is not the crisis. It's the conditions that caused the tent city that's the crisis. (Homeless advocate Eric Rubin, *St. Petersburg Times*, 6 January 2007)

Ben Ehrenreich is of course correct when he argues that Sacramento's Tent City was not *only* a symbol of the current economic crisis, but part of the 'back story' of that crisis, the result of a long history of disinvestment, upward wealth redistribution, the attack on the state and the veneration of markets. It is proof-positive of the nature of the good life neoliberalism has made. It is also proof-positive that the bourgeoisie *still* has no more solution to the housing problem than it did in Engel's (1872) day. Sacramento's Tent City is a case in point. Transient encampments of greater or lesser extent had long existed on the wasteland by the American River that Oprah brought to the world's attention in early 2009. The iteration she found had grown to some 200–300 residents over the past year (out of more than 1200 homeless people in shelters or sleeping rough in Sacramento).

– tents – on the only space they could find: a couple of dead-end streets near to where the new baseball stadium was being constructed (Staeheli and Mitchell 2008).

Some residents had long been homeless in the city; others became homeless or moved to the city recently. Divided into self-governing 'neighbourhoods,' tent-city residents had self-sorted themselves based on interests, affinity, tolerance for drugs or alcohol and the like. Joan Burke, who works at the nearby Loaves and Fishes homeless services agency said:

> There is a sort of very pure democracy and self-governance at play. People are making up the rules of their clusters of tents, deciding what's permitted, just as in any sort of community ... You don't want to romanticize this – it isn't camping – but there is a community and a sense of helping others. We've had a series of storms here recently, and if there's somebody new who doesn't have a tent, people will take them in. It's that understanding that, you know, there's somebody worse off than I am. (quoted in Burkeman 2009: 27)

In other words, something like the ethos of the 'jungle' was being recreated, precisely *as* a means of survival.

The global attention it garnered therefore made it intolerable. New, (neo) liberal mayor Kevin Johnson therefore announced plans to clear out Tent City. Arguing that there has to be some compassion towards the homeless, Sacramento, he declared, also needed to exercise 'tough love' (Gonzalez 2009c; Adler 2009) – classic urban-right code for stripping homeless people of their autonomy and humanity – as well as adopt a 'zero tolerance' (Gonzalez 2009c) policy towards homeless encampments. He therefore announced a plan, in March 2009, to open a wintertime emergency shelter on the grounds of the California State Fair – a shelter that would be highly regulated, fenced and locked at night, but within which residents would not be separated from their partners and pets, and where there would be at least some provision for the safe storage of belongings (Gonzalez 2009b; McKinley 2009). Many of those resident in Tent City resisted this plan: 'People out here are not going to go anywhere where they are going to lock you in,' as one of them put it. 'Would you go anywhere where they are going to turn the key and lock you in at night? No' (quoted in Gonzalez 2009b). As another said, 'I'm not sure what's going to happen ... I'd just like to be left alone myself. I like it right here where I'm at. So I don't know what's going to go on ... I'm not really happy about it' (quoted in Gonzalez 2009b). But as the National Public Radio reporter covering the story, Richard Gonzalez, closed one of his stories, 'being left alone isn't in the cards,' given Mayor Johnson's talk of tough love and zero tolerance (Gonzalez 2009b).[10]

---

10   US Supreme Courts have more than once declared the 'right to be left alone' to be one of the 'most comprehensive of rights and the right most valued by civilized men' (c.f. Mitchell 2005: 80). There is much to question in this formulation – and some of its political implications are troubling – but it does point to an autonomy in social life that citizens of the USA seem to have by right unless they are homeless.

Sacramento's Tent City was duly closed at the end of March 2009 and some 200 homeless people – not all of them Tent City residents – moved to the winter shelter at the fairgrounds. On 1 July, the winter shelter was closed, and these residents found themselves back on the streets. In the wake of the closure, homeless people (including many who had never moved to the fairgrounds, but instead retreated more deeply into the bush) marched through Sacramento and demanded a right to camp. Setting up a symbolic tent in an empty lot next to a police station, they demanded 'a civil liberty that ought to already exist, which is [that] people have the right to be, to live without the threat of being incarcerated in their own country' (quoted in Gonzalez 2009a). One of those protesting described his life since Tent City was closed at the end of March:

> When we moved out, we moved over to a private area two fields over. They wanted us off of there too. Just like shuttling cattle, that's all it is ... We're supposed to be the eyesore, but actually we're citizens and we're human beings. We're supposed to have rights like everybody else; it don't matter what we have in our pockets. (quoted in Gonzalez 2009a)

He had spent his time one step ahead of the police, seeking out any sort of shelter.

He likely lived, off and on, in one or another of the dozen or so small tent encampments that 'continue to pop up, and just as quickly' are shut down by police (Adler 2009). Advocates for the homeless have thus been agitating for what they call 'safe ground, a legal campground, so they're not hounded from place to place. And they're not subject to citations and arrests' (quoted in Adler 2009). Mayor Johnson says he is open to the idea, but he also says 'I do not believe that people should be able to camp, you know, illegally, anywhere in the city at this particular time' (quoted in Adler 2009).

The creation of such 'safe ground' is not a novel idea. Twenty years ago the city of Miami was required by court order to create a safe haven for homeless people and eventually set aside an area under a highway overpass where homeless people could be free from arbitrary police sweeps, the confiscation of their belongings, arrest for loitering or sleeping in public, and – as in the event that led to the lawsuit from which the court order resulted – being roused from their sleep in a park and handcuffed while their belongings are thrown in a pile, and lit on fire (Pottinger 1991; Simon 1992).[11] They have, however, sparked new interest, as the question of the very survival of homeless people continues to force itself into the consciousness of city managers and the public alike. Homeless people

---

11 Such action is not representative of all police action and sentiment towards homeless people, of course. A long-time cop on Sacramento's homeless beat expressed his favour for a legal camping site in that city, commenting that with the closure of the winter shelter, 'You need something for that immediate need' for housing (Gonzalez 2009a). But it is also not uncommon, as in the famous case of Santa Ana's detention and deportation of its homeless population in 1990 (Simon 1992; Takahashi 1998; Mitchell 2003).

in Nashville, for example, have been living in encampments under an interstate overpass next to the Cumberland River for perhaps two decades. According to a City Council member there, the camp was 'pretty extensive' with some shelters possessing roofs and stoves, and pirated electricity occasionally available. 'Over the years,' he said, 'we're found that it is a lot of individuals who are trying to find some sort of refuge from the mean streets from the violence and disorder they see in other parts of the city as they're homeless.' Interstitial space in Nashville has served as a safe haven as the tent city's population has grown during the economic crisis; the city has decided not to raze it, but to 'monitor it' and to 'put case management services around these people' to help move them out of homelessness (Local Leaders 2009).

The problem of safe havens is a difficult one (Mitchell 2003). It is probably most difficult in how quickly such safe harbours can be hijacked, as the case of Ontario makes clear. A related problem is how tenuous they can be. If Nashville's tent city seems to have been granted at least a small degree of stability, the same has of course not been true of Camden's, Sacramento's – or St Petersburg's, where in December 2006, church groups gave out tents to some 30 homeless people living under Interstate 375.[12] At the New Year, the tent city – now called 'Coming Up' – moved across the street to a vacant lot owned by the St Vincent de Paul Society, were it grew to about 140 residents.[13] Residents (the majority of whom worked full time) signed a contract with each other pledging four hours of community work a week keeping the grounds clean, cleaning the portable toilets, cutting hair, mediating disputes, and so forth. Such self-organization quickly prompted city officials (over the objections of some council members) to declare a 'crisis'[14] and to order St Vincent de Paul to evict the residents under an old law prohibiting people from living in tents anywhere in the city, even on private property. The city pledged to find a vacant building to use as a winter shelter, but had no intention of delaying the eviction until it did, a position that led to strenuous protests by homeless people and their advocates, including one at the Mayor's church. Threatened with daily fines of $250 for code violations, St Vincent de Paul complied with city orders to shut down the camp. Some residents moved back to one of two camps under the overpass; others accepted one-time rent vouchers of

---

12　The following account of St Petersburg's tent cities has been pieced together from more than 50 news reports, published between the end of 2006 and mid-2010, mostly in the St Petersburg Times; a full bibliography or copies of the articles are available from the author upon request. The YouTube video referred to below is available at: http://www. youtube.com/watch?feature=player_detailpage&v=LrPdZmPB36U.

13　St Petersburg homeless population was estimated to be about 2,250 in early 2007; city shelters provided space for 250 on an emergency basis and there were 500 transitions housing slots.

14　To which residents responded: 'We are not a crisis. We are a success and a solution! … [F]or many of us the tent city provides not only protection, but also a nurturing community' (Grimmage et al. 2007).

$550 which would allow them to stay in a motel for two weeks or more. Others merely disappeared.[15]

Soon after the St Vincent site was closed down, two homeless men were murdered in a single night. An extraordinary city council meeting followed, shedding further light on the dangers faced by homeless people living on the streets. Even so, a week after the murders, with no suspects yet apprehended, city police entered the two small tent cities that had sprung up in the wake of the St Vincent closing, slashing the tents from their bases and moorings with knives, box cutters and scissors, and confiscating them. They claimed fire code violations (though precisely which ones and whether they actually applied or not remained unclear in official explanations). They claimed they cut up the tents to avoid 'physical altercations' with homeless people, who might have refused to let them confiscate them if they asked.[16] The move was ineffective; homeless advocates secured new tents within eight hours and the camps were reestablished.[17]

Moreover, videos of the raid were quickly posted on YouTube, attracting significant national attention, and encouraging furious backtracking by the Mayor and other city officials.[18] In turn, nearby businesses and residents organized to assure the permanent elimination of the tent cities, holding rallies and protests nearby where they claimed the tent cities encouraged crime, threatened property values and undermined business. As a result, the city held a 'homeless summit', one result of which was a change in city codes – outlawing tents on public rights of way, but allowing them under certain conditions on private property – and the opening of negotiations with St Vincent de Paul to have it host a tent city again on the site the city had forced to be closed only a few weeks before, this time as a collaborative effort among homeless advocates, the city and St Vincent.

In the meantime the city and various charities worked to move those living in the tent cities into other housing (and in some instances to provide jobs). By late February, more than 100 tent city residents and other homeless had been moved to apartments and treatment centres (with the aid of a $500,000 grant from the Catholic Diocese). But as every homeless person or couple was found a new place to live, another arrived – from somewhere – to take their place in a tent, doing

---

15   St Vincent de Paul's explanations of its own actions during these weeks do not inspire much confidence in that organization's ability to recognize homeless people as autonomous subjects capable of shaping their own lives.

16   Apparently it did not occur to city, fire and police officials that the operation entailed seizing and destroying private property, a significant constitutional violation. 'In hindsight we didn't discuss the actual property issue,' according to Police Chief Chuck Harmon (whose job it is to uphold the law), 'and we probably should have taken that into consideration.'

17   Two arrests were made in connection with the murders – robbery may have been the motive – nearly three weeks after the tent city was destroyed.

18   Eventually, the police major who came up with the idea for the raid wrote a report exonerating herself and her colleagues, claiming the slashing of the tents was legal and justified.

nothing to dampen the growing backlash. The city continued to work on tightening laws against camping and sleeping in public space and announced plans for a 'temporary use permit' for the St Vincent site, which would allow 75 tents for no more than 90 days.[19] Tent city residents and their advocates demanded, however, that the St Vincent tent city be allowed to remain open indefinitely: as long as there was need. They also demanded an equal voice in the running of the camp, the entrance of new residents as current ones departed, that the city abandon its plan to require all residents to wear identifying armbands and that none be placed in a new shelter being built which they felt would be unsafe and represent a great loss of autonomy. The city refused all demands, and threatened those who refused to move to the new tent city with arrest.

Nonetheless when the new laws were passed and the St Vincent tent city opened in mid-March, 'the two-satellite tent cities appeared abandoned' and the new site quickly filled. Other homeless people moved to a new tent city on church property in another district that parishioners created despite objections from neighbours. The second tent city on St Vincent property – called 'New Hope City' – ran by strict rules. The lot was fenced. Residents had to wear identifying wristbands at all times. Alcohol was forbidden. There was a midnight curfew (when the gates were locked). When a resident moved out a new one could not take her place. Together these rules posed a problem. Twenty-seven were evicted for drinking or violating the curfew (which is to say, it was not just that they could not enter or leave the grounds after midnight, it was that they could not be *out* after midnight). Seventy-two received housing vouchers for one month. As these ran out (or as others given at the previous tent cities ran out), former residents could not return; many ended up living furtively on the streets. By early May, New Hope City was empty, the homeless street population had apparently not shrunk at all and city council turned its attention to a new anti-panhandling law to police those still on the streets. Homeless people and an advocate set up a protest encampment on the site of one of the 'satellite' tent cities, leading to three arrests; and other homeless residents of the slashed tent city sued the city for damages, which the city sought to settle with a $250 payment. Over the summer, with no other place to go, dozens of homeless people took to sleeping on the sidewalk in front of city hall, which the city was unable to do anything about because its anti-camping ordinance could only be enforced if there were shelter beds available; there were not, not even in a tent city.

Determined to learn from this experience, the city of St Petersburg and Pinellas County began planning early for the following winter's homeless 'crisis'. They

---

19 Unlike many earlier anti-sleeping and camping laws around the USA, the proposed St Petersburg law made it illegal to sleep on public property only if shelter beds are available. Such a provision would seem to meet the test for a 'just' anti-sleeping law laid out by such analysts as Waldron (1991), Simon (1992) and Foscarinis (1996), and seemingly accepted by anti-homeless legal campaigner Tier (1998), though its provision that the shelter beds could be as far as three miles outside the city complicates matters, suggesting as it does the possibility of expulsion.

planned this time to 'encourage[e] the homeless to live in' a controlled encampment built 'so out of the way you will never see it unless you search for it'.[20] A central plank in the County's Ten-Year Plan to End Homelessness (a federal mandate), the 'Pinellas Hope' tent city, was to be built on 10 acres of litter-strewn scrub owned by the Catholic Diocese in an industrially zoned area miles from any city. It would consist of 125 tents (housing 225), three excess modular buildings donated by the school district for laundry facilities, a kitchen and administrative offices, two large communal tents for eating and socializing in, and it would be fenced; security guards would be hired. Background checks would be conducted on all potential residents. Neighbours – a scrap yard, construction companies, trucking companies and the like – raised concerns about theft and safety.

Despite concerns that homeless people would not accept the distant Pinellas Hope, with its strict rules and fences, the tent city quickly filled to near capacity (even as a fairly large encampment remained in front of city hall by those who refused to go and who were protesting city and county policies). Catholic Charities, which managed the site, nonetheless stuck to their promise to close it on 30 April. 'One of the things we want to do is have the people in Pinellas Hope think, "What's my next step." We are not trying to create a tent city that people can live in permanently,' in the words of the Catholic Charities president. By the time it was scheduled to close at the end of April, 2008, Pinellas Hope had housed 490 people, of whom 148 found other housing, 122 found jobs and more than 200 simply went missing – probably returning to the streets. Donations had also been raised to allow a scaled-down version of the camp, housing 50–75 people, to stay open through September. The reduction in size would be achieved by evicting homeless residents who 'show[ed] no signs of progress'.[21] So far, the camp, which now has an annual budget of $2.5 million, remains.

And indeed, officials think it is such a success[22] they have changed housing and zoning laws to allow for the creation of more permanent campgrounds like Pinellas Hope – seeking to replicate it at a sight in nearby Hillsborough County (home to the city of Tampa, which hosts the largest homeless population in the state) – despite the vigorous objections of various property owners and residents.[23]

---

20   Despite repeated promises, the city had made no progress on developing a permanent indoor shelter.

21   Meanwhile St Petersburg not only expanded its anti-panhandling law, but also passed an ordinance giving the police the right to confiscate homeless people's property without a warrant, as 'sympathy for the homeless wane[d]'. 'People are simply tired of these antics' – homeless people establishing their own tent cities and finding other ways to survive in an increasingly hostile city – according to a city council member.

22   County cities contribute $1 million to the Pinellas Hope budget – about $12/day per resident. Jail lodging for someone arrested for trespassing or public urination costs $126/day.

23   Opposition and fear bordered on the ridiculous. A resident living more than a mile away bought a Rottweiler; another installed surveillance cameras; a third bought a gun and threatened to use it.

In essence, with the support of some local officials, Catholic Charities has sought to create a local, scaled down and more authoritarian network of camps like those created by the Farm Security Administration camps in the Western USA during the Depression to house homeless migrants. They were not totally successful. Hillsborough County commissioners rejected a plan for a second Pinellas Hope-like encampment on their turf, much to the delight of area residents. But at Pinellas Hope something like the FSA pattern continues to be followed, as tents and casitas are now being replaced with small, subsidised apartments.

Conclusion

From Camden to St Petersburg: these mark out the ends of two trajectories of tent cities in the contemporary USA, and they represent two different outcomes in the ongoing 'war of position' that is the permanent condition of homelessness in capitalism's heartland. As homeless people have been chased from doorstep to public park, and from public park to abandoned lot or Interstate underpass, as shelters and soup kitchens – and now semi-permanent tent cities – for the homeless and hungry are now more and now less tolerated by city elites, housed residents and businesses, and as homeless people themselves have been variously positioned as either deserving aid (as in the wake of St Petersburg's first tent city) or not (as was the case only as year later), tent cities, shanty towns and new 'jungles' have remained a constant.

For many on the left, such encampments sometimes represent important interstitial spaces not only of survival, but of autonomy and organizing (e.g. Wright 1998). The space of tent city must, for that reason, be preserved. There is much to be said in favour of this argument. The history of homelessness in the USA has shown that jungles and camps have indeed been vital to poor people's (sometimes radical) organizing – and to their dignity. Indicatively, in St Petersburg, Pinellas Hope was promoted by some of its advocates precisely as a means of quelling more radical demands by homeless people and their advocates. Pinellas Hope would create a more orderly, more controlled, less political space; and to the degree that it did, then more radical encampments like the one of the city hall steps could be shut down. So too Sacramento's emergency shelter at the fairgrounds: it was (in part) a means of breaking apart both a social and a *political* community that had formed along the banks of the American River – and, of course, Camden's. These moves against the political encampment of homeless people argue that indeed such spaces need to be fought for and defended.

And yet, it must be remembered, as one St Petersburg tent city activist put it: 'Tent city is not the crisis. It's the conditions that caused the tent city that's the crisis.' At the same time the rights of homeless people to occupy and mobilize in the interstices is struggled for; in other words, we must recognize tent cities for what they are: evidence of the utter failure of the capitalist city to provide for its residents. Not only does struggling Rustbelt Camden make this clear, but so too does Sunbelt St Petersburg – to say nothing of once-booming Sacramento. What must be fought for, in other words, is not (only) the protection of tent cities, but (especially) the destruction of a system that has made them an *inevitable* part of the urban landscape. We need to start to find ways to eliminate tent cities from the urban landscape – not to clear them out as the neoliberal urban right would have us do, and not necessarily to replace them with fenced-off campsites run by charities, hidden away in the scrub, but rather to make them superfluous rather than necessary. If the bourgeoisie *still* has no solution to the housing problem, then we need to find a *non*-bourgeois solution. And here, ironically, tent cities, though they must be eliminated if a just city is to arise, provide the model: as a taking of land, as a non-commodified and cooperative form of property and social relations, as (potentially) an organization space, tent cities, and their progenitors like the hobo jungle, have much to teach us.

References

Adler, B. 2009. Sacramento's tent cities still bloom in secret. *National Public Radio*, 26 July.

Anderson, N. 1923. *The Hobo: The Sociology of the Homeless Man*. Chicago, IL: University of Chicago Press.

Anderson, N. 1940. *Men on the Move*. Chicago, IL: University of Chicago Press.

Bahr, H. 1970. *Disaffiliated Man: Essays and Bibliography on Skid Row, Vagrancy, and Outsiders*. Toronto: University of Toronto Press.

Bahr, H. 1973. *Skid Row: An Introduction to Disaffiliation*. New York: Oxford University Press.

Baum, A. and Burnes, D. 1991. *A Nation in Denial: The Truth about Homelessness*. Boulder, CO: Westview Press.

Bluestone, B. and Harrison, B. 1982. *The Deindustrialization of America*. New York: Basic Books.

Burkeman, O. 2009. United States: out in the open. Recession exposes America's homeless underclass. *The Guardian*, 27 March, 27.

Cresswell, T. 2001. *The Tramp in America*. London: Reaktion Books.

Dear, M. and Wolch. J. 1987. *Landscapes of Despair*. Princeton, NJ: Princeton University Press.

Dear, M. and Wolch, J. 1994. Herding the homeless is an unjust answer. *Los Angeles Times*, 14 November, B7.

DePastino T. 2003. *Citizen Hobo: How a Century of Homelessness Shaped America*. Chicago, IL: University of Chicago Press.

Dixon, P. and Allen, T. 2004. *The Bonus Army: An American Epic*. New York: Walker and Company.

Dubofsky, M. 1969. *We Shall Be All: A History of the Industrial Workers of the World*. Chicago, IL: Quadrangle Books.

Duncan, J. 1978. Men without property: the tramp's classification and use of public space. *Antipode*, 1(1), 24–34.

Ehrenreich, B. 2009. Tales of tent city. *The Nation*, 3 June. Available at: www.thenation.come/print/article/tales-tent-city [accessed: 1 September 2012].

Ellickson, R. 1996. Controlling chronic misconduct in city spaces: of panhandlers, skid rows, and public space zoning. *Yale Law Journal*, 105, 1165–248.

Engels, F. 1872. *The Housing Question*. Available at: http://www.marxists.org/archive/marx/works/1872/housing-question/index.htm [accessed: 1 September 2012].

Foner, P. 1964. *History of the Labor Movement in the United States, Vol. 4: The Industrial Workers of the World*. New York: International Publishers.

Foner, P. (ed.) 1981. *Fellow Workers and Friends: Free Speech Fights as Told by Participants*. Westport, CT: Greenwood Press.

Foscarinis, M. 1996. Downward spiral: homelessness and its criminalization. *Yale Law and Policy Review*, 14, 1–63.

Galarza, E. 1977. *Farm Workers and Agri-Business in California, 1947–1960*. Notre Dame: University of Notre Dame Press.

Gragg, R. 2002. Guerrilla city: a homeless settlement in Portland has its own government, urban plan, and skyline. *Architecture*, 91, 47–51

Gregory, J. 1989. *American Exodus: The Dustbowl Migration and Okie Culture in California*. Oxford: Oxford University Press.

Gonzalez, R. 2009a. Hundreds of Calif. homeless march for land rights. *National Public Radio*, 2 July.

Gonzalez, R. 2009b. In Sacramento, tent city dwellers want to stay. *National Public Radio*, 27 March.

Gonzalez, R. 2009c. Sacramento tent city reflects economy's troubles. *National Public Radio*, 16 March.

Groth, P. 1994. *Living Downtown: The History of Residential Hotels in the United States*. Berkeley, CA: University of California Press.

Harrison, B. and Bluestone, B. 1988. *The Great U-Turn: Corporate Restructuring and the Polarizing of America*. New York: Basic Books.

Harvey, D. 2010. *The Enigma of Capital and the Crises of Capitalism*. Oxford: Oxford University Press.

Hedges, C. and Sacco, J. 2010. City of ruins: Camden, New Jersey, stands as a warning of what huge pockets of America could turn into. *The Nation*, 22 November, 15–20.

Higbie, T. 2003. *Indispensible Outcasts: Hobo Workers and Community in the American Midwest, 1880–1930*. Urbana, IL: University of Illinois Press.

Hopper, K. 2003. *Reckoning with Homelessness*. Ithaca, NY: Cornell University Press.

Kasinitz, P. 1986. Gentrification and homelessness: the single room occupant and the inner city revival in: J. Erickson and C. Wilhelm (eds) *Housing the Homeless*. New Brunswick: CUPR, pp. 241–52.

Kawash, S. 1998. The homeless body. *Public Culture*, 10, 316–41.

Kusmer, K. 2002. *Down and Out, On the Road: The Homeless in American History*. Oxford: Oxford University Press.

Local Leaders 2009. Local leaders address homelessness/Tell Me More. *National Public Radio*, 17 August.

McKinley, J. 2009. Homeless in Sacramento tent city will be moved to state fairground. *New York Times*, 26 March, 17.

McMurray, D. 1923. The industrial armies and the commonweal. *The Mississippi Historical Review*, 10(3), 215–52.

McSheehy, W. 1979. *Skid Row*. Cambridge, MA: Schenkman Publishing.

McWilliams, C. 1939. *Factories in the Field: The Story of Migratory Farm Labor in California*. Boston, MA: Little, Brown.

Maharidge, D. and Williamson, M. 1996. *The Journey to Nowhere: The Saga of the New Underclass*. New York: Hyperion Books.

Mitchell, D. 1996. *The Lie of the Land: Migrant Workers and the California Landscape*. Minneapolis, MN: University of Minnesota Press.

Mitchell, D. 2003. *The Right to the City: Social Justice and the Fight for Public Space*. New York: Guilford.

Mitchell, D. 2005. The S.U.V. model of citizenship: floating bubbles, buffer zones, and the rise of the 'purely atomic' individual. *Political Geography*, 24(1), 77–100.

Mitchell, D. 2012. *They Saved the Crops: Labor, Landscape and the Struggle Over Industrial Farming in Bracero-Era California*. Athens, GA: University of Georgia Press.

Mitchell, D. and Heynen, N. 2009. The geography of survival and the right to the city: speculations on surveillance, legal innovation, and the criminalization of innovation. *Urban Geography*, 30(6), 611–32.

Monkkonen, E. (ed.) 1984. *Walking to Work: Tramps in America, 1790–1935*. Lincoln, NE: University of Nebraska Press.

Parker, C. 1917. The I.W.W. *Atlantic Monthly*, November, 651–52.

Pottinger 1991. *Pottinger v. City of Miami* 810 F. Supp. 1551, S.D. Fla.

Presthold, K. 1931. How we solved it at Oklahoma City. *The Nation*, 7 October, 361.

Rowe, S. and Wolch, J. 1990. Social networks in time and space: homeless women in Skid Row, Los Angeles. *Annals of the Association of American Geographers*, 80(2), 184–204.

Schneider, J. 1996. Skid row as an urban neighborhood, 1880–1969, in: J. Erickson and C. Wilhelm (eds) *Housing the Homeless*. New Brunswick: CUPR, pp. 167–89.

Schwantes, C. 1985. *Coxey's Army: An American Odyssey*. Lincoln, NE: University of Nebraska Press.

Simon H. 1992. Towns without pity: a constitutional and historical analysis of official efforts to drive homeless people from American cities. *Tulane Law Review* 66, 631–76.

Simon, H. 1995. The criminalization of homelessness in Santa Ana, California: A case study. *Clearinghouse Review*, 29, 725–29.

Spradley, J. 1970. *You Owe Yourself a Drunk: An Ethnography of Urban Nomads.* Boston, MA: Little, Brown.

Staeheli, L. and Mitchell, D. 2008. *The People's Property? Power, Politics, and the Public.* New York: Routledge.

Starr, K. 1996. *Endangered Dreams: The Great Depression in California.* New York: Oxford University Press.

Stein, W. 1973. *California and the Dustbowl Migration.* Westport, CT: Greenwood Press.

Steinbeck, J. 1939. *The Grapes of Wrath.* New York: Viking.

Takahashi, L. 1998. *Homelessness, AIDS, and stigmatization: the NIMBY syndrome in the United States near the end of the twentieth century.* Oxford: Oxford University Press.

Tier, R. 1998. Restoring Order in Urban Public Spaces. *Texas Review of Law and Politics*, 2, 256–291.

Waldron, J. 1991. Homelessness and the issue of freedom. *UCLA Law Review*, 39, 295–324.

Woirol, G. 1984. Observing the IWW in California, May–July 1914. *Labor History*, 25, 437–47.

Wolch, J. and Dear, M. 1996. *Malign Neglect: Homelessness in an American City.* San Francisco, CA: Jossey-Bass.

Wright, T. 1998. *Out of Place: Homeless Mobilizations, Subcities, and Contested Landscapes.* Albany, NY: SUNY Press.

Chapter 4

Spatial Justice in the Lawscape

Andreas Philippopoulos-Mihalopoulos

An interstice is not an in-between

The location of urban interstices is problematic. To think of interstices, faithful to its etymology as a standing-between or an interval between two things, is an attempt at redressing the problem of dualism. The problem, whose solution interstices purport to be, can be simplified as follows: rather than choosing this or that, one carves a space between them. This famous 'third space' (as pioneered by Ed Soja (1996)) is geared to accommodating both sides without losing anything but the claim to centrality that is inevitably attributed to the other two. Thus, the in-between is regaled with the enviable quality of a perpetually relevant marginality which, in its turn, endows the in-between with political kudos and aesthetic radicality.

While the above is obviously well-meaning, it has reached full circle. The various attempts at carving a space in-between have now become central in their marginality (if the pun is allowed) and consequently have lost their radical potential. In-betweens have become co-opted hubs of capitalist pacification. We can all fit in the limbo of the imaginary outside, which assuages the damned when the latter are faced with the impossibility of a Hegelian synthesis. By fitting in the third space, however, we are embodying the synthesis at which dualisms precisely aim. As Marcus Doel (1999: 120) writes, 'the addition of a third space does not disable dualism: it merely opens the metaphysics of binary opposition to a dialectical resolution of contradiction'. The production of an in-between is the dreamland of the dualist contradiction, in which both thesis and antithesis retain a stake while ostensibly becoming surpassed, resisted, refused. The fluidity of the in-between quickly solidifies despite intentions to the contrary. How often has the world witnessed much-hailed in-betweens becoming simplified spaces of oscillation, political negotiation, circumstantial manoeuvring and self-congratulatory compromise? Are we not governed by self-propagating in-betweens, be this socialism, neo-liberalism, sustainability, human rights, international law, happiness indicators, big society resuscitations, ethical consumerism and so on? Governed by distance rather than affinity, void rather than continuum, antithesis rather than a non-relativistic multiplicity of positions, dualism's deeper problematic structure is not exclusion but hyper-inclusion. The in-between becomes normalized as the inclusion of resistance, the important third party that brokers the agreement, the centre of power where power is diffused and control appears dissimulated as non-power (see Philippopoulos-Mihalopoulos 2011a).

All this, however, is of lesser importance when compared to what I consider to be the main pathology of the in-between: by offering a solution to the problem of dualism, an in-between reasserts and firmly establishes the dualist position. Even when the in-between genuinely manages not to become a synthesis, but stubbornly maintains its focus on the emergence of a different space, the initial rupture is taken for granted. Interestingly, the proliferation of in-between spaces has done little to alleviate the initial dualism. Rather, the various in-betweens form part of the phenomenon of the politics of centre/periphery, whose aim is to reduce the antithesis into an in-between, which ultimately, however, turns against itself and self-cannibalizes in a cloud of political apathy. In short, by accepting the possibility of an in-between, one accepts the ontological priority of the dualism and its subsequent epistemological necessity of a synthesis, however materialized. In fighting Hegelianism, the in-between manages to be Hegelian through and through.

For the above reasons, interstices must be disassociated from the in-between. In this context, the location of urban interstices is a matter of some delicacy. In the introduction to this volume, Andrea Mubi Brighenti talks eloquently about the urbanization of territory and the territorialization of the city, namely the sprawling control society on the one hand, and the urban 'civility' on the other. Sidestepping the temptation to juxtapose these as, say, reality versus wishful thinking, Brighenti correctly commits his contributors and readers to the *simultaneity* of these territorial manifestations through his employment of Deleuze and Guattari's approach and in particular the simultaneous generation of striated and smooth space, namely space respectively with and without the top-down hierarchical organization according to the logic of logos. What I think is particularly important here is the way the two are not to be separated in a dialectic way. This has proven to be hard even for Deleuze and Guattari, despite their frequent and explicit denunciations of dualist thought. But one has to resist falling into the trap. This should be fought even on the level of instrumentalism: to use dualist thinking in order to counterattack it (indeed what Deleuze and Guattari seem to be doing in *A Thousand Plateaus*, 1988) can also be found guilty of espousing dualism in the sense of the *a priori* separation. Indeed, more than dualism itself, the problem is the acceptance of a rift that needs/must/can be mended.

Thus, both aforementioned foundational problems of dualism risk re-appearing from the back door. One, therefore, has to follow very closely what Brighenti means when he writes 'the interstice is rather the outcome of a composition of interactions and affections of multiple parts that coexist in various ways within a given spatial situation' (Introduction, this volume). Rather than synthesis, an interstice is an emergence (which means that it lies beyond prescription, controlled mechanics and systematic articulation of the result). Rather than originating in a dualism, an interstice emerges from a multiplicity (which means that it is not an oscillation between two opposing poles, but an often arbitrary picking of various positions that form a surface on which one moves). To this I would add the following: rather than an outcome in the sense of causal link between affections and emergence, an interstice resists causality. Further, an interstice resists also attribution, namely post-facto causal linking that takes place on a virtual plane, itself potentially co-opted by its own striation. Finally, an interstice is not flanked by more or less potent bodies but emerges properly speaking *in the middle*.

One must be careful not to confuse the middle with the in-between:

> The middle is by no means an average; on the contrary, it is where things pick up speed. *Between things* does not designate a localizable relation going from one thing to the other and back again, but a perpendicular direction, a transversal moment that sweeps one and the other away, a stream without beginning or end that undermines its banks and picks up speed in the middle. (Deleuze and Guattari 1988: 28)

The middle (or *milieu*) is the space of revolt against the usual tools of origin, centre and boundary: 'One never commences; one never has a tabula rasa; one slips in, enters in the middle; one takes up or lays down rhythms' (Deleuze and Guattari 1988: 123). Just as the grass has no one root, central part or limits to its expansion, in the same way to begin in the middle is to find oneself folded between the multiplicity of the world without a discernible origin, a specific centre and determined territorial limits. To be thrown into the mobile multiplicity of the grass is to follow the blades waving in the wind: one loses one's origin, one's preconceived ideas of location and destination, one's belief in the importance of the centre. Grass is opposed to the tree with its defined root, trunk and volume. As Deleuze and Guattari write, 'arborescent systems are hierarchical systems with centers of significance and subjectification' (Deleuze and Guattari 1988: 16). For this reason, they urge to 'make rhizomes, not roots, never plant! Don't sow, grow offshoots!' (Deleuze and Guattari 1988: 24). Offshoots and rhizomes are characteristics of the planar mobility with which Deleuze and Guattari describe the world.

Rhizomes specifically encapsulate the ideas of horizontal, trans-species, heterogeneous growth that traverses Deleuzian–Guattarian thought, in that they do not constitute a linear, vertical construction but a surface where any modulation is absorbed, closed in and eventually spread in lake-like smoothness. However, even radical rhizomes have been routinely fetishized in the literature as the way to guarantee openness, flexibility and contingency. This marginalizes the fact that rhizomes can also be co-opted, overcoded and used in ways that go against the very idea of rhizome (Michulak 2008). This is an interesting example of the complexity of the middle: neither necessarily 'good' or 'bad', positive or problematic, the space in the middle is a space of struggle – in this case, against origins, boundaries, centres. Even better, the space in the middle is a space of *encounters* with other bodies, a space in which one's body affects and is affected by other bodies. It is not a space of judgement, of secure values, of fixed constructions. Rather, the space in the middle is precisely *in the middle*: neither this nor that side; but then again, not a boundary and therefore not flanked by sides. Likewise, it offers no direction: just as the leaves of grass move with the wind, the space in the middle consists of the encounter between the grass and the wind. An encounter for Deleuze pushes the encountered parties off their comfort zone of categories and identities, and throws them in a 'mad becoming' (Deleuze 2004a: 141). The grass becomes wind and moves along the wind's breath, the wind becomes grass and spreads itself on the ground: becoming itself is pushed deeper in the middle, as it were. Finally, the space in the middle offers no chronology and no external causality: all is interfolded in simultaneity and immanence. The wind becomes the grass, the grass becomes tomorrow's grass, its beginning is in the middle, in the space of here, manically flapping around its movement.[1]

Having established what this chapter understands by interstices, I can perhaps now embark on the more applied discussion demanded by the adjective 'urban'. In order to do this, I present a version of an urban interstice, namely the lawscape, which has been appearing in my work of the last few years. Simply put, the lawscape is the interstitial space of law and the city. The argument underlining the lawscape is that there is no difference between these two and that one conditions the other from within an extensive immanence. Thus, regulated city and urban law are simply ways of starting in the middle, covering the same distance albeit arguably from different perspectives. The lawscape is the breeding ground of the potential emergence of spatial justice, another concept that I have been trying to redefine in relation to more specific legal and spatial considerations. In that sense, the interstice begets an interstice. The connection between the lawscape and spatial justice is both fragile and solidly immanent, which means that there is no prescription that guarantees the emergence of spatial justice, yet the lawscape is the only ground on which spatial justice can emerge.

Lawscape

The lawscape is the epistemological and ontological tautology of law and the city (see also Philippopoulos-Mihalopoulos 2007). On some level, the neologism risks making the individual use of the terms redundant. For what is law without city or city without law? A city without law can only be this fetish of a holy city of justice, perpetually floating in a post-conflict space where everything is light and forgiveness. Likewise, a law without a city is a law without materiality, that other fetish (this time of legal thinking) that considers law to be an abstract, universal,

---

1   'The orchid deterritorializes by forming an image, a tracing of a wasp; but the wasp reterritorializes on that image. The wasp is nevertheless deterritorialized, becoming a piece in the orchid's reproductive apparatus. But it reterritorializes the orchid by transporting its pollen. Wasp and orchid, as heterogeneous elements, form a rhizome.' (Deleuze and Guattari 1987 [1980]: 10)

immutable, what? Thing? Breath? Divine will? Act of violence? Both law without city and city without law are fantastic beasts that operate at best as horizon and at worst as cheap rhetoric. However, one thing must be clarified: abstract law is very different to justice. Justice as horizon operates on an always-to-come space but through the calculation of law, a messianic justice that demands present legal calculation (Derrida 1992). After that, and once justice has been achieved (if ever), the law recedes for a well-deserved rest, since it becomes superfluous when the city becomes just. The law emerges in conflict, in quest (for justice), and in need to capture the future – namely at *all times* in the city. It becomes abundantly clear that none of these legal apparitions is law in abstraction. Law is always spatially grounded, epidermally embodied, materially present. Law as an abstract universal, free from the constraints of matter and bodies and space, is one of the illusions that law itself (and some strands of legal theory) insists on maintaining. Law as control is by necessity material (meaning spatial and corporeal), for it is only through its very own emplaced body that the law can exert its force. Law comes nowhere but from within the controlled, their bodies of appearance and the corridors on which they move, as post-colonial theory has taught us (Bhabha 2005). This is more than just biopolitical control, since it addresses the material nature of the law itself: only from within matter can law control. To posit a law without a city is tantamount to positing, say, a universal human right that applies to everyone without the need for contextualization. The latter is not 'just' the context. On the contrary, it is the supreme need to close in and eavesdrop on the particular body's specific circumstances. Even in the theoretical, indeed *horizon*tal, possibility of a just city, the law's withdrawal would be a material one, its movement traced on the skin of the city, its back turned to the urban deification. In its turn, a just city has captured time itself, engraved it right *here* in its Edenic *intramuros*. There is no other way: a just city is a theological concept and cannot accommodate anything that falls sort of divinity (*contra* Fainstein 2010). A just city does not belong to the lawscape except as a horizon. And the risk of course is that the horizon can always be co-opted on behalf of cheap demagogy.

Law in the lawscape is not just the standard, written law but also the diffused normativity that streams through everyday life – what Spinoza (2007) has called 'rules for living'. This includes human and other bodies as well as objects. Just as a body, an object is already functionalized, normalized, never independent of its normative position in the world. At the same time, the object determines the functions and normalization processes around it. In that sense, human, natural, artificial bodies come together in creating and being created by the law. For this reason, I would talk about the law as an expansive *institutional affect* that permeates the formal and the informal, the abstract and the material. What is remarkable, however, is that the latter diffused form of normativity exhibits the paradox of appearing both as a corporeally embedded preference for individual self-preservation, and a feature compliant with the current surveillance and control culture. This sense of normativity takes few risks and delegates conflict resolution to what it considers to be higher levels of judgement-making – indeed, to go back to Spinoza, a sort of guardian authority that pursues efficiently the individual interests of its subjects. The phenomenon of the 'nanny state' is both an anathema and a desire, a direct result of which is the perceived political apathy. It is not all bleak though. This is a comfortable sense of normativity that covers specific needs, such as issues of belonging, constructions of home and community, as well as emplacement. It is, properly speaking, a product of its own spatiotemporal conditions, and as such it manages either to preserve itself as a visibly unethical, oppressive, dictatorial, fascist and indeed illegal regime (which, however, engenders its own legality); or to make itself invisible and neutral, to recede from the surface and conceal its force in the folds of its own legality. The latter, a phenomenon of most Western societies, works both ways: legal subjects recede from actively questioning the law (complacency or reassurance), and the law recedes from claiming a role in the construction of the everyday. This does not mean that the law is not there – simply that it is not perceived as being constantly there. This is a strategic move that aims at diffusing and dissimulating the force of law, offering instead a smooth, anomic atmosphere. Even so, things can on occasion overflow, exceed themselves and embark upon a flight of radical self-redefinition. In such cases, the already 'contagious' (in the sense of epidemic imitating, see Tarde (1903)) nature of the normative doubles up and becomes rapid, horizontal and fiery, engendering such eruptions as demonstrations, revolts, revolutions, coups. In all these cases, the law does not leave the stage. It is merely supplemented by a different normative direction and sometimes a higher velocity.

City on the other hand is the thick spatiality of bodies (humans, nonhumans, linguistic, spatial, disciplinary), buildings, objects, animals, vegetables, minerals, money, communication, silence, open spaces, air, water and so on. This spatiality is a fractal manifestation of what I have elsewhere called 'open ecology' (Philippopoulos-Mihalopoulos 2011b), namely the assemblage of the natural, the human, the artificial, the scientific, the political, the economic and so on, on a plane of contingency and fluid boundaries, or as Brighenti (2006: 80) puts it, 'a series of territories, which can be thought of as superimposed ... or mutually exclusive ... or even criss-crossed and overlapping'. The open ecology of the city is simultaneously open and closed. Hinterlands, globe, outer space, hybrid technohumans, technologically manipulated meteorological phenomena 'and so on' (see Anna Grear's (2011) collapse of the anthropomorphic effigy) are all grounded on the urban materiality of *here*, itself open to any definition of materiality may come from over *there*. Thus, while infinite, open ecology is entirely immanent. Any transcending movement is inscribed within, in the recesses of the unknowable here. There is nothing that is not, actually or virtually, included in open ecology. And nothing that is not, actually or virtually, connected to everything else in some form of connection that enables everything to *become* everything else. This is a processual rather than value-based ecology and, to quote Deleuze and Guattari (1988: 4), 'we make no distinction between man and nature: the human essence of nature and the natural essence of man become one within nature in the form of production of industry'. Instead of a distinction, a fractal fluctuation between human/artificial and natural. Instead of one city, an infinite multiplicity that repeats itself as difference.

The lawscape therefore operates as a surface on which the open normativity of the law and the open ecology of the city emerge. Yet it does not constitute a new unity. Rather than positing an origin of a fusion between the two, it builds on an existing becoming (becoming lawscape entails that the city becomes law becomes city *ad infinitum*). It does not assume the role of a synthesis since it does not presuppose a dualism between city and law. On the contrary, it assumes that the two have always shared the same ontological surface and even the same epistemological lines of flight. In that sense, it is properly speaking an interstice, namely an always-already emergence of ontological and epistemological tautology. There is no causal link between city and law on the one hand, and the lawscape on the other, since there is no distance that needs to be bridged, no logical step that needs to be taken. Likewise, wherever one locates oneself on the lawscape, there can be no attribution – say law comes from the city, or city comes from law. City and law are necessarily observed in their tautology. To do otherwise means that the observer is constructing a different epistemological plane from which to observe the lawscape – but even then the tautology cannot be doubted.

There is, however, a further movement within the lawscape. The surface of the lawscape enables the reciprocal dissimulation of law and the city. Thus, in the lawscape, the city sheds its asphyxiating normativity just as the law sheds its ever-present materiality. Law and the city become mutually exclusive in their emergence, thus dissimulating and diffusing the otherwise oppressive nature of the lawscape. In that way they can both carry on with their self-perpetuating myths, such as the self-description of a city as an *accueil* of difference and the breeding ground of communitarian nostalgia, and of the law as a universal good that has the potential of universalizing values such as right and wrong. Some elements remain, however, despite the very grounded and strategically engineered attempts at dissimulation. These are elements of the lawscape itself, which however change in degree according to the conditions of the specific lawscape. First, the *inescapable* lawscape: wherever one is in the city (and arguably beyond it, in its global hinterlands), one swims with and against the various normative flows that constitute the materiality of its lawscape. Second, the *posthuman* lawscape: defining the city as a slice of open ecology means that the lawscape lies beyond such distinctions as human/natural/artificial (Wolfe 2009). Third, the *fractal* lawscape: while each lawscape is different, they all fractally repeat the reciprocally invisibilizing embrace between open normativity and open ecology. There is no global lawscape that operates as a semantic and material common surface for the totality of cities, yet there is a *plane of immanence*, not unlike the earth or nature, as Deleuze and Guattari put it (1988). This plane consists of lawscapes but also trammels the lawscapes, constantly pushing them along new *lines of flight*, namely internal planar movements that begin and end within the plane of immanence yet push the edges of the plane always further. An example of such a line of flight would be the creative or competitive edge of any city that wants to attract the globe and that, by placing itself alongside other cities, manages to develop creatively its own potential.

The above characteristics set the lawscape apart in relation to other fusions of the legal and the spatial, such as the *nomotop* (Sloterdijk 2006) or the *nomosphere* (Delaney 2010). The main difference between the lawscape and these other fusions is that the latter are characterized by a compartmentalization of the non-human in relation to a spatially determined human community. Sloterdijk (2006: 10) talks about 'the "tensegral" nature of human association in the nomotopic field'; Delaney (2010: 25) about 'cultural-material environs … and the practical performative engagements [with them]'. In both cases, the human remains a central figure of perception, performance or action. Even Sloterdijk's series of human 'islands', one of which is the nomotop, which moves further in the direction of a material emplacement of normativity through the use of architectural structures such as tensegrities (the thin but necessary structures that support air buildings), has a post-phenomenological structure that still retains the centrality of a human, anthropocentric and anthropomorphic subject. On the contrary, what is proposed here, largely following Deleuze and Guattari (1988: 314–17) on their 'alloplastic stratum', namely the level of creative construction of signs not limited to humans, is a proper decentring of whatever residue of centrality might remain in the configuration of the connection between the human and the environmental. This entails a radical opening of both understandings of the city and the law towards an unmediated wilderness. At the same time, however, not all bodies are equal. Human, animal, vegetable, inorganic, semantic and discursive bodies are characterized by different viscosities, different concentrations of power in relation to other bodies and consequently different affective abilities. Thus, in the lawscape human affective abilities are regularly stronger than animal affective abilities, but both are subject to the affective abilities of meteorological, geographical or even complex social phenomena that construct specific corridors of urban movement.

Spatial justice

The epistemological passage from lawscape to spatial justice is a smooth one, building on the interstitial process of 'becoming' already in operation within the lawscape. In other words, from one interstice to another: spatial justice emerges from the lawscape. In what follows, I would like to explore an understanding of spatial justice that emerges from the interstitial tautology of law and the city in a manner that does not build on origins, grounds and *Grundnorms*, but rather on the practice of normative repetition. In other words, I am interested in thinking of spatial justice, not so much as rupture (although it can also be that) but as a process of repetition that produces difference. In that sense, spatial justice is the interstice par excellence: it continues the interstitial tautology of law and the city through the repeating movement of its very own body of emergence. As I explain below, therefore, spatial justice is not the ground or indeed the final destination (in the sense of the just city) of various juridical claims. Rather, spatial justice is a movement, embodied, emplaced and thoroughly material. While following the texture of the lawscape and indeed repeating this texture through its own motions, spatial justice brings forth a new level of potentiality. It is in that sense that spatial justice has the potential of being the most radical spatial/legal concept of recent years, promising both destabilization of prefabricated understandings of law and urban space, and new emerging ways of dealing with old problems.

Before that, however, let me briefly introduce the way the concept has been dealt with so far in the literature. While the term itself has been around for a while, markedly since David Harvey (1973) introduced the concept in the 1970s, the way it has been employed since is either flaccidly uneventful or bombastically originary (for my analysis of this, see Philippopoulos-Mihalopoulos (2010a)). The main issue with both these approaches is that they carry on with preoccupations of *being* rather than *becoming*, namely origin and destination and boundaries (and consequently control and claiming) rather than emergences (and therefore, processes of speed and stasis) that often lie beyond mere human control. This happens for one of the two following reasons: either because the normative aspect of the concept of spatial justice gets completely swamped by political considerations; or because the spatial aspect is replaced by facile metaphors of a vague geographical nature or indeed by a geographical concreteness that does not lend itself to spatiality. Thus, in the first case, the omnipresence of law is marginalized, indeed ignored, and replaced by politics of rights to the territory, access to resources and democratic processes of participation – all relevant, yet none managing to capture the normative *force* behind the lawscape, namely the force with which the body of the law affects other urban bodies as well as the urban body as a whole in becoming the lawscape. In the second case, spatial justice becomes an anaemic metaphor that talks about social inclusion and equal distribution, managing thus to ignore the violent, exclusionary and directionless nature of space. Indeed, spatial justice becomes aspatial. Space is reduced to yet 'another' social factor, 'another' perspective which does not offer anything more than at best a context and at worst a background.

This is probably what Lefebvre (1991: 73) wanted to avoid when he wrote 'space is not a thing among other things, nor a product among other products: rather, it subsumes things produced and encompasses their interrelationships in their coexistence and simultaneity—their (relative) order and/or (relative) disorder'. In most current literature that focuses on spatial justice, space is replaced by geography. But geography, the imaging of the world, the *grapheme* (*-graphy*) of the earth (*geo-*), is a representation (Gregory 1993). As David Delaney (2002: 67, emphasis added) puts it, geography 'seems *to stand for* spatialities, places, landscapes, materiality, and the thick and sensuous domain of the visible'. Geography indeed *stands for* all that, itself an epistemological avenue through which some of these things are sketched. But where is space in geography? Where is the thing that still resists the violence of the geographical mapping, the geographical instructions on how to move, the barely concealed prohibitions and exclusions and scaled divisions that come with geography? This thing of course is none other than *space* – often the *grand manqué* of geography. Spatial justice has become a geographical justice, namely a possibly equitable way of redrawing maps of property.

There is good reason for this. Or at least, a sympathetic justification may be found. Space is a fearsome thing, hard to deal with, contain or control. Doreen Massey's (2005) description of space is by now well known: a product of interrelations and embedded practices, a sphere of multiple possibilities, a ground of chance and undecidability, and as such always becoming, always open to the future. The flipside of the above can be haunting, exclusionary, disorienting: interrelations and practices denote closure and difficulty of belonging unless partaking of such practices; the multiplicity of possibilities harbour unpredictability, uncertainty, lack of direction, guidance, destination; constant openness to the future may prove treacherous in that the *here* might never be proven adequate, thus always pushing one to a mindless, escapist movement. Space embodies the violence of being lost, of being uncertain about one's direction, orientation, decision, judgement, crisis. Unlike the linearity or the compartmentalization of time (depending on your preferred school of thought), there is no respite from the relentless and simultaneous spatial presence. And if this is true for a generic spatial experience, imagine how intensified this is in the context of the urban, where everything is taken to its extreme, and where fast can be vertiginous and slow can be a total stop.

On this platform, the interstitial emergence of spatial justice has the potential to be one of the most radical emancipatory tools within the ambit of the spatial turn in law, as well as the more generalized movement of local and specific spatiality focus, which has largely followed decolonization. Spatial justice has sufficient materiality and abstraction to appeal to the various levels of geographical and normative thought. It can be worked out in such a way that will include the violence of space as well as the disciplinary nature of the law. The challenge is to forge a concept that is both realistic and visionary, both actual and virtual, neither pure horizon nor pure process. In order to do this, I attempt a fusion of two concepts: repetition and withdrawal. To some extent, both stem from Deleuzian (and Deleuzian–Guattarian) thought, in its turn stemming from Nietzsche's concept of eternal return. Thus, in *Difference and Repetition* (2004a), Deleuze shows how repetition does not bring identity but difference. The repeated event is never the same. He gives the 'paradoxical' example of festivals: 'they repeat an "unrepeatable". They do not add a second or third time to the first, but carry the first to the "nth" power' (2004: 2). Repetition in the sense of difference is neither habit nor mere generality, which in their turn produce similarity and identity. Repetition does not produce commensurate events but rather singular differences 'without any mediation whatsoever by the identical, the similar, the analogous or the opposed' (2004a: 117). The repeated event is a monad that lies beyond representation, 'a unity that envelops a multiplicity' as Deleuze writes in his book on Leibniz, *The Fold* (2006: 25). Repetition is characterized by multiplicity both internally and externally since not only is the repeated event different from any other but it remains beyond comparison with others. Deleuzian repetition is difference because it 'constitutes the degrees of an original difference' (Deleuze 2004b: 48), which is not an origin in the sense of a being that remains unchanged but rather the difference that trammels all differences without making them commensurate.

Let me connect this to the discussion on spatial justice. The lawscape consists of paths of normative behaviour that establish themselves through repetition. Think of the way the law operates. When norms (or judgements) repeat themselves, drawing on each other and building on the previous ones, superimposing themselves on a spiral of self-referential production, repetition is every time different and given to the conditions that determine their singularity. Likewise, when one embodies the law by, say, respecting private areas within the city, traffic lights, flow of traffic when cycling or even when one finds a particular way of dealing with the law by circumnavigating it, say when cycling on the pavement which, depending on the jurisdiction, it might or might not be illegal; in all these cases, one deepens the normativity of the path by finding oneself in a situation of repetition along the various elements (the pavement, the tree on the pavement, the bicycle, the law, the perception of the law and so on). The law fragments up in its various perspectives, lends itself to the multiplicity of senses, spreads its body in time and then, arbitrarily at a given point, regroups and delivers a judgement or establishes a normative event. This might be an emergence of justice, always within the law, appearing dream-like from within the normative edifice and yet beyond prescription. Derrida has famously shown that justice, however to-come (*à venir*), comes from within the calculability of the law. One can take this even further: in its repetitive immanence, law is justice. Indeed, there is no dualism, no contradiction between the two. Law is so absolutely, incommensurately inscribed within its repetition that only by carrying on with its obsessive repeating can it allow justice to spring forth. This is what Deleuze means when he writes that repetition 'refers to a singular power which differs in kind from generality, *even when, in order to appear, it takes advantage of the artificial passage from one order of generality to another*' (2004a: 4, added emphasis). The passage from one spatial normative path to another, however close to generality or habit it might be, has the potential of giving rise to repetition as the difference of justice, where each case is looked at in its singularity, above and beyond comparisons with cases decided alike (yet in its emergence relying on this repetition). But at this point the arbitrariness of the law is revealed: as far as we are concerned, we who view the spectacle of the law in all its square claustrophobia, the law just *may* be just. There is no guarantee. The law is blind to its injustice.

The interstitial nature of spatial justice becomes apparent when one considers that it appears 'in the passage from one order of generality to another', namely building on the normative repetition (which might be mere production of sameness) and passing on, flowing along or indeed folding up as repetition of difference. What seems like dull normative sameness is the plane on which the repetition of spatial justice may emerge. Although immanently appearing within the lawscape, spatial justice is a *fold* of the lawscape, a doubling-up of difference that does not interrupt the lawscape but intensifies it by allowing it to slide next to itself. Alain Pottage has spoken about 'a fold in the fabric of contingency' (1998: 11), namely a continuation and a doubling up of contingency – and in this case, the contingency of the lawscape. This is how spatial justice emerges: contingently, immanently, on the basis of spatial normative repetition. The challenge, however, does not end there. As Deleuze writes, the problem is 'how to continue the fold, to have it go through the ceiling, how to bring it to infinity' (2006: 39). In other words, how to build on these emergences of spatial justice, how to carry on developing the fold?

This is where the concept of withdrawal comes in. It all begins with a betrayingly simple formation: one body and other bodies. And then, right in the middle of this, the desire for movement: I want to be where you are, exactly *there*, exactly *then*. The motives (greed, attraction, possessiveness, territorialism, reterritorialization) can be put aside for the time being, for what is important is the desire for justice, the act of moving, of passing, of being deterritorialized by the spatial position of the other – that is, by allowing the position of the other to make her territory out of my position. The gesture begins ontologically. As Graham Harman, drawing from Heidegger, puts it, objects withdraw from each other, indeed 'absolutely from every relation' (Harman 2005: 76). This is an ontological position referring to the lack of connectivity between 'objects', which, for Harman, are material, beyond representation entities that do not juxtapose themselves to 'subjects' but exist 'whether we like it or not' (Harman 2009: 195). In this object-oriented ontology, objects have no relation at all with other objects but dwell in an autopoietic closure that excludes the environment, namely the other, from coming in and taking up one's territory. There is, however, a twist in this since objects do communicate with each other after all. This happens through what Harman calls translation and which one could see as internalization of the other within the self in the direction of the self. This is a mendacious dichotomy, however, even in strict autopoietic terms, since, as Niklas Luhmann's (1997) theory of autopoietic closure abundantly shows, the other is the 'object' of the object, as it were. Closure is openness in the sense that the other is what the system is, what the system consists of (Philippopoulos-Mihalopoulos 2010b). Levi Bryant (2011) has put together Harman's withdrawal and Luhmann's closure in order to show how every object is self-othering through its very withdrawal. In that sense, self-othering or, otherwise put, withdrawal from the territory of the self by delving deeper into the self, is an ontological position. Spatial justice, therefore, points to the 'no-relation' between bodies, meaning that every body occupies a certain space (indeed, every body *is* a certain space) at any given moment and there can be no connection amongst the various spaces in that they all withdraw behind the contour of their skin and close themselves to the other in their attempt to immunity. Deep in this closure, however, is the other, the world through the skin and within the contours of the skin. Spatial justice refers to the simultaneous impossibility of sharing space and closing-off space.

Space both conditions and is conditioned by the desire to move, and move constantly. This movement is partly facilitated by what Deleuze and Guattari have famously called *smooth* (as opposed to *striated*) space, namely the space of the nomad as opposed to that of the state. Striated space is the organized 'space of *pillars*' and of homogeneity (Deleuze and Guattari 1988: 408), 'striated by walls, enclosures, and roads between enclosures' (ibid.: 420). Smooth space, on the other hand, is a variable open boundless space characterized by a 'polyvocality of directions' (ibid.: 421). Striation and smoothness are two values which, however, are never encountered in isolation but are always interfolded (thus, 'smooth or nomad space lies between two striated spaces' (ibid.: 424). The need for justice arises as soon as the lawscape emerges – namely, as soon as law and space become each other, partitioning space and territorializing law through paths of spatial normativity. A word of caution: there is no one originary point at which law and city merge but there are specific points at which the conflict between their various manifestations becomes apparent. Paths cross each other, bodies clash, geopolitical presences are not tolerated, homeless bodies are shoved under the bridge, veiled bodies are shut indoors, religious adversaries are housed next to each other, the industry moves into the forest, the ship moves into the fish stock: in all these movements, there is conflict. The conflict can be put in an ontological language as that between closure and openness or internalization of the other and withdrawal from the other. Spatial justice is the movement out of this conflict while delving deeper into it.

With this, we move into the other important role of spatial justice, that departs from a mere ontological position and urges instead for a transcendentally empirical position, indeed a political position: spatial justice is the emergence of resistance against the omnipresence of the law. If the lawscape is all there is, it means that the law is material through and through, and that there is no space free from law. Even a smooth space has its own, nomadic law, the nomos that moves on the surface of the earth. Law and matter flow together in a way that it is impossible to tell them apart, capturing all there is. So where is the space of resistance? Where can one find a sliver of escape from the rapturous nuptials of law and space? This is where withdrawal comes in: a removal from the space of the law, a movement of bodies away from the embrace. Withdrawal is not an isolated movement, at least in the sense of a directed displacement. Rather, it is a shift that mobilizes the space, the bodies on this space and the legality that trammels their connection. Withdrawal is a tectonic shift that takes with it the surfaces on which the law appears. A body withdrawing is lawscape withdrawing. But this is precisely the movement of *justice*. In order to employ the law *justly*, one (a judge, a lawmaker) needs to destroy the law, to let the whole legal edifice collapse, to withdraw from it – and only then will the law regroup and reach a judgement that might or might not be just. One moves one's body away from the law, withdraws one's corporeal attachment to it and sees the law in full materiality.

The withdrawal can only take place from inside and within the lawscape, hammering right at its foundations and up to its turrets. In withdrawing from the lawscape one does not move outside. There is no better place outside. There is no better law, better city, better justice. It is all part of an infinite plane of immanence on which withdrawal moves. If justice is to be materialized, withdrawal must be kept immanent. This amounts to more than a manipulation of the law, a new interpretation or a legal stuttering. Nor does it mean that one has to work with the system. Rather, it is a denial of the law, a questioning of its relevance, its validity and even its lawfulness. Withdrawal rides the waving banner of the unutterable legal paradox: is the law lawful? Take the example of a revolt against the government. Revolts work from outside the lawscape in that they assume the difference in materiality between 'us' and 'them'. The policeman is not us, the fellow citizen is not them. It is a necessary suspension, an inclusion of negation. Yet whatever change takes place with a revolt, it will have to be within the lawscape. Materiality reunited. Which lawscape is that? A brand new lawscape? No doubt; but also a very old lawscape. A piece of the lawscape must be preserved in order for the lawscape to assemble itself every time after every withdrawal. The withdrawal has to be registered by the lawscape: speak the law's language, enter the law's dreams, touch the law's extremities. Revolting is withdrawing, but withdrawing is immanent. One cannot achieve justice by revolting alone.

Spatial justice is disconnected from historicization and thrown in at the space of *here*, namely the space that vibrates with history through its material appearance. Not an abstract history but a history of the *here*. Not a history that legitimizes atrocities but a history that accepts the need for bodies to be here, exactly where other bodies might also want to be. Justice is a conflictual space, full of erupting laws and spreading normativities. For justice away from the law is not a lawless justice. It is certainly a risky, potentially dangerous space, emptied of pillared security and smooth lines. It is also a space of constant reconstruction, rapid concept formation, applied acrobatics of thought and action. A space of justice – and indeed spatial justice – is a space where the law is being erected at every moment as if for the first time. Like a group of nomads that must set up home every time they stop for the night, in the same way the law is re-erected through a repetition that might create difference. This is where we come full circle: withdrawal leads to repetition that leads to withdrawal. The two are not opposites but share one surface: that of *stasis*. Faithful to its etymology, stasis is both pause and revolt, withdrawal and return. Stasis is nomadic. For it is not the case that the nomad moves constantly. As Deleuze and Guattari (1988: 420) put it, 'it is false to define the nomad by movement'. It may be the case that the nomad moves from point to point to a further point, but the points are there by necessity. The nomad always moves along paths or trajectories that simply happen to include points. In that sense, the nomadic movement is, as the authors write while referring to Heinrich von Kleist, 'immobility and speed, catatonia and rush, a "stationary process," station as process' (1988: 420). The nomadic movement is the 'absolute movement', or the speed in which the body 'in the manner of a vortex' swirls in palpitating stasis. In that sense, the body carries the smoothness within, as it were, and moves between various positions in striated space.

Withdrawal takes withdrawing with it and leaves a space of perpetual *stasis*, namely a pause that pulsates with revolt, with turning. The shift is a forceful declaration of appearance, of being *here*, fully embodied: a lawscape moved by the spaces and bodies of its appearance. Spatial justice can finally be defined as the conflict between repetition and withdrawal, a conflict that shares one surface, that of stasis, and one political position, that of constructive, creative resistance that creates the lawscape through its very repetition. This way of approaching spatial justice serves a multiplicity of objectives. First, it establishes the interstice as a common surface of a multiplicity, in this case the multiplicity of law and the city. In that sense, spatial justice is not a synthesis but an emergence that *may* occur. This occurrence takes place irrespective of prescriptive policies. This does not mean, however, that one must give up. This is, counter-intuitively, the meaning of spatial justice as *withdrawal* – and the second objective of spatial justice: namely, spatial justice as withdrawal entails a constant awareness and action upon the conflict between closure and openness, property as exclusion and property as need for connection. This is played out entirely on the material, spatial plane of stasis – third objective: spatial justice is material through and through, between material bodies and involving real spatial arrangements that are informed by an ethical awareness of decentring. Fourth objective: the self is not the centre of the lawscape. This resolutely anti-anthropocentric approach makes the lawscape a fractal piece of the open ecology in which bodies circulate (as they do *de facto*) amidst other bodies. Spatial justice emerges as soon as the conflict becomes articulated (that is, immediately) and demands a radical decentralization, not only of the human or the self in general but of the centre itself. The result: a truly interstitial conceptualization of spatial justice as emergence.

References

Bhabha, H. 2005. *The Location of Culture*. London: Routledge Classics.

Bryant, L. 2011. *Democracy of Objects*. Ann Arbor, MI: Open Humanities Press.

Delaney, D. 2002. Beyond the world: law as a thing of this world, in: J. Holder and C. Harrison (eds) *Law and Geography*. Oxford: Oxford University Press.

Delaney, D. 2010. *The Spatial, The Legal and the Pragmatics of World-Making*. London: Routledge.

Deleuze, G. 1988. *Spinoza: Practical Philosophy*. San Francisco, CA: City Lights.

Deleuze, G. 2004a. *Difference and Repetition*. London: Continuum.

Deleuze, G. 2004b *Proust and Signs*. Minneapolis, MN: University Of Minnesota Press.

Deleuze, G. 2006. *The Fold: Leibniz and the Baroque*. London: Continuum.

Deleuze, G. and Guattari, F. 1988. *A Thousand Plateaus: Capitalism and Schizophrenia*. London: Athlone Press.

Derrida, J. 1992. Force of law: the 'mystical foundation of authority', in: D. Cornell, M. Rosenfeld and D. Gray Carlson (eds) *Deconstruction and the Possibility of Justice*. New York: Routledge, pp. 21–29.

Doel, M. 1999. *Poststructuralist Geographies: The Diabolical Art of Spatial Science*. Edinburgh: Edinburgh University Press.

Fainstein, S. 2010. *The Just City*. Ithaca, NY: Cornell University Press.

Grear, A. 2011. The vulnerable living order: human rights and the environment in a critical and philosophical perspective. *Journal of Human Rights and the Environment*, 2(1), 23–44.

Gregory, D. 1993. *Geographical Imaginations*. Oxford: Blackwell.

Harman, G. 2005. *Guerrilla Metaphysics: Phenomenology and the Carpentry of Things*. Chicago, IL: Open Court.

Harman, G. 2009. *Prince of Networks: Bruno Latour and Metaphysics*. Melbourne: re-press.

Harvey, D. 1973. *Social Justice and the City*. Oxford: Blackwell.

Lefebvre, H. 1991. *The Production of Space*. Oxford: Blackwell.

Luhmann, N. 1997. *Die Gesellschaft der Gesellschaft*. Frankfurt am Main: Suhrkamp.

Massey, D. 2005. *For Space*. London: Sage.

Michulak, M. 2008 The Rhizomatics of Domination, in: B. Herzogenrath (ed.) *An [Un]Likely Alliance: Thinking Environment[s] with Deleuze|Guattari*. Newcastle: Cambridge Scholars Publishing.

Philippopoulos-Mihalopoulos, A. 2007. *Absent Environments: Theorising Environmental Law and the City*. London: Routledge.

Philippopoulos-Mihalopoulos, A. 2010a. Spatial justice: law and the geography of withdrawal. *International Journal of Law in Context*, 6(3), 1–16.

Philippopoulos-Mihalopoulos, A. 2010b. *Law, Justice, Society*. London: Routlege.

Philippopoulos-Mihalopoulos, A. 2011a. Suspension of suspension: notes on the hybrid, in: N. Akestrom and I. J. Sand (eds) *Hybrid Forms of Governance: Self-suspension of Power*. Basingstoke: Palgrave.

Philippopoulos-Mihalopoulos, A. 2011b. '…the sound of a breaking string': critical environmental law and ontological vulnerability. *Journal of Environmental Law and Human Rights* 2(1), 5–22.

Pottage, A. 1998. Power as an art of contingency: Luhmann, Deleuze, Foucault. *Economy and Society*, 27(1), 1–27.

Sloterdijk, P. 2006. The Nomotop: on the emergence of law in the island of humanity. *Law & Literature*, 18(1), 1–14.

Soja, E. 1996. *Thirdspace: Journeys to Los Angeles and Other Real-and-Imagined Places*. Oxford: Basil Blackwell.

Spinoza, B. 2007. *Theological-Political Treatise*, edited by Jonathan Israel. Cambridge, UK: Cambridge University Press.

Tarde, G. 1903. *The Laws of Imitation*. New York: Holt.

Chapter 5

Coming up for Air: Comfort, Conflict and the Air of the Megacity

Peter Adey

The air of the city makes free. (Pirenne 1925, cited in Alsayyad and Roy 2009)

Introduction

Why has air escaped our enquiry? Perhaps, as Luce Irigaray (1999) has it, the air appears to have been forgotten. Air seems in-between; it is not quite there, translucent, often invisible. Air does not cry out for its analysis. Yet air cannot really be separated from the apparently more solid and persistent story of the city, nor can it be divorced from our understanding of social and political struggle. Those who seem to fall between the gaps of an inclusive and equitable society appear to live in quite different sorts of air and they are accused of producing air of the wrong kind. Whilst we might have forgotten air for now, our first cry for life was a gasp for breath. It should therefore come as no surprise that it is a materiality, like water, that is continuously fought over.

As a medieval Germanic legal principle, the airs of the city, were they breathed for a year, meant freedom (Alsayyad and Roy 2006). City air meant emancipation should one breathe the free air that could 'set them free'. But air has more often been associated with a history of labour, poverty and contestation. From the medieval urban to the industrializing metropolis, polluted air became a marker of uneven development and the urbanization of the working classes, so rendered visible in Britain by the portrayal of northern industry by writers such as Elizabeth Gaskell and Charles Dickens. In the choking air of the northern towns of Gaskell's 'Darkshire' (standing in for Britain's Lancashire cotton and textiles industry), air gained substance for the working conditions of factory labourers. Forced to endure extremes of heat and humidity, or the suspended fluff and cotton dust of the mills and their looms, air stands as a threatening atmosphere to health. Thus for nineteenth-century investigations of the working classes, air became an obvious signature of the commodification of the body and its 'sweated' labour by capital. Divisions and industrial disputes over the automation of the worker body present themselves as an air endurable only to a 'degraded' class. For Engels (1971), air is 'corrupted', 'poisoned', 'pestilent'; it is an atmosphere 'penned in as if with a purpose', forcing the poor into conditions which are 'incomprehensible'.

Today's megacities of the global south are told in a similar way through the linear narratives that underpin developmental ideologies from planning to journalism and travel writing. Travelogues describe an 'envelope' or 'atmosphere' of wreathing haze and dirty skies which constitute the environmental and atmospheric conditions of megacity life. The air of the city in these contexts seems to hang. It lies somehow apart as if a veil flung over the camera lens. The hazy conditions grey the sky. The noxious pollutants of rapid and unplanned industrial and residential development and inequitable waste management policies express a political economy and governance of air, yet the shrouding haze is seemingly insensible to negotiation or intervention. The inhabitants of these spaces are at a greater climatic risk than others, more sensitive to the seasons, heat-waves and cold snaps. Those truly homeless from the summer cyclones and floods further seek their way in the city as the climactically susceptible and homeless populous. Given the environmental policies that are now justifying urban rehabilitation and the dispossession of the poor, air really does matter, as Doyle and Risley (2008) note, to 'life and death, right now'. This is particularly the case for those who live in the in-between zones of 'illegal' urban slums reliant upon informal and improvisory infrastructure and sanitation. This matters in terms of health, as people are forced to live with the interior burning of fuel, lack of ventilation and the realities of a life literally lived – as various author have characterized quite bluntly – 'in shit' (Davis 2006; McFarlane and Desai 2011). Furthermore, air matters because various attempts to clean the city air go hand in hand with efforts to remove particular inhabitants and peoples from it.

In this chapter, I explore the struggle over air in the whirlwind-development of the megacity, focusing especially on the slums of Delhi and Mumbai. Whilst we might see that there is a long historical context to air's dispute and its governance, I suggest that in the modernization of India's economy and the massive urban development of its megacities, the urban political and social struggles for the city are being expressed and reproduced through the governance of air. I shall show how these issues orbit around a 'politics of comfort', a kind of domesticity redolent of a colonial and cultural imperialism of atmosphere, aesthetics and sanitation.

Making the air explicit: air, explication and atmosphere

Bringing the air to our notice follows a path blazed by philosopher Peter Sloterdijk (2009), who suggests that the air has been made explicit through a series of key technologies, sciences and knowledges brought to bear on the air. Ironically enough, this explicitness renders the air graspable so that it might be taken away. The key moment in this process, for Sloterdijk, is the German's release of poison gas at Ypres in 1915 during the hostilities of the First World War. Making the air explicit in this story serves to undermine the environmental conditions that life lives in, in order to subsequently deny those very conditions – a manner of violence he describes as 'atmosterrorism'. This characterizes several aesthetic and political as well as very practical changes in late modernity (particularly the conduct of modern war).

My concern here, however, is to push Sloterdijk beyond an exceptional moment of abandonment becoming the rule (in war at least) and closer to the domain of biopolitics. For we might see that Sloterdijk evinces a long background of research that has explored the social entanglement of the air through other technologies/techniques of explication that we can locate within liberal projects of biopolitical governmentality. Managing and administering air has been conducted over and over again as a way to act on the conditions that will make life live. For instance, David Gissen's (2006) work in urban studies suggests we take the air seriously in a different way as a malleable and governable object to condition and shape inhabitation. Elsewhere, Mark Whitehead's (2009) fantastic exploration of the 'atmospheric self' explores how we became governable subjects through which the State, atmosphere and the subject have existed together in mutual care. In fact his story is really one of the governmental appropriation of air through miasmic imaginations, public health programmes and sanitation debates in early twentieth-century Britain which have sought to envelop and cushion a population by and through air. I think we need to further take seriously just whose atmosphere has been governed, for whom and by who. Just which valued lives are protected by air, and who are not? What's more, what might it mean to be in or with, or even of, air?

We might turn to Tim Ingold's (2007, 2010) writing on weather to explore a more nuanced take on air. For Ingold, accounting for air involves a rethinking of our place on or within it, drawing on more processual and vitalist concerns. What Ingold expresses is a 'weather-world', where there is no distinct surface separating earth and sky, an inter-involvement of land and air, reciprocatingly vertical. 'Life is rather lived in a zone in which substance and medium are brought together in the constitution of beings' writes Ingold, 'which, in their activity, participate in weaving the textures of the land'. This is an open landscape of fluxes, mixtures and suspension, of binding mediums and substances, folds and envelopes, made not of inhabitants but 'exhabitants'.

But the slight swerve we might take here is to think through, conceptually and historically, the notion of atmosphere, whose affect in some respects resembles Irigaray's 'cry for air', for an 'aspiration of air' not by air's absence as if a void open, but because of the excess of air, what it suspends and what it evacuates. More specifically, the atmospheres of air I want to explore today seem to threaten. I'm not sure that this is quite the same as Irigaray's description of the air-borne, but it certainly is characterized by this sense of entry and movement not from the inside, but as the outside comes in: '[It] enters him, limitlessly. Outside, having entered into the outside, he is penetrated to his innermost by this outside: a horror, for him. That into which he enter and that which enters him are the same, and are present imperceptible, if not as excess' (Irigaray 1999: 41).

The atmospheres I want to explore gather together this sense of otherness, of being transported into these envelopes, of air flooding in almost immutable to intervention. This has a particular cultural and political history I want to bring together which is wrapped up in colonial history.

For instance, it could be easy to see the atmosphere's cataclysmic properties evident in examples such as Bhopal, the worst industrial accident in history which, in 1986, killed some 3,000 people and caused over half a million injuries in the densely populated city of Bhopal, capital of the Madhya Pradesh region in India. The Bhopal planners had failed to relocate their 'obnoxious industries' outside of the city (Bogard 1989; Cassels 1993), and thus the proximity of the Union Carbide chemical to the populous became deadly when the plant malfunction released a toxic gas cloud which spread through the neighbouring area and communities. Disasters such as the Bhopal incident present us with the scale of the megacities' atmospheric problems, but also with air's tensions that do not only occupy the suspending time–space moment of an exceptional emergency, but exist far more permanently in India's planning law and its tumultuous social changes.

Of course, the air of the Indian city for Dipesh Chakrabarty (2002) has similarly described the dominant narratives of Orientalism, understood through the grids of European intelligibility as a place of 'heat and dust'. An aesthetic cityscape of fever, stagnation and disgusting air – a stifling, humid air for Kipling that would feed his insomnia-led midnight walks in Calcutta. Air, then, seems to signify difference, and it would even characterize the inequalities of a caste system, inscribing polluting airs on castes tainted by faeces and smells (Douglas 1966). As Naipaul writes:

> Indians defecate everywhere. They defecate, mostly beside the railway tracks. But they also defecate on the beaches; they defecate on the streets; they never look for cover [...] But the truth is that Indians do not see these squatters and might even, with complete sincerity, deny that they exist. (Naipaul cited in Douglas 1966: 149)

Air symbolizes difference and quite different and marginalized social practices, whilst it also suspends something that threatens to move inwards and to overcome those whom it envelops, to disgust or smother. Not surprisingly then the processes this chapter will explore orbit around removal. But it is removal in relation to a kind of barrier or threshold of inside or outside. Despite air's apparent fluidity and effervescence, we will see how it is drawn down into a geometry of threat and safety which Sloterdijk characterizes as an immunological security sphere (Klauser 2010).

Since the Bhopal disaster, legal disputes are still ongoing and its example is compelling evidence for academic studies concerned with catastrophic accidents and social change, trans-national protest movements and urban industrial policy (Sarangi 2009, Walters 2009). According to Kim Fortun's (2001) wonderful excavation of the events, the Bhopal case saw a hearing in the US courts under Judge John Keenan in May 1986. The case was dismissed by the judge on the grounds of *forum non convienens* – a legal doctrine, writes Fortun, explaining that it would have been inconvenient or difficult for the court to secure both evidence and victims to testify. The Judge concluded with the following statement over a ruling on Indian safety. Retention of the case would

> be yet another act of imperialism, another situation in which an established sovereign inflicted its rules, its standards, and values on a developing nation. [...] To deprive the Indian judiciary this opportunity to stand tall and pass judgment on behalf of its own people would be to revive a history of subservience and subjugation from which India has emerged. (cited in Fortun 2001: 25)

This moment is interesting and important for our relationship with air because it seemingly expounds the kind of colonial authority with which air has been governed yet it seeks to rework. And it is this imperialist history of air that I don't think we can separate from our examination of the megacities of today. While this will become clearer when we examine the cultural imposition of, for instance, values surrounding comfort, ambience and atmosphere later, Bhopal also signals Sloterdijk's and Irigaray's points. A gaseous materiality like air seems to resist efforts to manage it, and it is this quality that may in fact offer one of air's redeeming qualities.

Air-filter, nuisance and smell

> The discursive and material domain of sanitation remains as fragmented, unequal and politicized as it was one and a half centuries ago. (McFarlane 2008: 432)

To talk of the air of India's megacities is difficult without the miasmic imaginations of germs and contagion that so animated earlier European discourse over air and its vectors of disease, madness and other social disorders (Rabinow 1989). Colonial city air was an atmosphere perpetual and growing. Air grew close with the proximity of its people crammed into too much space as air began to be thought of in terms of population security and sanitation. A primary concern was the survival of disease and 'air borne' threatening microbes within broader histories of climate and its relationship to health and race (Corbin 1986; Harrison 1999). Air seemed to denote an excess. Air was 'irritating' and city air had so much, too much suspended in it that one could not breathe.

As geographers such as Stephen Legg and Colin McFarlane have explored in the sanitation histories of colonial Delhi and Bombay, air was pathologized as a spatial imaginary that would act on the body corporeal and politic in several ways. As one of the primary spatial tropes to be forever rehearsed within sanitation politics, exposure to bad air could mean transmission, 'from cholera and plague to a range of indeterminate fevers', the threat of contagion was king. For commentators in the late nineteenth century, these were made manifest in the 'potential "cesspools" – open drains, that emanated smells into houses and over food' or the 'noxious matters', 'poisonous gases' and 'accumulated filth'. Within this context 'filthiness' was the worst of Bombay's 'many Evils' (cited in Mcfarlane 2008: 419).

Alternatively, odorous air could be breathed and taken within the sanctuary of the body or the home. The Indian's city's humidity would simply hang there, persistent and unmovable. It could easily sap the strength or vitality of a body by its ambient heat and the urging of the body's immoral secretions of sweat.[1] In post-mutiny Delhi, Sharan (2006) describes the management of vapours and nuisances which took on an insurrectionary odour. Regulations would seek to police 'unhealthy trades', 'bad air', 'badly constructed and ill-ventilated habitations', 'poor drainage' that would all contribute to an 'undesirable state of affairs', and the disaffection of a colonial and urban population (Sharan 2006: 4906).

Stephen Legg's examination of the evolution of tear gas as an urban disciplinary technology in Delhi tells us something about the nature of colonial air politics as sanitation sought to clean up the city in terms of biological, moral and social health that meant the efficient rationalization and separation of both waste and population. Learning from a paper describing crowd control in Shanghai, tear gas would be trialled, tested and put to use in Delhi. It was initially deployed from a motor lorry especially, for the very 'moral effect produced by it on crowds'. Not unlike the terrorizing prospect of gas warfare and terror bombing, atmospheric policing harnessed the principle of amplification by affect. This was not to simply envelope the Raj from its population, but to encase and divide the indiscipline and insurrectionary crowd – to remove them from their dangerous and threatening collaboration and proximity. The gas was not intended to kill as with Sloterdijk, but to separate a valued life from another.

Today the air is increasingly part of the generic solutions that seek to secure the megacity from other contemporary social and 'environmental type' threats (Massumi 2009). In fact the struggle over air is taken more along the lines of moral sanitation practices of the nineteenth century as air becomes a medium that has legitimized urban displacement, removal and the biopolitical 're-habilitation' of Delhi's and Mumbai's urban slums. Today we see air being legally redefined in a manner that has become the juridical basis for what Ghernter (2010) calls a new paradigm or 'nuisance law'. This notion of nuisance is serving as the foundation for an aesthetic rather than calculative rationality of governmental intervention on the lives on the poorest. Commenting on the 2001 removal of 98,000 small-scale and 'polluting' industrial units, similarly for Baviskar (2003), this is an advancement of a bourgeois environmentalist agenda of environmental and social purification: smokestack industries, effluent-producing manufacturing units and other aesthetically unpleasant sites that make the city a place of work for millions, which should be discreetly tucked away out of sight, polluting some remote rural

---

1   Of course the association between the climatic properties of the colonial city cannot be divorced from the relationship between racial stereotypes with the characteristics of the tropics: see for instance James Duncan's recent history of Ceylon (Duncan 2007).

wasteland. The workers who labour in these industries are banished out of sight. Even people whose services are indispensable for the affluent to live comfortable lives – domestic workers, vendors and sundry service providers, should live where their homes do not offend the eyes, ears and noses of the well-to-do.

In this context, the governing of megacity atmospheres and climates has been both troubled and solved (Foucault 2007) by the problematization of the environment or 'milieu' as both an effect and object of governing, bringing us somewhere between a neoliberal 'environmentality' identified by both Foucault and Agrawal (2005, 2009). This is a space where disordered housing, industry and mobility cause high toxin levels, which may lead to respiratory problems and raise temperatures. The quelling of such precipitous activities may create subsequent reductions in growth and development and putative threats to a population's welfare. In Delhi this resulted in significant riots and social unrest following the closures of the small-scale polluters (Baviskar 2003).[2] In other words, it is the megacity's environment of interdependencies and connections which are both the source of their success as well as risks to their growth. In order to act on this space of circulation, environmental law has created a space of intervention over which the megacity population and its industries may act.

Tracing the legal discussion and decisions over the relationship between slum populations and their apparent nuisance, Ghernter explores how Delhi has embarked on a decade-long period of slum clearance, contraction, removal and criminalization of the slum population by the new definition of a nuisance, defined as 'any act, omission, injury, damage, annoyance or offence to the sense of sight, smell, hearing or which is or may be dangerous to life or injurious to health or property' (Jain cited in Ghernter). In this evolving legal discourse, the *jhuggi jhompri* dwellings that make up the slums become inseparable from their status as social bother. But more perniciously is that the inhabitants of these dwellings become divorced from any categorization as reasonable citizens with rights over public land because only 'unreasonable' people are believed to live and pollute in this way. The Supreme Court's 2000 directive which called for 'all polluting industries of whatever category operating in residential areas' to be shut down was exemplary of this politics as Delhi's urban slums were identified as the birthplace of the city's environmental and social problems. Oozing liquids, fecal matter, informal industrial pollutants and household waste constitute the unsanitary threat to social order and aesthetic sensibility of the rising urban middle classes. Take how one lead petition in the Indian High Courts complained over a *jhuggi* located on vacant ground in front of a resident's welfare association (RWA) colony. There, the slum residents would use the ground to urinate and defecate during the day. For the RWA, this was making their life 'miserable' and had 'transgressed their

---

2   In his published lecture series Foucault (2007) famously uses the example of the town's concern with miasmas: bad and potentially noxious air that could cause death. Problematically it could reside from the rotting corpses not properly disposed of – people who may have succumbed to air-borne related illnesses in the first place.

right to very living' because 'thousand of people easing themselves pose such uncultured scene, besides no young girls can dare to come to their own balconies throughout the day [because] obnoxious smells pollute the atmosphere [thus] the entire environment is unconducive to public health and morality [*sic*]' (cited in Ghernter 2008: 60).

This is a juridical fulfillment of Sloterdijk's thesis: the atmospheric purification of nuisance or smell serves to legally define-out the very ways of living that produce that air. The ironic way this has come to a head in one way is at Mumbai's Chhatrapati Shivaji International Airport, where the slums on the edge of the airport come so close that some aircraft wings hang over the edge of the settlements. Examined by the documentary *Routes in the Runway*, the very workers who helped to build the now thriving international airport – essential to the city's extraordinary growth and its status as a 'world class city' – are being faced with removal and their homes destroyed as the slum is rehabilitated by HDIL, who plan to remove and resettle 20,000 occupants, although the total number of residents is looking more like 80,000 households or about one million people (thirdtreefromtheleft 2011). The case is being fought by the Airport Slum Dwellers Federation and on their behalf the Indian NGO SPARC on the grounds that the development has appeared to circumvent many of the planning guidelines and protections set up in the National Rehabilitation and Resettlement Policy (NRRP) of 2007. According to SPARC's *City Watch* journal, the airport development seems to have outsourced the slum rehabilitation process to a private company. This is problematic because the consideration of alternatives, a social impact assessment, an independent multi-disciplinary panel, an Administrator for Rehabilitation and Resettlement, a public hearing, survey and census of affected families, a grievance redress mechanism and an ombudsman, have not been forthcoming. As far as the federation is aware, 'none of these steps have been taken' (SPARC 2010). Indeed, the recent protests have demanded the proper rehabilitation of the slum's residents to government land, rather than their simple removal by private hands, without any of the responsibility.

What is so ironic is the juxtaposition of residential settlements with a fast expanding airport. Here it is the slums that are seen to encroach and suffocate the airport as opposed to the airport's usual characterization as some kind of hungry, polluting amoeba-like growth. The slums and their dwellers are treated as a temporary necessity for the airport's construction which should not stand in the way of the capitalization of the land's new economic and social value to the future of Mumbai. But there are other experiences of slum air that must be accounted for that tell a different side to the story of middle class notions of smell and disgust. For instance, by taking a subaltern perspective of those very dwellers forced to use the bad airs of slum sanitation infrastructures in Rafinagar, a slum in northern Mumbai, McFarlane and Desai discuss how

> the visual and olfactory experiences of bodily wastes in overloaded, poorly-ventilated and infrequently cleaned toilets provoked disgust to the point of it

being a potentially sickening experience. One resident expressed this when she explained that she would not be able to eat all day if she used the dirty public toilet block near her house in the morning, thus revealing that she used a private toilet block a bit further away. (McFarlane and Desai 2011)

For many others, open defecation was the only option given the inadequate provision of toilets in the slums, leading to high numbers of people attempting to use far too few toilets. Some are pay per use, whilst other toilets have seen social disorder including verbal abuse and violence coalesce around them. This is especially the case for women.

In this sense, open defecation becomes quite a rational outcome if one considers the poor provision of public sanitation infrastructures so that one has no place else left to go, forcing defecation into open areas, by roads and gardens, and wasteland near the toilet blocks. What's more, such practices bring further into question whether the elite perspectives on urban air should be used to cast judgment on the slum populations. Should the norms of air and defecation permeate perceptions and expectations of air and filth that are culturally mutable?

Conditioning, comfort and domesticity

People in air-conditioned, closed cars think the city isn't polluted and their children's respiratory problems do not make them see it either. For them, Delhi is those cars, their palatial houses and Punj baroque. (Tellis 2001)

As Mumbai's airport slums shrink, new residential developments and 'world class infrastructures' will be made possible from the land freed up – some 235 acres on the airport site positioned for hotels, apartment buildings and freeway construction. Nearby a vast condominium project Whispering Towers is being built by the same developers, a seemingly perverse twist of logic for those whose apparently polluting air comes at the cost of a middle-class haven with questionable environmental credentials. Perhaps the 'whisper' is intended to signify its supposed environmental non-presence, the seemingly low impact of the development which boasts high quality building materials, large sound-proof windows, air conditioned and elegant communal areas, landscaped gardens and CCTV. Or one whispers it quietly lest it become too common as outdoor swimming pools, gazebos, sun decks, yoga rooms, herb gardens, cricket pitches, even skating rinks and a meditation garden plus a forest walk, are all there to be enjoyed in a sort of gated bubble of greenness and sleek elegance. It is these sorts of airs, which the slum workers helped build the capacity to inhabit as they make up the majority of formal and informal construction workers, which is actually the megacity's more permanent dream.

These secessionary spaces appear to be emblematic of developments that various scholars are calling a manner of enclaveism – a neoliberalized security that Don Mitchell describes as SUV citizenship,[3] a regressive isolationism best characterized by the fortress interiority of the air-conditioned car 4×4 or sports utility vehicle (Mitchell 2005). As Mitchell writes,

> The rise of the sports utility vehicle (S.U.V.) over the past decade and a half has been attributed to any number of factors (and cannot only be explained in terms of consumer choice), but a central factor has been the sense of inviolability that a couple tons of steel and fiberglass can instill. Cocooned in a sealed chamber, behind tinted glass, with the temperature fully controlled, and the GPS system tracking, and sometimes dictating, our every turn, our every stop and start, we are radically isolated from each other, able to communicate only through the false connectedness of the cell phone. We ride high and sovereign; we are masters of space; we are safe against all who might intrude, all who might stand in our way (and against the weather, too) [...] We are now, truly, the liberal, autonomous subject. (Mitchell 2005: 96–97)

Except in the context of India's cities one's sovereign removal to a safer and purer air is not new, nor is it a metaphor for a legal bubble. For just as today's slum removal and rehabilitation projects form part of a longer historical background of sanitation planning and politics, the escape to the radical isolation of the SUV resembles an earlier form of colonial separation and escape to a better kind of air, extending and projecting Western forms of domesticity.

For the administrators of the British Raj, the solution was the hill stations such as Darjeeling and the Ooctamund, partly justified by the biopolitical administrative techniques that sought to study and know the nature of airy diseases (Kennedy 1996). Sanitation discourse would give rise to infrastructural improvements geographer Steven Legg (2007) shows in Delhi, whilst strategies of withdrawal were commonplace as the colonial administration retreated to the higher ground. The hills of the Nilgiri provided a tolerable climate, enabling the British elite to temporarily resettle for the summer months with the home-like qualities and the spatial organization of the Britain that they had departed. This would almost perfectly reconstruct the English country estate and planned communities: 'Patrons of the colonial hill stations liberally praised natural environments that were relatively cool, green, and unpopulated. The contrast with the lowlands seemed to provoke the question "could this be India?"' (Panter- Downes 1967 in Kenny 1995).

In the case of Ootacamund, assessments ranged from Tennyson's description of the '"sweet half-English air" to a later paean to its value as "an island of British atmosphere hung above the Indian plains", all communicating the site's

---

3   Matt Sparke has intelligently explored how these bubbles enable the inhabitation of asymmetric vectors of movement or tunnels that, in the context of extraordinary rendition and post-national citizenship programmes, he calls a form of 'gulfstream citizenship' (Sparke 2006).

superiority and the escape' (Kenny 1995: 699). The air and climate of the othered Indian landscapes of the plain is here inscribed with the characteristics of the safe, the familiar and the moral. Lord Lytton would describe the summer capital of the Madras Presidency as thus: 'I affirm it to be a paradise. The afternoon was rainy and the road muddy but such beautiful English rain, such delicious English mud'. It was a 'combination of "Hertfordshire lanes, Devonshire towns, Westmoreland lakes, Scottish trout streams and Lusitanian views"'. Even travelling to these sites reinforced the relationship between good climate and the comfort of travel as voyages on the railway to Darjeeling were rated in the quality of food and the standing of their wine.[4] Today, visitor guides enable tourists to discover the magic of 'Snooty Ooty', from St Stephen's Church – a stop on the architectural heritage trail – to the Victorian Government Botanical Gardens, to the Savoy Hotel.

What I think we are seeing today in struggles over India's air is some sort of reprisal of this colonial administrative and middle class past. The bourgeois elite's summer-long extrication from the city – also place for social gathering as Blunt (2004) suggests (paradoxical frivolity and excess in relation to their purifying and healthy nature) – finds itself reproduced in a much more permanent and diffuse geographical form of social secession or 'splintering' (Graham and Marvin 2001) of India's city life. This means not simply the removal of the poor, but the removal of the rich and middle classes who are extricated to a cleaner and different sort of atmosphere, a kind of domesticity (Gowans 2001, 2003; Stoler 2006) once seen in the hill stations of Simla and the colonial compound.

In the context of India's megacities, the air's differentiation and removal from the life of the populace permits a literal vertical hierarchy of air quality and atmospheric comfort that replays the vertical distance of the hill station and its isolated model communities into cocooned premium and elite spaces of the condominium or the car. Moreover, this model sees itself coupled with what Francisco Klauser (2010: 328) explains are 'the inherent atmospheric volume of the thereby created spaces of security', the 'relationship between the physical protection and the atmospheric self-encapsulation created by securitization strategies'. Whereas the removal of nuisance slums and inhabitations might then sort to purify air and space, the forms that are replacing those slums create their own climates of secessioned air, comfort and domesticity.

Delhi's own recent mega-event presents us with an ideal example where it was the precise nature of comfort which had raised such a furore amongst competitors travelling to the Commonwealth Games in 2010. The hastily constructed competitor apartments were accused of being less than habitable. Leaking air conditioning units and bare wires from other partially finished residential blocks and athlete sports villages were front page news. The event's comforting atmospheres were

---

4 The hill stations continued to function as middle class hideaways as narrated in Anita Desai's (1987) recollection of her childhood trip on the train from Delhi which is full of – to a certain extent – quite petty and idiosyncratic irritations and nuisances of smells, and the discomforts of jolts and bumps.

irrevocably connected to security and separation in the manner that Klauser (2010: 334) identifies in the secured spheres of security evident within the 2004 Greek Olympics, where 'toxic elements and people, as well as bad news and attempts at undermining, had to be kept out, in order to give the Olympic community a sense of physical and psychopolitical security and togetherness'.

The leaky air conditioning, which seemed to have threatened the Scottish athletic team's safety, was described by the UK's Health Protection Authority's instructions to travellers as the best form of 'room protection' from airborne mosquito viruses such as Dengue Fever, by creating an inhospitably cool atmosphere for mosquito survival. 'Highly secured spheres of emotion' and 'confidence' (Klauser 2010), were preserved within separated and securitized enclaves represented so well by the main Jawaharlal Nehru Sports Complex. The megalith was separated by its own climate of auto-sprinkling technology, an ozone system for air freshening, a low-power air conditioning system, lush natural grass and on-site and distributed security systems through the transit network. This example of what Sloterdijk (2008: 100) might call 'differently-attuned, differently enveloped and differently air-conditioned others' is becoming extremely common through developments such as this that privilege a politics of sensibility premised on comfort.

Geographer David Bissell (2008) describes comfort as an 'aesthetic sensibility' or 'affective resonance' induced between bodies, objects, environments and other people. This is of the kind associated with the sensibilities expressed within elite public spaces and spaces of travel when passengers are invited to relinquish, to lessen, and experience a 'soothing detachment', cushioned by the variegated air of atmospheric comfort and quality (Atkinson and Blandy 2009). Within the megacity, the model of the gated enclave and mega-event developments are developing in their own fashion into the high rise, preserving isolation by high value secessionary zones premised upon splintered infrastructural provisions of sanitation, energy and other air services (McFarlane 2008), but especially something as banal as building codes and specified levels of 'thermal comfort' in the new buildings that replace them (Cooper 1998). These may adversely affect the megacities' ambient air temperatures outside of those cocooned environments through their positive contribution to the cities' heat-island effect. But there is a deeper issue that concerns the imperialism of air and comfort too. For Stephen Healey (2008) this is an issue of the government of air through the standardization and normalization of what thermal comfort might actually mean, and how it can be governed through technical, administrative and institutional measures. These for Healy (2008: 312) reinforce 'technical definitions of thermal comfort, and the standards they inform' and thus work to 'condition both thermal norms and particular forms of life'.

Whilst numerous studies have shown how apartment dwellers appear to have sustained degrees of comfort that contrast greatly according to social and economic background and disposition, the overall levels of threshold thermal comfort in India depart dramatically from the associated standards. Part of this problem, for thermal engineers such as Indraganti and many other studies, is the seeming inability of the Indian high-rise to do anything other than emulate Western building types, especially as its building codes follow the dominant and international standards as set by the American Society of Heating, Refrigerating and Air-Conditioning Engineers (ASHRAE) (Indraganti 2010a, 2010b). 'Alarmingly', writes Indriganti, 'a growing number of apartments in the city' are 'designed to appear like their Manhattan counterparts, even if they are in Madhapur, Hyderabad' (Indraganti 2011). Authors like Indriganti argue that these building types 'are coming pre-fixed with oversized air conditioning systems, with little or no attention paid to thermal comfort or adaptation mechanisms of the occupants'. The literature strongly criticizes the overreliance on outdated international guidelines and 'comfort' levels or thresholds that reflect specifically western climates built on distinctively Anglo-European surveys and models of comfort.

According to the more technical literature, the dominant norms of comfort do not reflect the specific 'climatic and cultural context' of India, and it is the buildings that follow this standard which accounted for 46% of India's final energy use between 1995 and 2005. Studies of thermal comfort have shown that the comfort expectations of populations between temperate, cold climate and hot tropical climates are quite different. We should be careful here. And earlier explorations of comfort thresholds and adaptation distinctive to India were conducted with 'sweated' factory labour.

Easier questions might be asked of the consequences of imposing these sorts of standards of air. What is at stake for Healy are the conditions of comfort 'whose homogenous and enduring character is witnessed today in complementarily homogenous embodied dispositions, cultural norms, and built environments'. Healy (2008: 318) wants to push the debate so that critical questions over the 'resultant displacement of heterogeneous alternatives' and their potentially 'damaging consequences for energy use and problematic impacts on lifestyle and culture', are asked. Thermal monotony, in other words, might work to purify-out indigenous and culturally distinctive ways of living, yet with climatically damaging consequences for that very locality itself.

What seems to be crucial here is the 'attunement' Sloterdijk criticizes. Growing demand for these standardized levels of comfort appears driven by changing cultural economies of work in India which are shifting towards more office-based employment in closed and tightly controlled environments (Thomas *et al.* 2011). These are the kinds of 'Grade-A air conditioned office buildings. Buildings designed in the Dubai style'. Contemporary buildings like these are currently proliferating in India's rapidly growing urban centres and are characterized 'by extensive use of under-performing envelope materials (notably unshaded glass), fully sealed facades, and intensive air-conditioning' (Thomas *et al.* 2011: 7). The problem is perhaps one that brings us back to work. For it could be the culture of office work which is requiring the expectations of certain kinds of comfort in the air, and thus 'mimicking 20th century mistakes will simply elevate Indian comfort expectations to levels that require unsustainable energy inputs' (Thomas *et al.* 2011; 3). The inhabitants of air according to these studies, to reuse a metaphor, become air-conditioned towards particular levels of comfort.

Conclusion: exhausts, leaks and permeable boundaries

In the megacity the air continuously signs otherness. In the in-between and seemingly ephemeral materiality of air can be found the odious smells of a life forced to live without adequate sanitation. These are atmospheres that intrude onto the sensibilities of a bourgeois environmentally conscious middle class who are increasingly successful at removing the stench – and by implication, the people – from their environment. Air also denotes bounded enclaves of spherical security, a homogenous zone of thermal comfort but also monotony that once more illustrates a politics of difference managed by purification and intensive air design.

And yet these enclaves, islands and cocoons are not perfect. They leak, overspill and they expel and exhaust. Whilst these leaky boundaries are extremely problematic for those excluded from the interior spheres of security and domesticity, it is maybe in those boundaries that instances of possibility for survival exist. Whether the megacity's homeless sleep near exhausts, underground warm pipes or near road-sides during the winter to gain warmth, or informal and improvised sanitation and infrastructural practices mean residents of the slums are able to eke out an existence despite the crackdown of energy suppliers and the local state, air's refusal to accept its containment and purification, its harnessing and enclosing, may offer a means of living for those air-conditioned others found outside the boundaries of its secured spheres.

References

Adey, P. (2013 forthcoming) *Air*. London: Reaktion.

Agrawal, A. 2005. *Environmentality: Technologies of Government and the Making of Subjects*. Durham, NC: Duke University Press.

Alsayyad, N. and Roy, A. 2006. Medieval modernity: On citizenship and urbanism in a global era. *Space & Polity*, 10(1), 1–20.

Atkinson, R. and Blandy, S. 2009. A Picture of the floating world: grounding the secessionary affluence of the residential cruise liner. *Antipode*, 41(1), 92–110.

Baviskar, A. 2003. Between violence and desire: space, power, and identity in the making of metropolitan. *Delhi International Social Science Journal*, 55, 89–98.

Bissell, D. 2008. Comfortable bodies: sedentary affects. *Environment and Planning A*, 40(7), 1697–712.

Blunt, A. 2004. Imperial geographies of home: british domesticity in India, 1886–1925. *Transactions of the Institute of British Geographers*, 24(4), 421–40.

Bogard, W. 1989. *The Bhopal Tragedy: Language, Logic, and Politics in the Production of a Hazard*. Boulder, CO: Westview Press.

Cassels, J. 1993. *The Uncertain Promise of Law. Lessons from Bhopal*. Toronto: University of Toronto Press.

Chakrabarty, D. 2002. *Habitations of Modernity. Essays in the Wake of Subaltern Studies*. Chicago, IL: University of Chicago Press.

Cooper, G. 1998. *Air-Conditioning America: Engineers and the Controlled Environment, 1900–1960*. Baltimore, MD: Johns Hopkins University Press.

Corbin, A. 1986. *The Foul and the Fragrant. Odor and the French Social Imagination*. Cambridge, MA: Harvard University Press.

Davis, M. 2006. *Planet of Slums*. London: Verso.

Desai, A. 1987. Hill stations of the Raj. *New York Times Magazine*, 32.

Douglas, M. 1966. *Purity and Danger: An Analysis of Concepts of Pollution and Taboo*. London: Routledge & Kegan Paul.

Doyle, T. and Risely, M. 2008. *Crucible for Survival. Environmental Security and Justice in the Indian Ocean Region*. New Brunswick: Rutgers University Press.

Duncan, J.S. 2007. *In the Shadows of the Tropics. Climate, Race and Biopower in Nineteenth Century Ceylon*. Aldershot: Ashgate.

Engels, F. 1971. *The Condition of the Working Class in England*. Oxford: Blackwell.

Fortun, K. 2001. *Advocacy after Bhopal: Environmentalism, Disaster, New Global Orders*. Chicago, IL: University of Chicago Press.

Foucault, M. 2007. *Security, Territory, Population. Lectures at the Collège de France, 1977–78*. Basingstoke: Palgrave Macmillan.

Ghertner, D.A. 2010. Calculating without numbers: aesthetic governmentality in Delhi's slums. *Economy and Society*, 39(2): 185–217.

Gissen, D. 2006. Thermopolis: conceptualizing environmental technologies in the urban sphere. *Journal of Architectural Education* 60: 43–53.

Gowans, G. 2001. Gender, imperialism and domesticity: British women repatriated from India, 1940–47. *Gender, Place & Culture*, 8(3), 255–69.

Gowans, G. 2003. Imperial geographies of home: Memsahibs and Miss-Sahibs in India and Britain, 1915–1947. *Cultural Geographies*, 10(4), 424–41.

Graham, S. and Marvin, S. 2001. *Splintering Urbanism. Networked Infrastructures, Technological Mobilities and the Urban Condition*. London: Routledge.

Harrison, M. 1999. *Climates & Constitutions: Health, Race, Environment and British Imperialism in India, 1600–1850 Delhi*. Oxford: Oxford University Press.

Healy, S. 2008. Air-conditioning and the 'homogenization' of people and built environments. *Building Research & Information*, 36(4), 312–22.

Indraganti, M. 2010a. Behavioural adaptation and the use of environmental controls in summer for thermal comfort in apartments in India. *Energy & Buildings*, 42(7), 1019–25.

Indraganti, M. 2010b. Thermal comfort in naturally ventilated apartments in summer: Findings from a field study in Hyderabad, India. *Applied Energy*, 87(3), 866–83.

Indraganti, M. 2011. Thermal comfort in apartments in India: Adaptive use of environmental controls and hindrances. *Renewable Energy*, 36(4), 1182–89.

Ingold, T. 2007. Earth, sky, wind, and weather. *Journal of the Royal Anthropological Institute*, 13, 19–38.

Ingold, T. 2010. Footprints through the weather world: walking, breathing, knowing. *Journal of the Royal Anthropological Institute*, 16, 121–39.

Irigaray, L. 1999. *The Forgetting of Air in Martin Heidegger*. London: Athlone.

Kennedy, D. 1996. *The Magic Mountains: Hill Stations and the British Raj*. Berkeley, CA: University of California Press.

Kenny, J.T. 1995. Climate, race, and imperial authority: the symbolic landscape of the British hill station in India. *Annals of the Association of American Geographers*, 85(4), 694–714.

Klauser, F.R. 2010. Splintering spheres of security: Peter Sloterdijk and the contemporary fortress city. *Environment & Planning D: Society & Space*, 28(2), 326–40.

Legg, S. 2007. *Spaces of Colonialism: Delhi's Urban Governmentalities*. Oxford: Blackwell.

McFarlane, C. 2008. Sanitation in Mumbai's informal settlements: state, 'slum', and infrastructure. *Environment and Planning A*, 40(1), 88–107.

McFarlane, C. and Desai, V. 2011. The Politics of Open Defecation: Informality, Body and Infrastructure in Mumbai, Working Paper, Durham University.

Massumi, B. 2009. National enterprise emergency steps toward an ecology of powers. *Theory, Culture & Society*, 26(6), 153–85.

Mitchell, D. 2005. The S.U.V. model of citizenship: floating bubbles, buffer zones, and the rise of the 'purely atomic' individual. *Political Geography*, 24(1), 77–100.

Rabinow, P. 1989. *French Modern: Norms and Forms of the Social Environment*. Cambridge, MA: The MIT Press.

Sharan, A. 2006. In the city, out of place: environment and modernity, Delhi 1860s to 1960s. *Economic and Political Weekly*, 25 November, 4905–11.

Sloterdijk, P. 2009. *Terror from the Air*. Los Angeles, CA: Semiotext(e).

SPARC 2010. Mumbai airport slum dwellers rehabilitation? *City Watch*, June 14–15.

Sparke, M.B. 2006. A neoliberal nexus: Economy, security and the biopolitics of citizenship on the border. *Political Geography*, 25(2), 151–80.

Stoler, A.L. 2006. *Haunted by Empire. Geographies of Intimacy in North American History*. Durham, NC: Duke University Press.

thirdtreefromtheleft2011.RootsintheRunway–VoicesfromMumbai'sairportslums. Available at: http://www.youtube.com/watch?v=CyK5Td3SnFE [Accessed: 1 April2011].

Thomas T. *et al*. 2011. Adapting to Change: New Thinking on Comfort, Paper to the Conference *Adapting to Change: New Thinking on Comfort*, Cumberland Lodge, Windsor, UK, 9–11 April.

Virilio, P. and Degener, M. 2005. *Negative Horizon: an Essay in Dromoscopy*. London: Continuum.

Whitehead, M. 2009. *State, Science and the Skies. Governmentalities of the British atmosphere*. Chichester: Wiley-Blackwell.

Chapter 6

Automobile Interstices: Driving and the In-Between Spaces of the City

Iain Borden

The sheer physical effect of automobiles and driving on cities has been immense. Apart from the visible presence of automobiles themselves and the mass of traffic which they create, consider the whole range of roads, signs, lighting, street furniture and car parks, not to mention the general dispersal of car-centred buildings and urban form, whether these be in centralized European cities, gridded American cities, Asian megacities, suburbs or all manner of haphazard urban development (Taylor 2003). Already by 1922, no less than 135,000 suburban homes in 60 US cities depended wholly on cars for their transportation, while by 1940 some 13 million Americans lived in suburbs wholly devoid of public transport. In post-war Europe, the number of cars in the UK rose 55% in just 5 years and went on to reach 5.5 million in 1960 (Setright 1999: 72), while the 117,000 cars in Norway in 1950 had multiplied nearly eight-fold to 903,000 by 1970 (Ostby 2004: 247). The effects of these kinds of extraordinary traffic multiplication on the city were of course substantial and considerable, and, for example, by 1965 the one million plus vehicles which existed in Paris had turned it into 'an enormous car park' where 'trees are cut down and pavements trimmed to allow thousands of cars to circulate' (Evenson 1979: 54–55).[1] Today, around 25% of London and 50% of Los Angeles are devoted to car-only environments, while in Asia around 2,000 additional cars join the streets of Beijing every single day of the year (Sheller and Urry 2000: 746, BBC 2008, Wines 2010). These, then, are interstitial spaces, in that they are the spaces which are often considered to be leftover or in-between the buildings, parks and urban squares of our cities, but they are also far from being peripheral or secondary spaces. Indeed, these particular kinds of interstices are often some of the most significant, even sometimes most dominant, of our contemporary urban spaces.

How then do we understand these roads and their automobiles as spatial experiences in cities today? How is this interstitiality formed not only as a physical presence, but as an encounter with these spaces through the act of

---

1 See also Jean-Marie Delettrez, chief government inspector in finances, cited in District de la Région de Paris (1965: 131), quoted in Paskins (2011). See also Flonneau (2005).

driving? How, also, are these experiences represented and communicated among and between us?

In order to briefly explore these questions, I turn here to consider the experience of driving as represented in film over the last century or so. This is a subject which I have considered in different ways in a book-length study (Borden 2012), but here I turn to look at some films and ideas which are not covered in that publication, and in particular those which help us to explicate this notion of the interstitial in cities.

The arrival of the automobile

Turning to film, it is unsurprising that many of the automobile-based urban spaces identified above are readily visible in movies, from the earliest history of the cinema, right through to the 1970s when José in *The Gumball Rally* (Chuck Bail, 1976) declares that 'in this country you ain't nothing if you got no wheels,' and to recent films as diverse as *Happy-Go-Lucky* (Mike Leigh, 2008) and *Drive* (Nicolas Winding Refn, 2011). To begin with, pioneering documentaries by film-makers such as Sagar Mitchell and James Kenyon showed 1900s British city streets to be mostly populated by horse-drawn trams, buses and wagons which, along with bicycles and pedestrians, help to create urban traffic jams and bustling intersections controlled by helpful policeman. Across the rest of the world, other early twentieth century documentaries show similar scenes of downtown streets which are filled with horses and pedestrians as well as with cars and other motorized traffic. In such filmic depictions, automobiles, while undoubtedly present, are still something of a novelty, and indeed are often filmed as such, as with the gentle depictions of slow-moving cars in the Edison Manufacturing Company's *Automobile Parade* (1900) and *Automobile Parade on the Coney Island Boulevard* (1901). A decade or so later, however, and movies like *Tillie's Punctured Romance* (Mack Sennett, 1914) frequently present cars in a much more prominent role, here with Charlie Chaplin and wealthy farmer's daughter Tillie – who is inexperienced in city matters – nearly being run over by passing vehicles. Indeed, this film is far from exceptional in its treatment of the automobile, and between 1914 and 1920 over 300 American films made significant use of the car for the purposes of plot, theme and characterization (Smith 1983: 179). Charlie Chaplin himself made his first ever screen appearance in his now infamous tramp guise as a wayward spectator in *Kid Auto Races at Venice* (Keystone, 1914).

By the 1920s and 1930s, film-makers were showing the arrival of automobile traffic as part of the developing modernity of the city. Sometimes, this was as part of the general background to city life, as with the near abstract compositions of New York disclosed in the short artistic documentary *Manhatta* (Charles Sheeler and Paul Strand, 1921), in the colour shots of Cardiff, London and other British cities in Claude Friese-Greene's 24-part travelogue *The Open Road* (1925), in the everyday streets of Berlin in *People on Sunday* (*Menschen am Sonntag*,

Curt Siodmak, Robert Siodmak, Edgar G. Ulmer and Fred Zinneman, 1930), and in the bustling London traffic which occupies the opening sequences of *Piccadilly* (Ewald André Dupont, 1929) and the H.G. Wells science fiction film *Things to Come* (William Cameron Menzies, 1936), as well as in innumerable background appearances in films ranging from Fritz Lang's Berlin-based murder mystery *M* (1932) to Charlie Chaplin's *Modern Times* (1936), the latter, along with René Clair's *À Nous La Liberté* (1931), being one of the first filmic critiques of Fordist assembly-line production methods.

More creatively, however, many films of this period use automobile driving as part of a more dynamic depiction of the city, where the major new shifts which were occurring in people's everyday lives – the various interstitial times and speeds at which they worked and lived, the places and spaces they used, the foods, technologies and entertainments they were consuming – involved cars not only as an essential tool but as one of its most potent symbols. Seminal avant-garde documentaries such as Walter Ruttmann's *Berlin: Symphony of a Great City* (*Berlin: die Sinfonie der Großstadt*, 1927) and Dziga Vertov's *Man With A Movie Camera* (*Chelovek's Kino-Apparatom*, 1929), shot in cities including Kiev, Moscow and Odessa, along with other city portraits from the same period like *Moscow* (Mikhail Kaufman, 1927), all show city streets which are still largely dominated by pedestrians, horses, carriages and trams rather than cars, but they also go out of their way to depict cars wherever they can, and, in the case of Vertov's Kino-Glaz (Cine-Eye) *Man With A Movie Camera*, to heighten a sense of drama by intercutting automobiles with scenes of death, birth, injury and accident. As with many of the early films of D.W. Griffiths and others in America, the car is also used here to provide mobile tracking shots, adding to the sense of urban dynamism and modernity.

A few contemporary narrative films also adopted this sensibility. For example, *Asphalt* (Joe May, 1929), uses tilted camera angles to emphasize the dynamic, fast-moving nature of Berlin's interweaving cars, buses, trams and pedestrians, suggesting an intensity of speed and emotion which is always present and seemingly about to go out of control. Even more dramatically, in the silent masterpiece *Ménilmontant* (Dimitri Kirsanoff, 1928), two young country-dwelling sisters arrive in Paris where they are met with Kino-esque blurs, partial views and the distorted shapes of motorized traffic. As one of the sisters spends a passionate night with a young man, shots of her body are overlaid with those of cars speeding through Parisian streets; here, cars and movement are associated with independence, passion, sex and a headlong rush into the new and the unfettered. Later on, abandoned by her lover, and having given birth to a child, the same woman contemplates suicide next to the River Seine, while a maelstrom of people, cars, surfaces, cobbles and buildings rush across her face.

If these movies all tend to emphasize and even celebrate the arrival and visibility of the automobile in the intersections and interstitial spaces of the city, then a very different view is put forward in the propagandist *The City* (1939). Made for the New York World's Fair by pioneer documentary directors Ralph

Steiner and Willard van Dyke while working with urbanist Lewis Mumford, *The City* is essentially a 44 minute attack on unregulated city planning, combined with a passionate advocacy of Radburn planning principles involving a Garden City-style separation of traffic, residences, commerce and industry within smaller-scale settlements. An acerbic commentary written by Mumford together with strident music composed by Aaron Copland are deployed alongside damning scenes of children playing with motor traffic, car collisions and pedestrians unable to cross roads amid interminable traffic jams, pollution and congestion. In a much more humourous mode, the Disney short *Motor Mania* (1950) makes similar comments when it portrays the cartoon character Goofy's transformation, whenever he gets into a car, from the responsible and kindly 'good citizen' Mr Walker to the 'uncontrollable monster' and 'demon driver' of Mr Wheeler, who aggressively and impatiently treats the road as entirely his own domain.

Yet, despite the kind of argument put forward so forcibly by *The City*, the vast majority of films for the next 20 years or so simply reveal a reasonably trouble-free intersection of cars and cities, seemingly content to show how the interstitial spaces of roads, car parks and suburbia are gradually filling up with cars, traffic and drivers. Hence Alfred Hitchcock's *Shadow of a Doubt* (1943) portrays Santa Rosa as a small Californian town where policemen direct traffic in a friendly manner and where cars and pedestrians peacefully and harmoniously co-exist. Similar scenes of relatively genteel driving abound in other post-war films, ranging from Rome in *Rome, Open City* (*Roma, città aperta*, Roberto Rossellini, 1945), French village life in *Jour de Fête* (Jacques Tati, 1948), Vienna in *The Third Man* (Carol Reed, 1949) and London in *The Blue Lamp* (Basil Dearden, 1950), *Heavens Above* (John and Ray Boulting 1963) and *The Ipcress File* (Sidney J. Furie, 1965), to Naples in *Journey to Italy* (*Viaggio in Italia*, Roberto Rossellini, 1953), Paris in *The 400 Blows* (*Les Quatre Cents Coups*, François Truffaut, 1959), *Cléo from 5 to 7* (*Cléo de 5 à 7*, Agnès Varda, 1962) and *Band of Outsiders* (*Bande à Part*, Jean-Luc Godard, 1964) and Milan in *Yesterday, Today and Tomorrow* (*Ieri, oggi, domani*, Vittorio de Sica, 1963).

By the mid-1960s, however, signs of motoring strain are beginning to emerge. Given that many countries were by now beginning to experience frequently unpleasant traffic conditions – for example, in 1962 the lowest ever average traffic speeds were recorded in London; the UK's longest ever traffic jam, stretching 35 miles along the A30 from Yarcombe to the seaside at Torquay, occurred in the summer of 1964; and by the end of the 1960s, over 95% of American cities had introduced zoned parking restrictions (McShane 1997: 119, Ferguson 2004: 178) – it is unsurprising that humorous scenes involving traffic delays quickly became commonplace in many films of the 1960s, including, for example, *Kaleidoscope* (Jack Smight, 1966) and *The Sandwich Man* (Robert Hartford-Davis, 1966). The British comedy *The Fast Lady* (Ken Annakin, 1962) was one of the first to invoke a traffic jam as a source of frustration, as hapless Murdoch Troon (Stanley Baxter) tries to wrestle an unwieldy 1927 Bentley 3/4½ down a crowded high street.

More sophisticated comments regarding the physical impact of traffic upon urban life are made by French film-makers in this decade, notably Jacques Tati, whose magisterial *Playtime* (1967) pokes great fun at the car-borne residents of its modernist city, who cram car parks with endless rows of neatly ordered and near identical vehicles. In his later and often overlooked *Trafic* (1971), Tati concludes the film with another form of congestion, this time a rain-swept and grid-locked car park full of Fords, through which pedestrians with umbrellas pick their way. In a different vein, Jean-Luc Godard had already in his first full length new wave film *Breathless* (*À Bout de Souffle*, 1960) used Michel's fleeting and uncaring inspection of an injured pedestrian to reveal an uncaring attitude to fellow Parisians. But it is in the black comedy *Week End* (1967) that Godard makes a particularly overt reference to urban traffic, notably in the massive traffic jam encountered by the bickering and murderous couple Roland and Corinne as they try to escape Paris, and which contains various breakdowns, bumps, crashes, blaring horns, people shouting, zoo animals, children, picnics, chess-playing, reading, boats, jostling, and dead and injured people. Essentially, all of Parisian life is depicted here, condensed into a single tracking shot sustained over several minutes.

Other films show the presence of automobiles and the in-between spaces of the city road in a number of different ways, which I can only touch upon here. Some, such as the original version of the crime thriller *The Thomas Crown Affair* (Norman Jewison, 1968) starring Steve McQueen and Faye Dunaway, uses traffic almost metaphorically, with a parking meter 'violation' sign signalling to the audience that a more serious legal infraction – a bank robbery – is underway, while the unpredictable nature of city traffic adds tension to the robbers' escape. Other films adopt a more straightforward attitude, and disclose the impact of automobiles through new car-based buildings and urban developments, such as, to cite but a few examples, the American car parks, diners, gas stations, motels and bowling alleys of *Five Easy Pieces* (Bob Rafelson, 1970), the famous 1950s Mels Drive-In diner of Modesto in *American Graffiti* (George Lucas, 1973), the modern industrial estate, roundabouts and access roads of 1970s Britain in *Villain* (Michael Tuchner, 1971) and the beautifully expansive shots of Los Angeles surface streets, lights and freeway networks which provide the urban context for *Collateral* (Michael Mann, 2004). Other films use the drama and occasional violence of car-borne traffic as a backdrop to their main narrative, as in an opening scene of the Mexican road movie *Y Tu Mama También* (Alfonso Cuarón, 2001) where a voice-over describes the life of immigrant worker Marcelino Escutia, who has been killed trying to cross a busy road, or a radio recounting 200 fatalities during the summer vacation as part of the set up to *Red Lights* (*Feux Rouges*, Cédric Kahn, 2004).

Perhaps most insightful of all in their depictions of the physicality of motor vehicle-based society that often goes unnoticed, occupying as it does the oft-forgotten interstitial spaces of roads, are the pair of psychogeographic documentaries made by Patrick Keiller in the 1990s. In *London* (1994), we see automobiles largely as accident signs, traffic, billboards and IKEA car parks; that is, as incidental occasions and events interwoven into a rich tapestry of buildings, spaces, ideas, arts, landscape and inquisitive inspections. In the subsequent sequel *Robinson in Space* (1997), which extends Robinson's investigations into 'the problem of England' outside of the British capital, we are introduced to a much wider range of car- and truck-based spaces, most of which lie invisible within everyday life. Hence we are shown the national urban interstices of vast car plants, busy trunk roads and motorways set within a broader context of ports, ferries, containers, trains, literary associations, local histories, developer housing, automated plasterboard factories, prisons, satellite communications sites, defence and research establishments, shopping developments, Tesco distribution centres, old canals and power stations. As director Keiller himself explains, he is searching here for 'the passing of the visible industrial economy' and longing for 'an authenticity of appearance based on manufacturing and innovative modern design', but instead finds only constant movement and hidden services which are cloaked in conflictual and multivalent aesthetics. In many ways, then, *Robinson in Space* is not so much about directly seeing the full spectrum of cities around us, but of finding a way to see and understand that urban world – using driving to set facts, thoughts and ideas against places, sites and views, and so creating a way of looking, noticing and thinking that constantly hovers between the factual and the interpretive.

Returning to more mainstream movie making, by the mid-1970s it was possible for the very ubiquity of automobile urbanism to be the basis for a film, such as the extensive array of Long Beach parking lots, downtown streets and alleys which form the setting for H.B. 'Toby' Halicki's hugely indulgent car chase epic *Gone in 60 Seconds* (1974). In such places, as young Hunter, the estranged son of the main character Travis, remarks in *Paris, Texas* (Wim Wenders, 1984), 'nobody walks, everybody drives'. In an even more extreme version of this car-centred logic, Peter Weir's schlock-horror *The Cars That Ate Paris* (1974) imagines a small Australian town where the whole community – its economy, technology, politics and entertainment – are predicated upon automobiles and fuel, and which ultimately descends into a bloody internecine battle.

A different but in its own way no less apocalyptic approach to the ubiquity and seemingly unavoidable nature of car-based cities and society is presented in *Falling Down* (Joel Schumacher, 1993), where the central character of William Foster (Michael Douglas) is a recently divorced, recently unemployed defence industry worker. In recognition that the promise of limitless freedom seemingly offered by the automobile as it moves through the in-between spaces of the city is frequently illusory, Foster finds himself stuck in a cheap Chevette without air conditioning during a hot Los Angeles traffic jam. In a kind of typical modern urban hell, he endures smoke, fumes, flies, tacky Garfield toys, roads signs and technological failures while being assaulted by a cacophony of heated arguments, annoying radio adverts, beeping horns, shouting kids and pneumatic drills. Growing ever more claustrophobic and angry, Foster decides to abandon his car, walking across LA to attend his daughter Adele's birthday party. Along the way, he becomes successively intolerant, abusive and ever more determined and violent in his quest, including at one point blowing up a construction site with an anti-tank weapon. In many ways this is more than just an anti-car film, with Foster seeking revenge not just on cars themselves but on a car-based society which, in his view, has failed to provide a fair, responsible and equitable way of life. The unavoidable and interminable traffic jam at the start of the film is at once the symbol of all that has gone wrong, and the catalyst for Foster's maniacal response.

If the above sketches out briefly some of the ways in which film has identified and explored the impact of driving upon the urban environment over the last century or so, it also suggests that there is far more to driving than simply traffic configurations, new building types and car parks. As *Falling Down* indicates, urban driving brings with it an onslaught of ideas and experiences from city life, and is not just confined to objects as cars, roads and buildings. Indeed, all the films described so far in their own way address more dynamic, cultural and expressive aspects of car urban driving. So what are these less immediately visible aspects of driving? What are the social experiences which we gain through driving in the interstices of the city, and how does film explore them?

The quiet life

In many films, driving can be seen as a way of finding an appropriate setting within the world that allows the driver to disappear into the background of the urban environment, or to simply be comfortable within it. In this sense, the car promises the driver the chance to be removed from the city, to find an in-between world apart where they can escape from the intensive spaces, gazes, noises and exchanges of urban life.

The idea of invisibility is particularly strong within this thematic of urban escape, with cars often providing police, detectives and criminals alike with a way of seeing without been seen. An early film noir like Fritz Lang's *You Only Live Once* (1937) thus shows a bank robber watching a rain-swept branch of Fifth National Bank through a small slot in the screened-out rear window of a parked getaway saloon car, while similar scenes occur in countless surveillance scenes from *Walk East on Beacon* (aka *The Crime of the Century*, Alfred L. Werker, 1952), *99 River Street* (Phil Karlson, 1953), *Never Let Go* (John Guillermin, 1960), *Payroll* (Sidney Hayers, 1961) and *The Ipcress File* (Sidney Furie, 1965) to *French Connection* (William Friedkin, 1971), *Brannigan* (Douglas Hickox, 1975) and *Traffic* (Steven Soderbergh, 2000).

In other films it is not so much invisibility as a general ability to be unnoticed, to disappear into the backdrop of the city, which the car provides. In this respect driving helps further one of the great advantages of modern urban life, as identified by social theorists like Georg Simmel (1903), namely the right and capacity to be anonymous, to be unknown to and unrecognized by others and to adopt a blasé attitude towards them. Hence in Nicholas Ray's first feature, the 1948 film noir *They Live By Night* (later remade as *Thieves Like Us*, Robert Altman, 1974), the central couple are the falsely imprisoned Bowie and his wife Keechie, who along with accomplices Chicamaw and T-Dub are able to move between different small towns without anyone seeing or knowing them. In such a world, all places are the same, and driving helps people disappear into that uniform state.

Alternatively, many films use urban car driving as a way of increasing the tension between the conditions seeing and being seen, between discovering and being discovered. Alfred Hitchcock's *Vertigo* (1958), for example, depicts Scottie (James Stewart) using his 1956 DeSoto Firedome to follow Madeleine Elster (Kim Novak) in her European green Jaguar MkVIII through the streets of San Francisco. Conducted at very low speeds, these scenes use vision, concealment and curiosity to help construct a growing mood of unease and tension. The very distancing of one driver from another creates a sense of the unknown, and, given that Scottie later falls in love with Madeleine, a frisson of as yet uncertain attraction.

In *Vertigo*, Scottie's concealment is necessarily broken when he has to rescue Madeleine, who is apparently trying to commit suicide into the waters below the Golden Gate bridge. In other films, however, driving leads not to this kind of dramatic event but to a relatively quiet form of life, that is, where driving is a way to find an attitude or approach to the surrounding world. For example, in Godard's *Breathless*, one of the first films where city driving plays a central part of the milieu in which people relate to each other, Michel and Patricia drive through Paris, surrounded by other traffic, as they argue about the veracity of Michel's affections for Patricia. 'I can't do without you,' says Michel. 'Yes you can,' says Patricia. 'Maybe,' responds Michel as they negotiate boulevard traffic, 'But I don't want to.' A few years later, Wim Wenders, at the start of *Alice in the Cities* (*Alice in den Städten*, 1974), the first of his 'Road Movie Trilogy', devotes 13 minutes to simply recording main character Phil driving around in a 1973 Plymouth Satellite, yielding a matter-of-fact and largely windscreen-based view of buildings and signs, the linear perspective of roads, stopping at motels and gas stations, listening to the radio and, on finally arriving at New York, passing through the Lincoln tunnel. The rest of the film portrays similarly relaxed views of equally anonymous and in-between spaces in Germany, as Phil uses a 1973 Renault 4 Export to travel wherever he wishes in his search for an address which has been only ambiguously identified by the young Alice. The interstitial spaces of the road and the automobile here provide time and space in which to think and contemplate, to consider the world and other people, and to find a way to settle in with them.

A similarly gentle striving for connection takes place in the more dreamlike context of Wenders' later *Wings of Desire* (*Der Himmel über Berlin*, 1987), when angels Damiel and Cassiel sit inside BMW 320i convertible to report on what they have seen. Here they describe the myriad of extraordinary yet everyday incidents which they have witnessed, while lamenting their ultimate separation from human life. 'Stay alone. Let things happen. Keep serious. We can only be savages in as much as we keep serious,' comments Cassiel of their situation, 'Do no more than look. Assemble, testify, preserve. Remain spirit. Keep your distance. Keep your word.' All of this takes place not on city streets but within a car showroom, emphasizing their disjuncture from humanity as an interstitial existence in between heaven and earth. Alternatively, some drivers are quite content with their lot, so content in fact that they turn down even what others might consider to be a highly tempting offer. For example, in the Los Angeles tale within *Night on Earth* (Jim Jarmusch, 1991), taxi driver Corky declines the opportunity of a movie screen test from one of her customers. 'I'm a cab driver,' Corky explains, 'this is what I do.' The interstitial world of urban driving here offers stability and security, something valuable enough for Corky to reject a role in Hollywood which, by contrast, is 'not a real life'.

Other worlds

Corky's refusal of an opening into the big-time world of Hollywood suggests that the interstitial world of driving is at once a place of reality and of escape, and it is this tension between the real and the imagined which pervades many cinematic portrayals of automobile driving. However, in other cases, it is undoubtedly the latter – the world of fantasy, imagination and release – which is most overtly entered into.

In particular, although some have argued that the 'ecstatic dimension' to speed and acceleration can only be felt through first-hand experience (Beck and Crosthwaite 2007: 25), it is also exactly this aspect of high speed driving which is dynamically expressed in many films, indeed so thrillingly that the viewer actively imagines themselves participating in the exhilaration of velocity. There are innumerable movie explorations of this thematic, so many in fact that it is worth briefly noting here some of the most notable examples. In chronological order, these include: the very early *The Runaway Match, or Marriage by Motor* (Alf Collins, 1903) and *Dashed to Death* (Edison Manufacturing Company, 1909); D.W. Griffith movies such as *The Drive for a Life* (1909) and *Intolerance: Love's Struggle Throughout the Ages* (1916); the interwar *Emak-Bakia* (Man Ray, 1926), *La Glace à Trois Faces* (Jean Epstein, 1927), *Ménilmontant* and *The Crowd Roars* (Howard Hawks, 1932); post-war films such as *The Killers* (Robert Siodmak, 1946), *They Live By Night, Gun Crazy* (Joseph H. Lewis, 1949), *The Blue Lamp* (Basil Dearden, 1950), *To Catch a Thief* (Alfred Hitchcock, 1955), *Thunder Road* (Arthur Ripley, 1958) and *Les Tricheurs* (Marcel Carné, 1958); the 1960s with various James Bond films as well as *Payroll, The Killers* (Don Siegel, 1964), *Catch Us If You Can* (John Boorman, 1965), *Pierrot le Fou* (Jean-Luc Godard, 1965), *Bonnie and Clyde* (Arthur Penn, 1967), *Robbery* (Peter Yates, 1967), *Week End, The Italian Job* (Peter Collinson, 1969) and *Winning*; 1970s road movies like *Duel* (Steven Spielberg, 1971), *Two-Lane Blacktop* (Monte Hellman, 1971), *Vanishing Point* (Richard C. Sarafian, 1971), *The Getaway* (Sam Peckinpah, 1972), *Gone in 60 Seconds, Dirty Mary Crazy Larry* and *The Gumball Rally*; the 1980s and 1990s with *Goodbye Pork Pie* (Geoff Murphy, 1981), *Tron* (Steven Lisberger, 1982), *Thelma & Louise* (Ridley Scott, 1991) and *Freeway Speedway 6* (Nikkatsu

Corporation, 1996); and most recently with films such as *Changing Lanes* (Roger Michell, 2002), *Minority Report* (Steven Spielberg, 2002), *The Transporter* (Louis Leterrier and Corey Yuen, 2002), *The Italian Job* (Gary Gray, 2003), *I, Robot* (Alex Proyas, 2004), *The Fast and the Furious: Tokyo Drift* (Justin Lin, 2006), *Death Proof* (Quentin Tarantino, 2007), *Death Race* (Paul W.S. Anderson, 2008), *Speed Racer* (Larry and Andy Wachowski, 2008), *Fast and Furious* (Justin Lin, 2009) and *Tron Legacy* (Joseph Kosinski, 2010).

Together, all of these movies – and many more besides – depict a vast range of speed events including bumps and bashes, crashes and smashes, curves and corners, running traffic lights and stop signs, jumps and leaps, near misses and slender gaps, overtaking and undertaking, races and chases, slides and spins, twists and turns, undulating roads and switchback bridges, as well as extreme shocks and vibration. Audio is also an important addition, through the sound of accident impacts, blaring sirens, clunking gear-changes, echoes and reverberations through tunnels, revving engines, shouting voices, squealing tyres, turbo and supercharger effects and a general impression of sonic mayhem. Advanced filmic techniques further help to convey the sensation of speed, such as close-ups, fast editing, in-car shots, long lenses, low angles, montage, pans, rhythm editing, single-point perspectives, tracking shots, undercranking and overcranking, vehicle-mounted cameras, wide angles and zooms as well as computer generated imagery (CGI) and other post-production special effects. For example, in the London-set action movie *Brannigan* (Douglas Hickox, 1975), where visiting Chicago cop Brannigan (John Wayne) commandeers a yellow 1974 Ford Capri MkII to chase a 1964 Jaguar S-Type, the impression of speed comes not from any particularly high speeds being attained but rather from an expert portrayal of tight corners, sinuous S-bends, the rushing road surface, enclosure from surrounding buildings, close and swerving cars and even an improbable leap across the partly-raised Tower Bridge. Camera techniques utilized include multiple car-mounted cameras and road-level tracking shots. Other notable examples of sophisticated portrayals of high speed driving range from the various highly sophisticated yet nonetheless reality-dependent representations of motor racing in *Grand Prix* (John Frankenheimer, 1966) and *Le Mans* (Lee H. Katzin, 1971) and the *verité* authenticity of *Gone in 60 Seconds*, to the video game-influenced stylizations of *The Fast and the Furious: Tokyo Drift*, *Death Race* and *Fast and Furious*, and the merging of digital and live action in *Tron*, *Tron Legacy* and *Speed Racer*.

Yet, as overtly entertainment-oriented movies from the many James Bond escapades to *Gone in 60 Seconds*, its later remake, *Swordfish* (Dominic Sena, 2001) and *The Fast and The Furious* series all make clear, velocity and performance are not in themselves enough to transport the cinematic experience of driving into other worlds. So although we have in these films a great sense of speed while cars are variously raced, chased, stolen and crashed, often with an impressive range of advanced stunt driving and complicated filmic trickery, we have to turn elsewhere to locate a richer and more satisfying immersal into the interstitial sate of psychological as well as physical high velocity.

In particular, many other movies exploit high speed driving to more stimulating effect, invoking a sense of alternative and modified experience. This thematic is explored in many art projects, such as that entitled 'The Royal Road to the Unconscious' in which conceptual artist Simon Morris and film-maker Daniel Jackson recorded an instance of driving as a deliberate yet 'seemingly random act of utter madness'. In this project, Morris took a cut-out of every single word from Sigmund Freud's Interpretation of Dreams, and, on Sunday 1 June 2003, proceeded to throw these words out of the side window of a Renault Clio Sport travelling at 90 mph, at a site 122 miles southwest of Sigmund Freud's psychoanalytical couch in London. In the words of the artist, this action 'freed the words from the structural unity of Freud's text as it subjected them to an aleatory moment', but it also served to underline the way in which driving itself can throw the driver into an alternative psychological state, that is by invoking a sense of the illogical, irrational and accidental (Morris 2003).

Perhaps of more immediate significance to this study of urban everyday driving, however, is the more mainstream yet still highly mediated films such as those created by experimentally minded directors David Lynch and Oliver Stone in the 1990s. For example, Lynch's road movie *Wild At Heart* (1990) follows Sailor Ripley (Nicolas Cage) and his true love Lula Pace Fortune (Laura Dern) in their struggle to remain together despite the best efforts of Lula's mother, the mob and the police. During their various journeys around America, the couple experience a number of increasingly fantastical events, including a night-time trip mid-way through the film during which Lula sees a black-robed witch riding a broomstick alongside their open-topped 1965 Ford Thunderbird. As the road ahead dives beneath the arc of the Ford's headlights, and the dark expanse of the desert similarly disappears from view away from the side of the road, Lula pronounces that 'it's just shocking sometimes, when things aren't the way you thought they were', before adding that 'we're really out in the middle of it now'. Soon after, the pair of lovers come across the surreal aftermath of a car accident, with clothes and other debris strewn across the highway, dead bodies lying prone and unmoving, while car lights blink on and off and overturned wreckage creaks with heat and distorted metal. As Sailor and Lula tentatively investigate the scene, a bloodied young women behaves eccentrically while searching for a bobby pin, then collapses and dies theatrically in front of them. After many further twists and turns, *Wild At Heart* culminates when Sailor, lying horizontal on the highway after being beaten up by an Asian gang, has a vision of the pink 'Good Witch' – hovering within a bubble against the bright blue sky – who tells him that 'if you're truly wild at heart, you'll fight for your dreams' and 'don't turn away from love'. He then dashes after Lula, where they are reconciled in the middle of a traffic jam as Sailor croons Elvis Presley's classic *Love Me Tender*.

A similar sense of dislocation lies at the heart of many other depictions of high speed, from *Gun Crazy*, where Bart believes that it is as if 'nothing were real any more', to the literal intoxication of Thornhill in *North By NorthWest* (Alfred Hitchcock, 1959) who barely survives a mountainous journey after being force-fed liquor, and the opening sequence of *Shallow Grave* (Danny Boyle, 1994), where the rushing view from the front of an unseen car speeding through Edinburgh's New Town area signifies the film's later transition from domestic flat-sharing tranquility into a world of death, deceit, revenge and distrust.

Many of these movies are based on a film noir sense of a rushing trajectory, in which the drivers and other characters are propelled fatalistically to a future and end that is largely out of their control. By contrast, another aspect of driving interstitiality occurs when the drivers take a more deliberate course of action, using the in-between spaces of the city as a zone in which to test, challenge and even cross-over the legal and ethical mores of urban life. This is immediately evident in innumerable films, from the desperate manoeuvres of Riley and Spud in *The Blue Lamp* and the moonshine-running antics of *Thunder Road*, to the comic police-baiting of *The Gumball Rally* and *Cannonball Run* of the 1970s and early 1980s, and through the freedom-chasing drivers of *Goodbye Pork Pie* and *Thelma & Louise* to the counter-authority rebels of *Minority Report*, *I, Robot* and the Gallic *Taxi* series (Gerard Pirès and Gérard Krawczyk, 1998–2007). The combination of driving with drugs and sex is also a frequent theme in these dynamic automobile interstices, such as the sexualized encounter between Johnny and Sheila while driving on a racetrack in the 1964 version of *The Killers* (1964), or the scenes of drug- and alcohol-affected driving in *Pulp Fiction* (Quentin Tarantino, 1994), *Repo Man* (Alex Cox, 1984), *Withnail and I* (Bruce Robinson, 1986), *Open Your Eyes* (*Abre Los Ojos*, Alejandro Amenábar, 1997), *Y Tu Mama También* and *Red Lights*. Most dramatically, in *Basic Instinct 2*, (Michael Caton-Jones, 2006) the intoxicated and overly sexualized crime novelist Catherine Trammel (Sharon Stone) pleasures herself while driving a Spyker C8 Laviolette sports car at high speed through the subterranean world of London's Limehouse Tunnel. Soon after, on the very point of orgasm, she crashes into one of the docks of the nearby Canary Wharf office development, and in doing so drowns her drugged-up boyfriend.

Most telling of all, however, are not these somewhat excessive or fantastical filmic representations, but those films which depict – with varying degrees of authenticity and originality – real-life high speed city driving and in which the in-between spaces of the city become a place of overt irresponsibility and illegality. For example, *Freeway Speedway 6* (1996) shows a large number of real-life windscreen views of cars such as a highly modified Toyota Supra, offering in excess of 600 bhp, as the drivers negotiate Tokyo's expressways and other urban roads at very high speed, overtaking and weaving between city traffic in order to maintain momentum. Based on the exploits of the Mid Night Club and other notorious night-time street racers, the *Megalopolis Expressway Trial* series of documentary-esque films has subsequently been banned in Japan, while the genre has become known globally through street racing video games such as the *Midnight Club* series (Rockstar Games, 2000–08), as well as the *Wangan Midnight* manga comic book series and its various spin-off video games, movies and television programmes. For example, the fourth game of the Midnight Club video game series, *Midnight Club: Los Angeles* (2008), available on PlayStation and Xbox formats, enables the game player to roam freely around a highly detailed Los Angeles cityscape, both driving to and participating in various competitions, freeway races and 'pink slip' contests (after which the winner takes ownership of the loser's car), and in doing so, as one reviewer explains, 'transforms the bumper-to-bumper crawl of Los Angeles' street life into a roaring blur of rubber and metal' (Reinier 2009). The constant sense of illegality is further heightened by the appearance of the police, who constantly chase and, where possible, arrest and fine the driver. Other video games based on or incorporating illicit street racing include the *Grand Theft Auto* series (DMA Design and Rockstar Games, 1997 onwards) and *Need for Speed* series (Electronic Arts, 1994 onwards), as well as *Burnout* (Criterion Games and Electronic Arts, 2001 onwards), *Juiced* (THQ, 2004), *Cruis'n* (Nintendo and Midway Games, 1994 onwards) the German *Emergency 3* (Sixteen Tons Entertainment, 2005), and the Japanese *Initial D* (Sega Rosso, 2001–2004) and *Wangan Midnight* (Sega and Namco, 2001 onwards). Some of these games are also massively popular worldwide. For example, although not based on illegal city driving, the ultra-detailed and complex *Gran Turismo* driving simulation video game for the Sony PlayStation (Polyphony Digital, 1997 onwards) has attained global fame, with over 60 million copies sold by 2011.

The rise of the real-life Japanese car import scene in the USA, UK and other countries has also been important here, much of which relies on a subcultural spirit in which social underdogs or outsiders heavily tune and modify their cars in order to overstep normative social codes regarding personal expenditure, aesthetic style and driving behavior (Kwon 2004). Numerous depictions of this street racing and its associated subculture emanate from around the world, such as the Swedish *Getaway in Stockholm* series (Duke Marketing, 2000 onwards) and *Ghost Rider* series (Team Ghost Rider/Müller Productions, 2002 onwards), both of which are commonly available in DVD and on the internet.[2] Most freely available of all, YouTube and other internet-based movie-clip sites offer an enormous range of examples of illegal driving and racing, from high velocity freeway drives and overtaking to dangerous turns, spins, braking and other anti-social manoeuvres on the public roads. Returning to mainstream movies, films inspired by the *Megalopolis Expressway Trial* series, the Mid Night Club and the global street racing scene in general include the Hong Kong director Andrew Lau Wai-Keung's *The Legend of Speed* (1999) and *Initial D* (2005) and the Malaysian Syamsul Yusof's *Evolusi KL Drift* (2008) and *Evolusi KL Drift 2* (2010), as well as the American *The Fast and The Furious* series, *Biker Boyz* (Reggie Rock Bythewood, 2003), *Redline* (Andy Cheng, 2007), *Street Racer* (Teo Konuralp, 2008) and *Fast Track: No Limits* (Axel Sand, 2008).

As the sales and reception of *Gran Turismo* indicate, many of these films, video games and other depictions of illegal street racing have been hugely successful. For example, the *Grand Theft Auto* and *Need for Speed* series have sold well over

---

2 See www.getawayinstockholm.com and www.ghostridermovie.net [both accessed: 3 January 2011].

100 million copies each, while the notorious *Ghost Rider* motorcyclist series is particular popular on YouTube where, at the time of writing, the *Ghost Rider – Fuck Police* clip has been viewed over 14.5 million times.[3] This five-minute movie shows the anonymous Ghost Rider travelling at ultra high speeds along Swedish *motorvägs* (freeways), dual carriageways, country roads and city streets, where he overtakes much slower vehicles at tremendous velocities, squeezes between passing trucks, performs extended wheelies, smokes in front of public buildings, jumps over a line of fire, out-accelerates the chasing police, by-passes road-blocks and passes through red lights. Front- and rear-facing bike-mounted cameras provide a highly realistic sense of the on-board experience, while occasional external views of the rider provide an added sense of context and authenticity.

Conclusion

It is then, perhaps, in these kinds of filmic depictions of driving that we find one of the most significant themes of city automobile driving, namely that it offers, through its very state of interstitiality, a series of contradictory conditions and experiences. In these interstices we encounter at once enclosure and openness, slow speeds and high speeds, the quiet life and the tumultuous rapidity of cities. Here, we enter into a world of reality and unreality, of thrilling release and reprehensible risk-taking, individual independence and urban context.

Nor are these experiences wholly new. In his celebrated work of 1904, *The Complete Motorist*, the early Edwardian motorist A.B. Filson Young described high speed driving in the following terms. The 'ineffable thrill and exhilaration of such a flight,' Filson Young (1905: 285) extolled, is like 'the exaltation of the dreamer, the drunkard, a thousand times purified and magnified,' and the frontispiece of his book thus appropriately shows Paul Gervais' painting *L'effroi* (*The Terror*, exhibited at the Paris salon, 1904), in which the trajectory of a speeding car generates a state of panicked fright among a crowd of centaurs and nymphs. Today, the interstitial spaces of automobile driving continue to offer both sides of this equation – thrill and terror, safety and risk, quietude and release – in equal and enduring measure.

References

BBC (2008) Record Car Ownership in Beijing. Available at: www.news.bbc.co.uk [accessed: 12 February 2011]

Beck, J. and Crosthwaite, P. 2007. Velocities of power: an introduction. *Cultural Politics*, 3 (1), 23–34.

---

3   See www.ghostridermovie.net [accessed: 11 February 2012].

Borden, I. 2012. *Drive: Journeys through Film, Cities and Landscapes*, London: Reaktion.

District de la Région de Paris 1965. *Paris en Question: Une Enquête du District de la Région de Paris*. Paris: Presses Universitaires de France.

Evenson, N. 1979. *Paris: A Century of Change*, New Haven, CT: Yale University Press.

Ferguson, E. 2004. Zoning for parking as policy process: a historical review. *Transport Reviews*, 24(2), 177–94.

Filson Young, A.B. 1905. *The Complete Motorist: Being an Account of the Evolution and Construction of the Modern Motor-Car, Etc.* (revised 5th edn). London: Methuen.

Flonneau, M. 2005. *Paris et l'Automobile: un Siècle de Passions*. Paris: Hachette.

Kwon, S. A. 2004. Autoexoticizing: Asian American Youth and the Import Car Scene. *Journal of Asian American Studies*, 7(1), 1–26.

McShane, C. 1997. *The Automobile: a Chronology of Its Antecedents, Development and Impact*. London: Fitzroy Dearborn.

Morris, S. 2003. *The Royal Road to the Unconscious*. London: Information As Material.

Ostby, P. 2004. Educating the Norwegian nation: traffic engineering and technological diffusion. *Comparative Technology Transfer and Society*, 2(3), 247–72.

Paskins, J. 2011. The Social Experience of Building Construction Work in and around Paris in the 1960s. PhD Thesis, University College London.

Reinier, A. 2009. Second Opinion, addendum to M. Helgeson, Midnight Club: Los Angeles. *Game Informer*. Available at: www.gameinformer.com [accessed: 6 February 2012].

Setright, L.J.K. 1999. *Mini: The Design of an Icon*. London: Virgin.

Sheller, M. and Urry, J. 2000. The city and the car. *International Journal of Urban & Regional Research*, 24(4), 737–57.

Simmel, G. 1903. Die Großstadt und das Geistesleben [The Metropolis and Mental Life], republished in English in: P.K. Hatt and A.J. Reiss (eds) *Cities and Society: the Revised Reader in Urban Sociology*. New York: Free Press, 1951, 635–46.

Smith, J. 1983. A runaway match: the automobile in the American film, 1900–1920, in: D.D. Lewis and L. Goldstein (eds) *Automobile and American Culture*. Ann Arbor, MI: Michigan University Press.

Taylor, N. 2003. The aesthetic experience of traffic in the modern city. *Urban Studies*, 40(8), 1613–14.

Wines, M. 2010. Multiplying Drivers Run Over Beijing Traffic Plan. Available at: www.nytimes.com [accessed: 2 March 2012].

Chapter 7

Interstitial Space and the Transformation of Retail Building Types

Mattias Kärrholm

The aim of this chapter is twofold: to start and develop a conceptual discussion on interstitial space as an important issue of territorial change in the use of everyday urban spaces, and to describe the relationship between interstitial practices and the territorial transformation of retail spaces.[1] Today, retail has become an increasingly ambient part of our public spaces, and new retail environments and building types are evolving faster than ever before. This proliferation of new retail spaces both uses and undermines interstitial spaces and practices. In this chapter I initiate a discussion about how interstitial urban practices affect and are affected by the evolution of new territories of consumption such as pedestrian precincts, retail parks, airport malls, museum stores, railway-transport-oriented retail, concept stores, etc.

The chapter is divided into three parts. In the first part I give a theoretical introduction to interstitial space, using two cases, the disturbed but spatially inventive children at Bruno Bettelheim's school in the 1940s and the spatial transformations of the nineteenth century book collector Thomas Phillipps. I conclude this discussion with three points, putting interstitial space into a context of territorial theory (Brighenti 2010, Kärrholm 2007, 2012). In the second part, I discuss and give examples of new urban types of retail that displace or colonize both the in-between spaces of the old city centre and the in-between times of our everyday lives. In the third part, I use the concept of singularization as a way of dealing with the formation and evolution of new retail building types. This process involves a singularization of spaces, often making good use of interstitial space and practices. However, in order to capitalize on these new spatial innovations the process is often quickly followed by desingularization, where the fluid rules of interstices and territorial sorts become stabilized into firm and ordered territorial types. In short, interstitial practices are used by retail businesses to temporarily destabilize and transform territorial structures, but these are then often restabilized as new territorial types.

---

1 This chapter is a development of Chapters 5 and 6 in Kärrholm (2012) as seen from the perspective of interstitial space.

Notes on interstitial space

In-between space as a concept was imported from Martin Buber into an architectural discourse by the Dutch architect and co-founder of Team X, Aldo van Eyck, in 1961 (Lefaivre 2002: 24). Buber used the concept of *zwischenmenschliche* in his preface to the book *Die Gesellschaft* in 1906 and then came to develop the in-between as a dialogical relatedness between 'I and Thou' as well as between 'I and It' (Praglin 2006). To van Eyck, and later his colleague Herman Hertzberger, the in-between was, simply put, a place of two spatial programmes, often indicating a meeting of private and public spaces, e.g. something like a threshold that 'depending on how you interpret it, belongs more to the house or more to the street and hence is a part of both' (Hertzberger 2000: 215). The work of Hertzberger and van Eyck represents explicit examples of an architect's perspective on the in-between, where the focus most explicitly lies on interstitial material places (the front garden, *de stoep*, the porch) rather than on interstitial practices. Hertzberger devotes whole chapters to the subject in his books on space for students in architecture (Hertzberger 1991, 2000). Lefaivre has pointed out that van Eyck's more than 700 playgrounds made during the post-war period were unique in the way in which they were integrated into the 'living fabric of the city' (Lefaivre 2002: 28 ff.) on the many empty sites left after the bombing of Amsterdam during the Second World War. Van Eyck's playgrounds, placed as they often were in the middle of urban traffic spaces, might seem somewhat oddly designed to us today, but the lack of clear territorial boundaries also allowed for a kind of loose space (Franck and Stevens 2007), where it became possible to question any dominant function in a given situation, the walking commuter was, for example, not by default given privilege over the playing child.

Despite the interest shown by some architects in the concept of the in-between and the interstitial, the concept has not been theoretically developed or thoroughly investigated in terms of its function for urban life. The importance of architecture and the built environment when it comes to producing in-between or interstitial spaces must not be neglected. It should not be reduced to simply the physical (geometrical) space between two other spaces or buildings, or to the meeting place of public and private activities. In order to make the concept of interstitial space effective in discussions of architecture and everyday life, we need to be more precise about its meanings and objectives.

Bruno Bettelheim and Thomas Phillipps

Before it was ever used in architecture, the psychologist Bruno Bettelheim, who studied under Freud, pointed out the importance of in-between spaces in his book *Love is not Enough* (1950). In this book, Bettelheim wrote about life at the Orthogenic School for emotionally disturbed children, one of the laboratory schools at the University of Chicago during the 1940s. Bettelheim discovered that the preferred places of play often were in-between spaces like stairways and hallways, rather than bedrooms or dining rooms (Bettelheim 1950: 116). When the School decided to equip a nice living room for the kids, it was transformed as soon as the kids were allowed to take over:

> It became an in-between room. Something between a living room, a play room, a room for indoor sports, for music and for what not. Only then did the children like to use it [...] It was as if it were contrary to the children's desire to admit any clear-cut division of functions between rooms or to take up activities in line with what a room is designed for. (Bettelheim 1950: 117)

The same held true for more private spaces. The private dormitories soon became deprived, enabling the children to shift from rest to play, etc. (Bettelheim, 1950: 117 ff.).

In his therapy, Bettelheim allowed some children to break with strong territorial expectations and rules that could seem oppressive to them, like the need to eat in the dining room. Sten Andersson, Bettelheim's Swedish translator, has suggested in an essay called *The Psychology of Things* that Bettelheim regarded things as inscribed with meaning. Certain things, like a knife or a fork, thus seem to contain certain demands on their users (Anderson 1980: 50; c.f. Werne 1987). To me, however, it seems clear that the phenomenon Bettelheim describes is primarily spatial. It is in the spatial distribution of the artefacts that a certain territorial expectation becomes stabilized. It is not primarily in the fork or knife itself, but in the ways that a certain set of artefacts becomes associated with a dining situation or space, that certain behaviours and expectations become stabilized and can thus act oppressively or seem oppressive (Kärrholm 2004). One makes an association to a certain sort of territory as well as to the rule commonly associated with this kind of territory (c.f. Barker 1968). Bettelheim's therapy empowered the children to undermine these disciplinary rules and associations. By allowing them to eat in bed, territorial associations were deterritorialized. Bettelheim helped the children to produce an interstitial space which gave them the possibility of appropriating and associating to a territory of their own.

In-between spaces, or interstitial spaces as I also will call them here, play important roles in human life. One is the ability to create a space wherever one might want to, in order to develop actions of one's own rather than just reacting to strong territorial strategies, and their regulation. This has especially been studied in children and young people and their ways of appropriating public spaces that belong to the world of adults (c.f. Lieberg 1992), but is important in relation to all human beings.

Another role of interstitial practices, and this is the role that has been most developed by commercial agents and retailers, is the possibility of charging a certain space or territorial situation with potentially new and atypical performances. This kind of interstitial practice has a great deal to do with the addition of new rules and things to an existing territory; the adding of new things to a space where they, at least at first, do not seem to belong (like the living room produced by Bettelheim's children) is one possible and very basic strategy of interfering with an existing territorial order. This brings me to my second example of interstitial practices/ spaces: the case of Thomas Phillipps.

The industrial expansion during the nineteenth century was an era of increasing production as well as of evolving consumption. One of the more extreme examples of more scaled-up consumption was the English baronet and book collector Thomas Phillipps, famous for his utterance 'I want a copy of every book in the world' (an ambition not far from that of certain commercial websites of today, such as Googlebooks, Amazon or Bookfinder). Thomas Phillipps bought important books and manuscripts at a pace that did not even leave him time to unpack them. Wooden boxes filled with books were piled everywhere, and the house soon became an important destination for visiting scholars from abroad. Through this excessive accumulation of books, Phillipps managed to undermine and break all the meticulously constructed territorial rules of the Victorian home. He deterritorialized the spatial divisions of maid's chambers, parlours, billiard rooms, dining rooms, etc. Phillipps himself wrote in a letter to a friend in 1856: 'We have no room to dine in except the Housekeeper's room! ... Our Drawing Room & Sitting Room is Lady Phillipps' Boudoir!!' (Munby 1971: IV, 86).

The dining was further obstructed by the uneven floor which had sunk under the weight of the books, and there was trouble putting up a table. On his last visit to Middle Hill, Sir Frederick Madden, Keeper of manuscripts at the British Museum, describes a house where not even paths were maintained between the piles:

> I never saw such a state of things! Every room filled with heaps of papers, MSS., books, charters, packages, & other things, lying in heaps under your feet; piled upon tables, beds, chairs, ladders, & c. & c. and in every room, piles of huge boxes, up to the ceiling ... It is a literary charnel-house! (Munby 1971: IV, 88 ff.)

An important nineteenth-century concept was 'character', and it was demanded of both people and architecture (Forty 2000: 120–30; Hetherington 2007: 138). The main idea of the Victorian home was to safeguard the private sphere; it was a place of refuge and retreat that excelled in physical separation (c.f. Girouard 1985; Evans 1997: 79 ff.). It was also, as Hetherington argues, an important space for the projection of the moral character of the family, as well as a space in which the activity of taking possession of the world was manifested through consumption and collections (Hetherington 2007: 131 ff.). Phillipps never managed or wanted to live up to the Victorian standards. The resources for running a family and a household at Middle Hill were at best bleak, in terms of both space and money, and although collecting in general can be regarded as 'taking possession' it seem, in Phillipps' case, to have been much more used as a way of losing control. Phillipps' gradual erasure of Victorian territorial rules and conduct was not limited to the home. In fact, at the same time as he reconstructed his home into a public institution/library/archive/charnel-house he was also working at the other end of the private–public spectrum, with the privatization of a public institution:

the Bodleian at the University of Oxford. Phillipps had plans of selling his large collection to his alma mater for £30,000. This offer was, however, coupled with a list of demands. Phillipps wanted to be able to freely use the collection, to have his own keys so that he could go there after closing hours, etc. Later he also demanded to be Bodleian's head librarian, with the existing head librarian working as his assistant, that the entire Ashmolean building should be used for his collection only, and that he himself would be invited to live in the Ashmolean basement with a housekeeper. After a correspondence of some 150 letters over 35 years the negotiations finally broke down and came to nothing (Munby 1971: V, 2–8).

Three points on interstitial space

In the case of Phillipps we have ordinary rooms, associated with everyday Victorian territorial sorts such as parlours and sitting rooms, turned into interstitial spaces by means of the amassment of artefacts and the unconventional spatial practices resulting from this accumulation. Interstitial space, in this sense, is not about either the topological order of rooms (like Hertzberger's thresholds or van Eyck's playgrounds) or the activities taking place there; it is always a socio-spatial or socio-material process. Both Bettelheim's children and Thomas Phillipps transformed certain territorial sorts such as living rooms and bedrooms, by means of materialities, things, actions, rules and associations. Interstitial space can thus be described as spatial production through territorial transformation. Interstitial space has to do with territorial orders produced by an assemblage or network of people, objects, spaces and rules (Latour 2005; Kärrholm 2007), and interstitial space is thus in my opinion an integral part of the field of research Brighenti has discussed as *territoriology* (Brighenti 2010). Interstitial space adds to territorial complexity, e.g. by producing new territorial associations, appropriations and tactics, as well as by challenging the hierarchy of existent dominating territorial productions at that place (Kärrholm 2004). By way of comparison with interstitial space we can take Marc Auge's related yet wholly different concept, non-place. To Augé non-places like airports and shopping malls are areas without sufficient significations to be regarded as places (Augé 1995). In some cases these non-places really lack clear, dominant territorial production, and thus they can be seen as places of weak or heterogeneous territories in-between stronger and more homogenous territorial productions. In other cases, however, the territorial production might be very strong (such as at certain areas of the airport), and whether or not they are interstitial spaces remains to be investigated from case to case, and from moment to moment. My *first point* is therefore that interstitial spaces are dependent on, and can even be defined in terms of, how they relate to one or more stronger adjacent or overlapping territorial productions. This indicates a double identity of being (a) and also being (b). It also implies a sequential transformation from (a) and (b) and then on to something else, (c).

My *second point* is that interstitial spaces are not predefined or located at certain predefined spaces such as hallways, staircases, residual spaces (c.f.

Wikström 2005), etc., but can be found or produced at any place. Bettelheim describes in-between space as ill-defined and as the 'absence of stability' (Bettelheim 1950: 116), and this is true in the sense that interstitial spaces lack or defy a dominant territorial strategy as well as an easily associated territorial sort. Interstitial spaces defy classification and can in this sense be described as a kind of *terrains vagues* (Solà-Morales 1995). However, a *terrain vague* here must be understood as something applicable to all places, not just to the vague or *unheimlich* places outside traditional cities, such as industrial areas, ports and contaminated sites, as Sola-Morales seems to suggest. They can, in fact, also be produced within spaces of strong, strategic territorializations in city centres, in shopping malls and even inside the private home.

Finally, and in line with this, my *third point* is that there are at least two kinds of interstitial spaces. First, there are the ones that take advantage of weak or heterogeneous territorial programmes in between stronger ones, and second, there are also the ones that 'carve' out space within strong territorial strategies, through associations made to other sorts of territories than the ones supported by territorial strategies. This second type creates uncertainties and new rules that defy existing classifications and regulations within the 'territory of the enemy'. Thus, interstitial practices and in-between spaces might, as in the case of Thomas Phillipps, also be produced as an association to a certain strong territorial sort ('my home') or inside the borders of a strong territorial strategy (the Bodleian library).

The ambience of retail

Retailers have always made at least rudimentary use of interstitial practices and in-between spaces. This was certainly true of the ambulatory and periodic retail trade of the nineteenth century and earlier, when market days often doubled as festivals. In some respects, however, this can even be said of a more modern retail organization such as the shopping mall. The spatial logic of the mall was made up of three entities: the anchor (in the early days often a super- or hypermarket, but later also multiplex cinemas, airport gates, etc.), the entrance (e.g. the car park) and the in-between (the mall). The mall part was often maximized and designed as labyrinthine circulations spaces to encourage impulsive shopping (Goss 1993; Dovey 1999). However, after starting out from a kind of architectural 'in-between space concept', malls seldom became arenas for interstitial practices. On the contrary, territorial productions of the mall are stable, and events are predictable and schematized. Dovey gives us an example of how disruptive youth actually manage to change the territorial strategy of a certain mall, causing a relocation of game arcades and cinemas, previously deep in the spatial structure acting as anchors, to a place closer to one of the mall entrances (Dovey 1999: 135 ff.). Such examples are, however, exceptions. In fact, it seems that only the configuration of stores and special events might shift over time, whereas the territorial productions of everyday life remain quite repetitive and predictable. During the last decades, researchers have described a *mallification* of some cities, turning the city centres into mall-like structures with large parking facilitates, a pedestrian mall and with central shopping malls, bar districts, etc., acting as anchors (Graham and Marvin 2001; McMorrough 2001). In this development of an increasingly ambient retail trade, I describe two strategies that seem to affect the production of interstitial spaces: displacement and colonization.

Displacement

Retail trade was rationalized and concentrated all over the Western world during the twentieth century. In general, the number of street vendors declined, and production and distribution improved, promoting low-cost goods. Retail also moved indoors, forming large territories such as department stores, malls and supermarkets. The collective and more uniform consumption of the mid-twentieth century has since become much more individualized, but although the style of and reasons for shopping have changed dramatically during the post-modern period, some tendencies remain: the territories of retail and consumption become fewer and larger. New urban types such as retail parks, theme parks, pedestrian precincts and BIDs (business improvement districts) are cases in point. The malls have become larger and even moved outdoors to become lifestyle centres or 'malls without walls' (Graham and Marvin 2001).

In my earlier research I have dealt with the evolution of a large pedestrian precinct in the city centre of Malmö, Sweden (Kärrholm 2008, 2012). Pedestrianization coupled with commercialization is not an uncommon development in Western European city centres, and this case is also useful as an example of displacement. Malmö is a town of over 300,000 inhabitants (in 2011) in the south of Sweden, and part of an urban landscape or region of about one million people. This region is (as in many other parts of Europe) also characterized by the proliferation of new retail spaces and territorialization of retail on new and ever-larger scales in both outlying locations and in some of the larger old city centres, such as Malmö. The commercialization and homogenization of large parts of the city centre also means that certain aspects, such as sales, consumer and citizen behaviour, are becoming more predictable. Activities that used to be part of seeds for change in city life such as kids, skaters, graffiti artists, festivals and local groups are on their way out of the territory. Malmö has been relatively good at acknowledging and tolerating alternative urban practices but these have often been relocated outside the commercial city centre. *Stapelbäddsparken* is a large, international skate park that was inaugurated in 2006 and located in the old harbour. The graffiti wall of the parking garage, *Anna*, was the first legal graffiti wall in Sweden, inaugurated in 1983, and has now been followed up by a new legal wall at the Folkets park. Both are located outside the old city centre and well outside the pedestrian precinct. The last central public playground disappeared when an old 'vacant' lot in the middle of town was built on to develop the shopping centre Baltzar City in 2002. Even the annual Malmö City festival (established in 1985), with its events, retailers and food stalls, now (in 2009 and 2010) seem to have taken a step from the commercial centre to the harbour area. Some of these events can be seen as an expulsion from a retailized city core and others as part of a colonization of other spaces (and in the case of the City festival perhaps as both).

I could continue to list things that suddenly find themselves in or out of place in these ongoing processes of territorialization. In short, however, it seems as if retail tends to agglomerate into large mono-functional areas of consumerism, while the non-commercial and potentially interstitial practices of these places move or are moved elsewhere. The process of territorialization is not just to larger territories; these territories also tend to be more effectively controlled and functionally homogenous than, for example, the old city centres.

Colonization

In-between spaces are often related to in-between times. At the age of five, my oldest child was very good at taking advantage of in-between times when I collected him from day-care. During a short moment of time (often only minutes, sometimes seconds), there could be a confusion as to whether he was under the jurisdiction of the personnel or the parent (me). He immediately recognized this confusion and fully exploited the moment in order to break as many official rules of the day-care centre as he could (going to places where the children were not supposed to go, going outside without his winter jacket on, etc.). It took a couple of meetings and a collaborative effort before the personnel and I could work out a strategy to forestall this behaviour.

In-between times could also be used as a way of detecting interstitial spaces. Time is actually always of the essence when it comes to interstitial practices (c.f. Bettelheim 1950: Ch. 5), and people with a lot of time on their hands often have better opportunities for creating interstices. For retail businesses the places of waiting, drinking, eating, etc., are increasingly exploited (Cronin 2004), as retail tends to synchronize with the rhythms of urban life (Kärrholm 2009). The attempt by retail business to capitalize on urban rhythms is not only a matter of synchronization but could also be described as the colonization of in-between times, i.e. times of a certain social quality. In the short story 'The highway of the south', Julio Cortázar describes a traffic jam on a highway south of Paris. The waiting time is unsettling and seems to go on forever. Over the hours and days of waiting, new couples, friendships and routines are formed, matters of life and death are handled, etc. However, when the waiting time is over everyone just gets their cars and drives on. Although Cortázar's story might seem absurd, the phenomenon he describes is actually one of everyday life. The situation produced during these kinds of unsettling circumstances could be both stable and transient at the same time, and typical of an unsettled in-between time that anything or nothing (or both as in Cortázar's story) can happen. Owing to the difference from continuous relations at work, school, home, etc., the fact that no promises are given and no obligations could be expected produces a very special kind of sociality – the sociality of the (expected) sudden break.

Today, retail seems to be pinpointing (or even creating) these kinds of events in order to capitalize on them. The ongoing commercialization of different kinds of waiting spaces such as lobbies, waiting rooms, departure halls, museums, railway stations, libraries and airports, could be regarded as a kind of commercial colonization of in-between times and moments (c.f. Kärrholm and Sandin 2011). Moments that used to be quite weak in terms of territorial programme are inscribed with a kind of shopping logic. Airport shopping facilities are a good case in point, since they have even taken matters one step further. By actually creating, adjusting and monitoring the time between check-in and departure, in-between moments are created only to be filled with shopping (and security controls). Airport passengers only have a limited amount of time, so the strategy is for the airports to make as much high profit as possible in this time. This implies a focus on known brands (quick and easy to recognize), recognizable shop types, expensive commodities, large entrances, no shop windows (no window shopping), and a lot of product exposure. Queues are minimized and shops must be spatially intelligible, so the customers can see the scope of the retail space and the exit upon entering (Freathy and O'Connell 1998, Lloyd 2003).

Retail spaces affect interstitialities in different ways, and recent trends point out how the potential for interstitial practices, spaces and times seem to be declining. Above, I suggested that interstitial space is a movement that deterritorializes strong territorial strategies, often adding to the territorial complexity of a place. In Malmö city centre one could see how the one dominant theme in terms of use (consumerism) continues to grow increasingly in the city centre, whereas usages that cannot be defined in terms of consumerism are moved out or erased. One could also see how in-between times were colonized by shopping opportunities. However, the recent evolution of retail spaces is not all about destruction or elimination of interstitial space. It must be borne in mind that retail feeds on variety. Retail needs transformation, refurbishing and make-overs to survive. It needs new concepts and things that break with the old (Bauman 2007). In fact, new retail concepts may very well evolve as interstitial practices, and new kinds of retail spaces continue to be produced. In order to account for this we need to examine the process of transformation more carefully.

The evolution of retail spaces

How do you start something new? You never start from a *tabula rasa*; you start in an interstitial space. In his book, *The Trouble with Being Born*, the philosopher E.M. Cioran tells us about the Jewish expression *sim-zum*, or *tzimtzum*. The concept, literally meaning contraction, is used to explain how a ubiquitous God had to leave/create space in order for the world to take place. The world was then present in that space, but also a partially absent God (c.f. also Buber who discusses this as the eclipse of God in Buber (1953)). Humankind was thus born from something that both belonged and did not belong to God. For a pessimist such as Cioran, the sacrifice of God seems to have been a mistake that never should have occurred (Cioran 1986: 125). To me this story, or myth (or whatever one likes to call it), seems suggestive insofar as it acknowledges the precedence of an in-between space. Place making always starts in the in-between, in the middle of thing, *in medias res*, or *in mitten drinnen* to use a Yiddish expression (c.f. Connor 2002). The world as we know it is old and territorialized and thus nothing ever starts from a *tabula rasa*, all creation starts by means of an interstitial position. Interstitial practices start by surpassing existing rules and typologies, and give new meanings that defy any association with a previously given classification.

Singularization

The evolution from a certain type, classification or category towards a new and unique identity may be called *singularization* (c.f. Kopytoff 1986; Casey 2007), and this is, consciously or not, what most interstitial practices aim at – to singularize a place through de- and re-territorialization of its codes and meanings, and to turn it into something unique. Most things that meet us in the world have singularity, and this holds even for the most reproduced of commodities. When we confront a certain place, such as a Toys-R-Us store, we can in one glance identify it simultaneously as a toy store, as an example of a retail building type (for example, the category killer), as a 'Toys-R-Us-store', etc., but also as a genuine place of its own, beyond all stereotypes; it is something that is impossible to reduce to a type or to any another place (c.f. Casey 2007: 269 ff.). Every place and object, although connected to a lot of different things, also has a singular quality that makes it irreducible to anything but the place itself.[2]

In his seminal article 'The cultural biography of things', Igor Kopytoff discusses singularization as a decommodifying process and as a way of parting an object from the capitalist logic of exchangeable goods (Kopytoff 1986). Singularization is thus the process of defying classification, and can as such be initiated by, for example, religious or cultural institutions that want to keep certain object 'sacred'. In *Capitalism's Eye* (2007), Hetherington describes how objects are transformed and singularized into museum artefacts. The object is detached from the market, kept static and made 'invaluable' (Hetherington 2007: 171 ff.). Singularization can also be used in the production of symbols of power. Kopytoff gives a number of examples of how people in authority reserve certain artefacts for themselves only: 'The kings of Siam monopolized albino elephants. And the British monarchs have kept their right to dead whales washed ashore' (Kopytoff 1986: 73). There could also be objects that are forbidden to resell such as medicine or the indulgences of the Roman Catholic Church. Finally, there could be objects that are singularized

---

2   The singularity of a certain place or landscape could in this sense be related to the concept of 'mood' (Stimmung) as used by Simmel (2007: 27–28).

and decommodified since they are regarded as worthless, these may be common everyday things and non-commodities like individual stones, individual matches or scraps of food (Kopytoff 1986: 74 ff.). To make something useless is thus just as much a process as doing something 'invaluable'. Both cases imply that the things become impossible to trade.

Interstitial spaces are always part of a singularization process. When something becomes 'other' to the ordinary territorial sorts or types of halls, benches, parking lots, cafés, malls, etc., it also gets an identity of its own, it becomes singularized: 'It is the parking lot where those skaters usually come,' 'Those are the benches where that gang of youth always hang around and listen to music on Saturday evenings.' Interstitial space and singularization imply transformative and transgressive practices, but the process should not necessarily be regarded as a dialectic of dominance and resistance (or, for example, as the tactics and strategies of Certeau 1988). In fact, a better description of interstitial space would be as an actant of change in a transformative set of events. Hetherington has noted that resistance also produces order; it adds a new order, and it is this adding rather than the resistance part that is characteristic of interstitiality and its transformative qualities (Hetherington 1997: Ch. 2). In the case of Phillipps, we could see how Phillipps tried to introduce new orders, overwriting the home with the library and vice versa. In the less extreme but better case of John Soane's house at Lincoln's Inn Fields in London, such an order also became singularized as a building type. Soane built number 12 as a home and office in 1792, and later also bought numbers 13 and 14, and had them rebuilt. At the time of Soane's death in 1837, his house could be seen as a hybrid building, an example of a dwelling, an architect's office, an educational institution, an archive, a library, a museum, a mausoleum and a public institution (Furjan 2009). Soane singularized his home, transforming it by adding one function after another, and finally by the innovation of a new kind of building type: the private home and its collections as a public museum.

In the Western society, the singularization of built spaces for certain usages began to evolve quite rapidly during the eighteenth and nineteenth centuries. The development of modern capitalism and bureaucracy also transformed and gave birth to a proliferation of new territorial strategies and building types (Sack 1986). These new territorial strategies can be seen as part of a singularization process, where certain functions were pinpointed (singularized) and designed, and then *de*singularized into new kinds of buildings or room types.[3] Territorial control became more abstract and impersonal, but at the same time more effective since there were specific territories for every use, class, gender, age, mental state etc. (c.f. Markus 1993, Hacking 2002). The construction of a finely meshed territorial mosaic was an important part of the efforts to rationalize, control and capitalize major functions in society. Architecture played an important role in this evolution,

---

3   One could perhaps also compare this desingularization to types with Simmels concept of style – and how the notion of style always involves a process of desingularization (Simmel 1994: 15).

where spatial innovations, such as Bentham's Panopticon, Soane's art gallery, Boileau's department store etc., were made in order to support and stabilize new territorial productions. Thus the industrial era also saw the origin of a lot of new building types, such as factories, museums, schools, prisons with blocks of cells and different kinds of institutions that were meant to facilitate, directly or indirectly, the production of goods, money and educated, healthy and moral citizens useable in the workforce, etc. (Foucault 1977; Sack 1986; Markus 1993). Also indoors we saw this plethora of territorial sorts divided in terms of function, gender, social status, etc. Girouard notes an example of the late Victorian Pakenham Hall, Ireland, where tea was served at eleven different places depending on the social status of the people drinking it (Girouard 1985: 28).

Many of these territorial divisions have disappeared today, while others live on and new ones have been added. One can, however, talk of a qualitative and quantitative increase during the nineteenth century as regards building and room types that were intended for aspects of production (Markus 1993). This was perhaps most evident in the public institutions built by the State. During the twentieth century, some territorial divisions based, for example, on social status tended to decrease. Others, especially the territorial division of urban and regional space, increased owing to zoning regulation and the spatial differentiation of different means of transport.

In the territorial division of urban space in our Western world one can see changes that indicate a transformation from a society of production to a society of consumption (Bauman 2007). New building types and territorial productions of consumption and the experience economy, including factory outlets, entertainment retail, theme parks, multiplex theatres, lounge malls, lifestyle shopping centres, farmers' markets, flagship stores, etc., seem to be evolving all the time.

From sort to network to type

What interests me here, as mentioned above, is not the singular as such, but the process of singularization. Singularization is a prerequisite for desingularization and for the production of a building type, and as such it lies at the very heart of architectural practice as well as of spatial production in general from the Renaissance until today (c.f. for example Lefebvre's genealogy of abstract space, in Lefebvre (1991: Ch. 4)).

Today we see a commodification of space that is without precedence in history. Restaurants and cafes now also include McDonalds, Starbucks, espresso bars, food courts etc., and the number of new territorial types is adding up quickly. One of the primary means of singularization is theming, and the use of space as a medium (Lonsway 2009: 29 ff.) is one of the main ways of commodifying space. The Director of Architecture of Environmental Design at Walt Disney Imagineering, W. Dye, calls this 'architecture *with* a plot, not architecture *on* a plot' (Dye in Lonsway 2009: 51). Theming might affect the production of interstices since they often come without thresholds; no in-between seems to exist as the visitor is moved from scene to scene without any interruptions or places of weak programmes. The 'total environment' comes in all guises; themes might be defined in terms of aesthetics, strategic rules and categories. Most franchise shops have strict rules concerning advertising, what goods to sell and what atmosphere to induce in the customer. The category killer aims at being a place of all tastes within a category, not as much a general archive of goods as the old department stores, but deeper in its area of expertise. It is not the pedagogical museum with a little bit of everything, but a specialist collection that resembles the exclusive private collections aiming to comprise everything within their field or theme.

Building types could, according to Guggenheim, sometimes work as technologies, or in Latourian terms as black boxes defined by the fact that they have determined or predictable input and output. But sometimes they also work as mere 'masses of material' (Guggenheim 2010: 165) freed from their network stability. I agree with Guggenheim that this uncertainty is what makes the urban space so enjoyable: 'We orient ourselves with types and we enjoy being surprised by the failing of our own classification of types' (Guggenheim 2010: 175). However, one could take Guggenheim's description of building types a step further and try to make it more precise. What does it mean that we recognize or do not recognize something as belonging to a certain type? This recognition (or the absence of it) could easily and in an instant override a meticulously well-constructed and stabilized network (c.f. Guggenheim 2010: 166). In actor-network theory terms this could be described as the effect of fluid stabilization (De Laet and Mol 2000; Law 2002). The singularization/desingularization process turns the fluidity of a territorial sort (a mutable mobile), into a territorial strategy and a stabilized network. The stabilization makes the building type mobile (an immutable mobile), transforming it into a reproducible type (e.g. a global building type; see King 2004). The more one can describe an object as the effect of network stabilization, the more predictable it becomes and the less we can enjoy the feeling of 'being surprised'.

Fluid topologies can be described as a family of possible networks or assemblages that all produce similar effects. Different actors of a territorial production can thus be replaced (within certain limits) without affecting the territorial outcome. Territorial sorts can also take on different forms and network topologies and still work: different bus stops, pedestrian crossings, outdoor cafés etc., might produce similar territorial effects irrespective of whether or not they have an actor or material denominator in common. No specific combination of actors is privileged. Furthermore, a fluid continuity can change bit by bit but not in great leaps. Of course, we might reach a point where the territorial sort could no longer be recognized, where too many actants have been replaced, or something too unfamiliar to this specific sort of territory has been introduced (De Laet and Mol 2000; Law 2002). The association to a specific sort of territory can then no longer be made. The interesting thing about fluidity, however, is that as fluidity increases and more and more different actors can be connected to a specific territorial sort, the number of possible variants of this sort increases, and the more moveable it becomes. Whereas Latour, in his logic of the immutable mobile, states that things become moveable through a stabilized network topology, a territorial sort becomes mobile owing the mutability of its network – it can keep its identity, even though actors are lost or swapped. One could take an open air market as an example. Since it is fluid, i.e. it can change actors and take on a number of different forms, it can also be easily adjusted to the specific circumstances of different places. An open market can change the design or number of stalls, the spatial layout, etc., but still remains the same recognizable territorial sort: the open air market. This fluidity also makes change seem natural and makes interstitial practices less threatening.

When building types become specialized, themed and branded, like Starbucks or IKEA, the fluidity, still present in types such as 'the café' or 'the store' becomes less fluid or flexible, whereas the network topology becomes stronger. The first Starbucks opened in Seattle in 1971, and has been described as one of the first 'total experiences' (Klingmann 2007: 36). The concept was not just to sell coffee but a whole environment with smells, music, themed merchandise and a Starbucks atmosphere associated with a certain lifestyle. Indeed, one could argue that the brand was singularized as a specific kind of territorial sort and then desingularized into a specific building type. A 'Starbucks' was created by means of the fluidity of the territorial sort 'café', but as it was desingularized the territorial stabilization became less based on a fluid topology and more on a network topology. The possibility of altering, transmuting or hybridizing the type becomes less and less obvious. The possible outcomes of the Starbucks type are probably less, and definitely more predictable, than the outcomes of the café type in general. The difference could be compared with that between a low-tech and a high-tech object: robustness, accessibility and uncertainty are traded for more elaborate, specific and predictable results (c.f. Nilsson 2010).

Concluding remarks

So where do these arguments take us? In this chapter I have described interstitial space in terms of territorial transformation, and as an intermingling of at least two different and in some sense synchronic (co-temporal) and synchoric (co-spatial) territorial productions, producing a new singular place defying classification. This production is often likely to start in spaces or cracks in between stronger territorial programmes, but they can also take place within strongly regulated territories, where the tension or feeling of an in between is created by way of association to a strong territorial sort (that is literally out of place). Taking a cue from Bettelheim and others, interstitial space is thus not to be understood as a predefined space, but as a spatial effect that could be produced anywhere. The rapid retail expansion of later years (in Sweden and elsewhere) has brought about larger and more homogeneous territories. This seems to counteract the production of non-profitable in-between times and spaces. In this development, interstitial strategies might have been used as a way of creating and singularizing new kinds of urban places and spaces. In order to capitalize on these innovations, these spaces have, however, also been through a process of desingularization, producing more and more specific and reproducible building types and even urban landscapes. Desingularization is, as Kopytoff teaches us, a way of commodification. An ongoing decrease of the fluidity of territorial sorts is paralleled with a proliferation of stabilized territorial networks and onto immutable mobiles in the form of global building types that seem to leave less room for interstitial practices.

The lack of heterogeneous everyday practices might in turn create problems, not only for public space but actually for retail itself, since stagnation equals death, especially for business. The role of interstices needs to be addressed more explicitly by researchers on public space and everyday life. The production of interstices is a basic and immanent part of human existence. It is tempting to use Serres' concept of noise as an analogy to interstices. At the end of *Genesis*, Serres notes that the tower of Babel was not a failure. On the contrary, the ruins of Babel showed us that we need understanding without concepts. 'A tower plus *noise*', writes Serres, 'a system plus noise, tremendous architectures of walls, plus wailing walls where the moans, groans, and weeping can cleave the stones already loose. Then we understand. History begins.' (Serres 1995: 124). Interstices are important as the pre-requisites of something new, something pre-conceptual, and they play a fundamental role in all kinds of appropriation as well as in the ongoing production of heterogeneous public space.

References

Allen, J. 2006. Ambient Power: Berlin's Potsdamer Platz and the Seductive Logic of Public Spaces. *Urban Studies* 43(2), 441–55.

Augé, M. 1995. *Non-places: Introduction to an Anthropology of Supermodernity*. London: Verso.

Barker, R. 1968. *Ecological Psychology*. Stanford, CA: Stanford University Press.

Bauman, Z. 2007. *Consuming Life*. Oxford: Polity Press.

Bettelheim, B. 1950. *Love is Not Enough:, The Treatment of Emotionally Disturbed Children*. Glencoe: The Free Press.

Brighenti, A. M. 2010. On territoriology, towards a general science of territory. *Theory, Culture & Society*, 27(1), 52–72.

Buber, M. 1953. *Eclipse of God: Studies in the Relation Between Religion and Philosophy*. London: Gollancz.

Casey E. 2007. *The World at Glance*. Bloomington, IN: Indiana University Press.

Certeau, M. de 1988/1980. *The Practice of Everyday Life*. Berkeley, CA: University of California Press.

Cioran, E.M. 1986/1973. *Om Olägenheten i att Vara Född*. Stockholm: Bonniers.

Connor, S. 2002. *Michel Serres's Milieux*, paper to the ABRALIC conference *Mediations*, Belo Horizonte, 23–26 July 2002.

Cortázar, J. 1986. *La Autopista del sur y Otros Cuentos*. London: Penguin.

Cronin, A. 2006. Advertising and the metabolism of the city: urban space, commodity rhythms. *Environment and Planning D: Society and Space*, 24, 615–32.

De Laet, M. de and Mol, A. (2000) The Zimbabwe bush pump: mechanics of a fluid technology. *Social Studies of Science*, 30(2), 225–63.

Dovey, K. 1999. *Framing Places: Mediating Power in Built Form*. London and New York: Routledge.

Evans, R. 1997. Figures, Doors and Passages, in: *Translations from Drawing to Building and Other Essays*. London: Architectural Association.

Forty, A. 2000. *Words and Buildings, A Vocabulary of Modern Architecture*. London: Thames & Hudson.

Foucault, M. 1977. *Discipline and Punish*. New York: Pantheon Books.

Franck, K. and Stevens, Q. 2007. *Loose Space, Possibility and Diversity in Urban Life*. London and New York: Routledge.

Freathy, P. and O'Connell, F. 1998. *European Airport Retailing: Growth Strategies for the New Millennium*. Basingstoke: Macmillan.

Furján H. 2009. Exhibitionism: John Soane's 'Model House', in: V. Di Palma, D. Periton and M. Lahtouri (eds) *Intimate Metropolis, Urban Subjects in the Modern City*. London & New York: Routledge.

Girouard, M. 1985. *The Victorian Country House*. New Haven, CT & London: Yale University Press.

Goss, J. (1993) The magic of the mall: form and function in the retail built environment. *Annals of the Association of American Geographers*, 83 (1), 18–47.

Guggenheim, M. 2010. Mutable immobiles: building conversion as a problem of quasi-technologies, in: I. Farías and T. Bender (eds) *Urban Assemblages,*. London: Routledge.

Hertzberger, H. 1991. *Lessons for Students in Architecture*. Rotterdam: 010.

Hertzberger, H. 2000. *Space and the Architect*. Rotterdam: 010.

Hetherington, K. 1997a. *The Badlands of Modernity, Heterotopia and Social Ordering*. London & New York: Routledge.

Hetherington, K. 1997b. Museum topology and the will to connect. *Journal of Material Culture*, 2(2), 199–218.

Hetherington, K. 1999. From blindness to blindness: museums, heterogeneity and the subject, in J. Law and J. Hassard. (eds) *Actor Network Theory and After*. Oxford: Blackwell.

Hetherington, K. 2004. Second-handedness: Consumption, Disposal and Absent Presence. *Environment and Planning D: Society and Space*, 22(1), 157–73.

Hetherington K. 2007. *Capitalism's Eye. Cultural Spaces of the Commodity*. London: Routledge.

King, A.D. 2004. *Spaces of Global Cultures*. London: Routledge.

Klingmann, A. 2007. *Brandscapes, Architecture in the Experience Economy*. Cambridge, MA: The MIT Press.

Kopytoff, I. 1986. The cultural biography of things: commodization as process, in: A. Appadurai (ed.) *The Social Life of Things*. Cambridge, UK: Cambridge University Press.

Kärrholm, M. 2007. The materiality of territorial production. *Space and Culture*, 10(4), 437–53.

Kärrholm, M. 2008. The territorialization of a pedestrian precinct in Malmö. *Urban Studies*, 45(9), 1903–24.

Kärrholm, M. 2009. To The Rhythm of Shopping – on synchronisations in urban landscapes of consumption. *Social & Cultural Geography*, 10(4), 421–40.

Kärrholm, M. 2012. *Retailising Space*. Aldershot: Ashgate.

Kärrholm, M. and Sandin, G. 2011. Waiting places as temporal interstices and agents of change. *TRANS, Internet Journal for Cultural Studies*, 18. Available at: http://www.inst.at/trans/18Nr/II-1/kaerrholm_sandin18.htm [Accessed: 1 September 2012].

Latour, B. 2005. *Reassembling the Social*. Oxford: Oxford University Press.

Law, J. 2002. Objects and spaces. *Theory, Culture & Society*, 19(5–6), 91–105.

Lefaivre, L. 2002. Space, place and play, or the interstitial/cybernetic/polycentred urban model underlying Aldo Van Eyck's quasi-unknown but, nevertheless, myriad postwar Amsterdam playgrounds, in: L. Lefaivre and I. De Roode (eds) *Aldo Van Eyck, the Playgrounds and the City*. Amsterdam & Rotterdam: NAI & Stedelijk.

Lieberg, M. 1992. *Att ta staden i besittning, om ungas rum och rörelser i offentlig miljö*, rapport R3:1992. Lund: Byggnadsfunktionslära, Arkitektursektionen.

Lloyd, J. 2003. Dwelltime, airport technology, travel, and consumption. *Space & Culture*, 6(2), 93–108.

Lonsway, B. 2009. *Making Leisure Work, Architecture and the Experience Economy*. London: Routledge.

Markus, T. 1993. *Buildings and Power, Freedom and Control in the Origin of Modern Building Types*. London: Routledge.

Munby, A.N.L. 1971. *Phillipps Studies, (I. The Catalogues of Manuscripts and Printed Books, II. The Family Affairs of Sir Thomas Phillipps, III. The Formation of the Library up to the year 1840, IV. The Formation of the Library from 1841–1872, V. The Dispersal of Library)*. London: Sotheby Parke-Bernet Publications.

Nilsson, E. 2010. Arkitekturens kroppslighet/Stadens som terräng, PhD dissertation at LTH, LU Lund.

Praglin, L. 2006. The nature of the 'in-between' in D.W. Winnicott's concept of transitional space and in Martin Buber's das Zwischenmenschliche. *Universitas*, 2(2), 1–9.

Sack, R. 1986. *Human Territoriality, Its Theory and History*. Cambridge, UK: Cambridge University Press.

Serres, M. 1995. *Genesis*. Ann Arbor, MI: The University of Michigan Press.

Simmel, G. 1994. The Picture Frame. An Aesthetic Study. *Theory, Culture & Society*, 11(1), 11–17.

Simmel, G. 2007. The philosophy of landscape. *Theory, Culture & Society*, 24 (7–8), 20–29.

Solà-Morales Rubió, I. de 1995. Terrain Vague, in: C. Davidson (ed.) *Anyplace.* Cambridge, MA: The MIT Press.

Wikström, T. 2005. Residual space and transgressive spatial practices – the uses and meanings of un-formed space. *Nordic Journal of Architectural Research*, 18(1), 47–68.

Chapter 8

Interim Users in Residual Spaces: An Inquiry Into the Career of a Pier on the Hudson Riverfront

Stéphane Tonnelat

In this chapter, I borrow the sociological concept of 'career' from Goffman (1961) to describe two simultaneous but distinct processes of construction of an urban public space, in both the spatial and the political sense, in the same location, a former derelict pier on the New York City Hudson riverfront. Officially, the pier was reclaimed from a derelict past as an 'open space' managed by a semi-public partnership. It benefited from a large 'community involvement' in numerous meetings and other participatory venues. I call this side of the story the 'institutional career' of Pier 84 and I equate it with a notion of local democracy infused with the notion of the public sphere. But the pier also bears striking resemblances to its former supposedly abandoned state, when residents used it for gardening, rowing or fishing. It hosts a collectively run community boathouse and a community garden, which were fought for, not only through official participatory channels, but thanks to a relentless advocacy for activities that already existed at the time of the project. I call this part of the story the 'experiential career' of Pier 84. I equate it with another tradition of local democracy infused with the notion of the common good. Although less visible than the institutional career, I contend that the experiential career is more apt to understand the influence of residents on the final design of public space.

Urban interstices

Urban interstices are pieces of land seemingly abandoned for more or less durable periods of time throughout metropolitan areas (Tonnelat 2003). They are the varied collection of leftovers and by-products of urban development and decay. They are sites that are temporarily devoid of official function. Usually cast aside as land reserve by their owners, they dot the urban fabric of 'wastelands', 'brown fields', 'fallow lands', 'embankments' and other administrative and technical ways of describing uselessness (Bowman and Pagano 2004). Some of these sites are difficult to reclaim as they are cluttered with so many legal and technical constraints. They remain interstitial for long periods of time and are usually occupied by marginal and invisible activities (Tonnelat 2008). Others, on the other hand, are merely waiting to ripen for re-investment after periods of neglect, most often in areas targeted by renovation, gentrification (Smith 1996) or development (Davis 1998; Hayden 2003). These processes often give rise to conflicts as it happened in New York City with the empty lots that residents had reclaimed as community gardens in the 1990s.

The official story of Pier 84

Pier 84, on the Manhattan Hudson Riverfront in the re-branded (Greenberg 2008) Clinton District (previously Hell's Kitchen), was one of these sites. Without an official function for a long time, it was recently renovated and touted as one of the largest open spaces of the new Hudson River Park. Its official history is written in a few key steps on glossy paper in a brochure of the Public Trust, in charge of its maintenance and development. It culminates with the adoption of the bill that created it in the New York State Assembly.

> Situated between the Intrepid Sea-Air-Space Museum and the well-traveled Circle Line and World Yacht Cruise ships, Hudson River Park's Pier 84 has a long history. Prior to falling into disrepair in the 1980's, when it was used by the City as a parking lot, Pier 84 was one of the Cunard Line's passenger ship piers, making it the arrival place for thousands of immigrants to the U.S. in the early 20th Century. From there they were shuttled by ferry boat to Ellis Island for processing. In the 1990s a group of community activists created the *Friends of Pier 84* to advocate for its reopening to the public as *open space* and for incorporation into the Hudson River Park plan. As a result, the Pier was designated a new public park pier in the Hudson River Park Act in 1998. (Hudson River Park News, summer 2007)

The institutional career and public space as an 'open space'

This short official story sketches what I call the institutional career of Pier 84. Much like the moral career of an individual subject to mental disorder, it is made up of specific stages, usually going from pre-patient, to patient to post-patient. These reflect the official steps that lead from sanity to sickness, to treatment, to recovery. In the same way, the official history of Pier 84 is built out of generic statuses going from a port, to abandonment (or a parking lot), to a park. Of course, the story is more complex and the recycling of a derelict space needs to take into account the residents concerned with its use. The institutional career thus also needs to enroll the users in its version of the story in order to be accepted. How does it happen?

A slightly fuller account could go like this: In 1994, a group of residents in Hell's Kitchen, a neighbourhood on the west side of midtown Manhattan, got

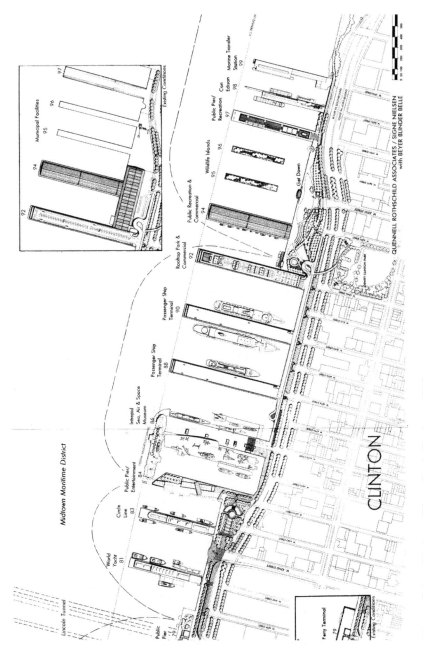

Figure 8.1   Hudson River Park Project, 1998.

together to oppose the taking over of a derelict pier on the Hudson waterfront by a heliport boat, the Guadalcanal, moored perpendicular to the aircraft carrier known as the Intrepid Museum.

The residents eventually won the fight, which led to the creation of a local grassroots organization, Friends of Pier 84 (FOP84), and opened the site to a host of activities such as gardening, rowing, fishing, dog running and more. These uses in turn made the pier a known new public space in the neighbourhood and transformed Friends of Pier 84 into a recognized interlocutor of the City and State administrations. Pretty quickly, the leaders of Friends of Pier 84 enrolled their group in a participatory process which allowed them to defend the pier as a 'public space' in the future park project. For this, however, they had to format their discourse and actions to make them compatible with the planning process. It is this process, I argue, which constitutes the steps of the institutional career of Pier 84 on the residents side.

Three steps of integrating residents in the development project

Three steps can be distinguished. First, FOP84 enlarged its original goal of using the pier to defending its accessibility for the whole neighbourhood. This step required a reframing in terms of public access that allowed it to grow in generality (Boltanski and Thevenot 1991) and gave it a new legitimacy. Second, FOP84 became a member of the Hudson River Park Alliance, a not-for-profit organization created to support the park Project. At its meetings, it had to find a vocabulary of advocating for a public pier shared with environmental organizations ranging from regional to national in their scope. This step lead to a dilution of their demands into a more abstract conception of the park and the pier that took it further away from specific uses.

Finally, the leaders were enrolled to stand in several public stages next to elected officials and park defenders. The most notable one saw them in April 1998, on the pier itself, contrasting its derelict state with a gleaming project on a prospectus (Figure 8.1).

These successive steps enrolled FOP84 into a specific vision of public debate that sees public space as guaranteed by a social contract with state institutions in charge of their maintenance. It marks a clear divorce from the group's original vision of an actually used public space. That same day, the president of FOP84 went to the State Legislature in Albany along with the Senator and Assembly members who were going to vote in favour of the Bill which created the Park (Figure 8.2). Coincidentally, the vote of the Hudson River Park Act, which officially marked the return of the pier to official life after years of dimmed existence, also corresponded to a closing of its physical space well before reconstruction. City officials said that the wooden piles were eaten up by worms called marine borers, and that the pier was in danger of collapse. It was a matter of public safety. It was quickly closed and fenced off to neighbourhood residents and activists. The leaders of Friends of Pier 84 felt powerless. They cancelled all the upcoming summer activities

Figure 8.2　　Political rally on Pier 84 with a State Senator and an Assembly Member: 'We are now calling the Governor and the Mayor to join us in what will be a marvelous waterfront which will stop the rotten piers, the derelict waterfront and will give us the Hudson River Park'. (Photo by Stéphane Tonnelat).

and reverted to a sustained push for a public pier, although then only on paper. They found refuge in an imagined space, a new design, that they advocated in the participatory process put together by the Hudson River Park Conservancy to insure community input. They thus moved from a users' and managers' perspective to a planner's perspective. Their role was indeed instrumental in bringing grassroots support to the plan and bringing both Governor Pataki and Mayor Giuliani to put their signature on the Bill.

In 2006, another eight years later, the rebuilt pier finally opened as one of the main 'open spaces' of the new Hudson River Park. Since then it has been managed as a quasi-public space (Mitchell and Staeheli 2006) by a public authority, which periodically rents it out for private parties aimed at financing the facility. Friends of Pier 84 is now a defunct organization. They never regained the influence they had built over the pier, its activities, its maintenance and its social order. A contested history of the site was thus erased and a new design was able to unfold on a supposedly clean slate. The words of its leader, back in 1998 when the pier was closed, still ring true although they have acquired a different meaning:

'We have a park pier but we have no pier!' Indeed, former Pier 84 members are now guests in the very site they contributed to save and maintain.

An interesting framing process is thus highlighted by the concept of institutional career. It was observable through the successive actions of the leaders of Friends of Pier 84 on different public stages where they each time aligned their own frame of motivation (Benford and Snow 2000), used to recruit members, with the institutional vision defended by the Hudson River Park Conservancy. The leaders of the group were brought to redefine the pier and their own relation to it in a way that lead to the erasure of the interim years of informal uses and progressively changed the users into guests or even consumers of a space open to them by a public authority. This process, bringing together the representation of space of the planners and the representational space of the users into a new design and practices (Lefebvre 1974), denotes the important work necessary to recycle the interstitial years of the pier and integrate them into the definition of a new space acceptable by all parties involved, from elected officials to local residents.

The result is a victory for people, mostly planners and activists, whose conception of democracy is in the hands of elected officials who in the end prefer an 'open space' run by their semi-public administrations to a truly public space.

The experiential career and public space as a common good

But not everybody was sold to the participatory process put together by Public Authorities and developers. Missing from the institutional career are the users, regular folk who actually engage with the built environment on a daily basis. Their influence on design, maintenance and management, despite being quite real, is commonly ignored or even erased in order to make way for institutional visions (Scott 1998).

Interestingly, although credit was only given to Friends of Pier 84 for saving the pier from dereliction, the layout of the pier today bears an intriguing resemblance to the wasteland years. A community boathouse, a community garden and a dog run shelter activities that all predate the park and mark a strong continuity with the interstitial years of official abandonment. How did they re-surface and how did they manage to find place in the new design?

The institutional career cannot explain how the community garden and the boathouse were able to find a home on the pier, despite plans that originally did not include them. In many cases, the users' and the developers' perspectives are irreconcilable. People are evicted or projects scrapped altogether. The career of the site is then identical to a one-sided history (most of the time, the history of the evicted is erased and thus needs to be redressed). In some situations, however, negotiations happen and concessions, big or small, are granted (or won) on all sides and perspectives are redefined both at the institutional and at the more individual and subjective user levels. It is this mutual reworking of perspectives, re-definitions of the situation, which define the career of a site and marks the

Figure 8.3   Community rowing from Pier 84 (photo by Stéphane Tonnelat).

significant steps that lead to a new place. Thus the concept of career is more complex. In the sociology of deviance, it encompasses another level, this time subjective, of perception of change by the individual or patient herself within the scope of her own life. In the case of a piece of land, I want to argue that this other side of the career is made out of the perspectives built by users over a long period of time, which bridge and overlap the more official stages of the site's career. Whereas the official career is made of discrete statuses, clearly identifiable, the subjective career reveals more durable user involvements, activities and projections that sometimes end up bearing a stronger influence on the evolution of the built environment than is usually recognized.

My point is that some users relied on a different conception of space, one less easily co-opted by dominant views and, more importantly, one that resisted the closing of the pier in 1998. I suggest that the rowers and the gardeners were in fact able to keep the pier with them under the shape of an 'embodied space' (Csordas 1990; Low 2003). The plants and the boats were transferred to nearby land areas and other sites in the city where the same body movements reenacted the space of the pier (Duranti 1997; Low 2009). Subsequently, these users were able to defend their vision for a boathouse and a garden in a variety of local political arenas using arguments based on actual shared experience, and not just on future projects. The open letter sent by the leader of a rowing group illustrates this point well:

As most of you know, through personal experience, grape vine or the press, community volunteers working with Floating the Apple (FTA) have been building Whitchall boats, of a type traditional to NY Harbor [...] Some of you rowed during the past two summers with FTA's fee-free community rowing program. Those who have frequented Pier 84 since last June, have seen the temporary boat-housing comprised of 40-foot cargo containers. (Open Letter to Members of Clinton's Block Associations, February 1998)

Their fight, detached from the group's own defence of abstract public space, fed off a continuing practice of gardening and rowing that they were able to present neither as a projection of future needs, nor as an expression of public reason but as already existing activities, and this despite the lack of a physical location from spring 1998 to 2006. This is, I suggest, what explains the presence of these amenities today (Figure 8.3).

Two conceptions of public space and democracy

Obviously, the subjective or user career is tied to the institutional career. The official stages of a site's career are marked by events, either negotiated or imposed, which bring together the main institutional players and local users. The closing of the pier in 1998 was one of these defining moments, imposed from the top and forcing local residents to reconsider their involvement with the site and ally with the planners. Users thus worked with a dual vision that encompassed both the institutional, more abstract, perspective imposed by the planning world and a more engaged experience within the site. In a sense, the career is a concept that allows identifying both perspectives, each one corresponding to a different conception of public space in the same physical site. On the one hand, an 'open space' is managed by public authorities and made accessible to a generic public who, precisely because it is not incarnated in existing people, have no control over the site. On the other hand, the boathouse and the community garden are amenities run by and for residents of the neighbourhood and open to visitors. The public is made of regular users who become co-hosts of a place itself regarded as a common good, just as they were doing when the pier was an urban interstice.

To conclude briefly, I would like to stress how these two sides of the career of Pier 84 are illustrative of two ways of thinking about public participation in design and maintenance processes. The dominant one, inherited from enlightenment philosophers (Kant 1932; Habermas 1989; Rawls 1999) is predicated on the use of public reasoning. It has been slowly integrated into the laws and practices regarding the design of public spaces. Although it offers a measure of participation, I contend that it still contributes to marginalize users' initiative and experience in profit of a more abstract and economically driven conception of space. The second, an underdog perspective, is based on the idea of actual experience and on a process of inquiry which posits both public space and its users as problems to be solved, much in the tradition of radical pragmatism advocated by Dewey (1989). This perspective is contested today, as are the boathouse and the garden on Pier 84, as it gives a new visibility to users until now excluded from the structures of power.

References

Benford, R.D. and Snow, D.A. 2000. Framing processes and social movements: an overview and assessment. *Annual Review of Sociology*, 26(1), 611–39.

Boltanski, L. and Thevenot, L. 1991. *De la Justification: les Economies de la Grandeur*. Paris: Gallimard.

Bowman, A. and Pagano, M. 2004. *Terra Incognita. Vacant Land and Urban Strategies*. Washington, DC: Georgetown University Press.

Csordas, T. J. 1990. Embodiment as a paradigm for anthropology. *Ethos*, 18(1), 5–47.

Davis, M. 1998. *Ecology of Fear: Los Angeles and the Imagination of Disaster*. New York: Metropolitan Books.

Dewey, J. 1989. *Public and Its Problems*. Athens, OH: Ohio University Press.

Duranti, A. 1997. Indexical speech across Samoan communities. *American Anthropologist*, 99(2), 342–54.

Goffman, E. 1961. *Asylums. Essays on the Social Situation of Mental Patients and Other Inmates*. Garden City, NY: Anchor Books.

Greenberg, M. 2008. *Branding New York: How a City in Crisis was Sold to the World*. New York: Routledge.

Habermas, J. 1989. *The Structural Transformation of the Public Sphere: An Inquiry into a Category of Bourgeois Society*. Cambridge, MA: The MIT Press.

Hayden, D. 2003. *Building Suburbia*. New York: Vintage Books.

Kant, I. 1932. *Critique of Pure Reason*. London: Macmillan.

Lefebvre, H. 1974. *La Production de l'Espace*. Paris: anthropos.

Low, S.M. 2009. Towards an anthropological theory of space and place. *Semiotica*, 175 (6), 21–37.

Low, S.M. 2003. Embodied Space(s): Anthropological theories of body, space, and culture. *Space & Culture*, 6(1), 9–18.

Mitchell, D., and Staeheli, L.A. 2006. Clean and safe? Property redevelopment, public space and homelessness in Downtown San Diego. In: S. Low and N. Smith (eds), *The Politics of Public Space*. New York: Routledge.

Rawls, J. 1999. *A Theory of Justice*. Cambridge, MA: Belknap Press.

Scott, J.C. 1998. *Seeing Like a State: How Certain Schemes to Improve the Human Condition Have Failed*. New Haven, CT: Yale University Press.

Smith, N. 1996. *The New Urban Frontier: Gentrification and the Revanchist City*. New York: Routledge.

Tonnelat, S. 2003. Interstices Urbains Paris/New York: entre controle et mobilites, quatre espaces residuels de l'amenagement urbain. PhD Dissertation, Université Paris 12/CUNY Graduate Center, Institut d'Urbanisme de Paris/ Department of Environmental Psychology.

Tonnelat, S. 2008. Out of frame: The (in)visible life of urban interstices: a case study in Charenton-le-Pont, Paris, France. *Ethnography,* 9(3), 291–324.

Chapter 9

The Urban Fringe as a Territorial Interstice: On Alpine Suburbs

Andrea Mubi Brighenti

The urbanization of the Alpine region

During the course of the last century, Alpine cities have experienced a tension between, on the one hand, strong traditional local identities and solidarities and, on the other, the requisites of modernity and late-modern urbanism. Various competing models of development for Alpine space have been proposed and applied; however, as a general trend, the infrastructures of physical and informational mobility of the industrial and post-industrial capitalist model seem to finally have overcome all resistance and alternatives, at least on a large scale. In this chapter, I focus on one spatial and territorial outcome of such processes in the Alps, turning to the case of suburbanization, or peri-urbanization. While, as is well known, the European urban pattern is substantially different from the Northern American one (Secchi 2005) in Europe, too, some trends toward suburbanization are visible today. In Italy, for instance, a 'Po megalopolis', mainly deriving from urban sprawl, has been described and analysed by geographer Eugenio Turri (2004). These trends, as I will try to show, are also linked to increased spatial segregation, although once again Europe is far from the American levels.

In the case under scrutiny, an additional complexity derives from the fact that while in the USA the suburb is in many cases built on previously blank rural space (Ingersoll 2006; Beauregard 2006; Bruegmann 2006), in Europe, and more specifically in the Alpine city, suburbanization essentially takes place as a residential expansion around ancient rural villages surrounding major cities. Consequently, middle class newcomers settle in newly built houses just outside the small core of the old, in most cases medieval, historic village, or even in restored traditional houses. Examining the case of the city of Trento, in the Italian North-Eastern sector of the Alps (located approximately between Verona and Bozen, along the Adige valley), I seek to understand what kind of cleavages, solidarities and, ultimately, what kind of neighbourhoods and territorial configurations do emerge from this specific pattern of suburbanization. My basic assumption shares Savage *et al*.'s (2005: 7) view of an 'ongoing significance of territoriality for social relationships' and, in particular, for relationships of neighbourhood and belonging. In this chapter, I present the results of a fieldwork focused on the experience of settlement and the relationship between older and newer inhabitants in the Alpine suburbs surrounding Trento.

Geographic and planning scholarship on the Alpine region (Dematteis 1975; Diamantini and Zanon 1999; Camanni 2002; Bätzing 2002, 2005; Beattie 2006; Schonthaler and von Andrian-Werburg 2008; Dematteis 2009) have explored the tension between tradition and modernity in this area. Literature tells us that the major national and regional patterns of development are mirrored in the urban and cultural features of the Alpine city. As first observed by Giuseppe Dematteis (1975), the Alps are, in a meaningful sense, an urban region. Yet, arguably, most of the Alpine territory is not simply urban; rather, it has been *urbanized* – a process that largely occurred over the course of the last century. Bätzing (2002) has observed that the Alps became marginal in the European space only with the advent of industrialism in the early nineteenth century. The steps to bridge that gap began with the development of communication infrastructures. In the Dolomites sector we are considering, for instance, the Brenner railway was completed in 1867.

Tourism and the war – in particular the First World War – represented two other major forces in such a trend towards the urbanization of the Alpine space. Indeed, these events brought typically modern and industrial technologies into the heart of the Alps, leading to the building of typically urban infrastructures such as paved roads, which were subsequently essential to support twentieth-century trends of urban development in the Alps. Alpine cities and centres share crucial characteristics with the rest of the European urban space, such as bureaucratic regional administration, advanced capitalist economy, tourism, transport and communications infrastructures, but also typical urban environmental problems of pollution, noise, lack of ground permeabilization, loss of biodiversity and bad land use. At the same time, they also share important features of their specific territory (in particular, a certain *Zeitgeist*, a series of cultural values, traditional attitudes etc. – see in particular Arnoldi 2010). Today Alpine cities find themselves at the point of convergence and tension between different social forces, whose spatiality mirrors the constitution of a discursive social field in which different development, mobility, cultural and urban models are argued for and debated.

Alpine suburbanization

In this context, the dynamics of suburbanization have received less attention than other social and territorial transformations. To my mind, suburbanization is particularly interesting because it questions the boundaries of the urban as well as the features and physical setting of the modern Alpine territory. In the American case, Bruegmann (2006: 51) has argued that, 'with the penetration of urban functions far into the countryside, the old distinctions between urban, suburban, and rural have collapsed'. In Europe, sprawl is present but less pronounced. In Italy, the phenomenon of sprawl has been extendedly described by Turri (2004) as concerns the Po plains, and has only been hinted at in the case of the mountain area of the Lessini in Veneto:

> If we consider the impact on the landscape and their statistical impact we can affirm that the Lessini have become an extension of the Po megalopolis, via both the spread of industries and residential areas in its valleys, and the growth of that diffused city that results from the urbanisation of the upper hill and determines commuting towards the city and, lastly, tourist settlements on the highland, where the ancient ties between the city and the countryside are perpetuated, though mainly according to an urban style. In short we can say that the city has projected itself into the mountain, or that the mountain has been metabolised by the city, that has turned it into its own space. The phenomenon of cities devouring space is by now huge and invasive of the whole Po area and, peculiarly, it also involves the pre-Alpine mountains, which is a wildlife to be protected, even though by now it has lost all the productive potentials which made it attractive through its diversity [...] Today the upper hill, abandoned by its inhabitants fifty years ago, is looked for the settlement of city-users who take advantage of its easy accessibility from the city and the lower valley, and are willing to commute just to have the possibility of living in an environment far from the metropolitan nuisances. (Turri 2004: 207–8, my translation)

My hypothesis is that a similar pattern of urbanization can also be found elsewhere in the Alpine arc. More specifically, I am particularly interested in exploring the Alpine suburb as a sort of urban interstice or urban fringe, an often blurred borderland not so much between the urban and the non-urban, but rather between different imaginations of the urban, where different territorial components and modalities of making the urban intermingle. As ancient villages have become technically and structurally urbanized, a degree of anonymity typical of urban life has also appeared; but the social organization of local life has not become urban, both because new inhabitants are in fact suburbanites rather than urbanites and because old inhabitants have tried to protect a sense of local belonging which is essentially communitarian, grounded in the ideals and values of a peasant society that no loner exists, and can ultimately be characterized as anti-urban.

The modern Western city is both a site of settlement and a site of circulation, where the settlement of communities coexists with the flowing of individuals, goods, services, money and images. If large cities exhibit such features to their the utmost intensity (see e.g. Urry 2007; Adey 2009), relatively marginal spaces such as the Alpine region have also experienced a stealth increase in the construction of infrastructures for material (new speedway-like roads, tunnels, bridges, bypasses etc.) and immaterial mobility (communication and information networks, internet providers, wi-fi spots etc.). Nowadays the Alpine arc is no longer a disadvantaged region; rather, it is a complex and diversified European transnational macro-region with important supply functions. More precisely, there appears to be a sort of dual development at play, whereby some sectors such as the French and part of the Swiss Alps are experiencing strong demographic growth, while in parts of the Italian Alps – particularly in the regions of Piemonte, Veneto and Friuli – as well as in several Eastern Austrian districts and in some parts of the Swiss Alps many valleys are experiencing the effects of depopulation and economic marginality. Notably, mobility plays a crucial role in this trend, the disadvantaged zones being precisely those not well connected with major communication axes. Wherever it has materialized, enhanced mobility has also made possible new lifestyles for the inhabitants of the Alps, including the twin processes of suburbanization and commuting. The suburbanization of the middle class in the Alps is essentially based on the possibility for people to live in smaller mountain towns and work in the service sector in major cities and regional capitals, as well as peri-Alpine large cities and metropolitan areas.

I am not going to venture here into the huge debate about the (un-) sustainability of suburbia as a pattern of territorial development. Suffice to recall some aspects of the complex relationship between suburbs and the city at the cultural and social levels. Bruegmann (2006) argues that a sternly negative view of suburbia has been dominant in the American literature. According to this author, intellectualist criticism has produced only a stylized, cliché-like depiction of suburbia and has prevented the carrying out of accurate research on the topic. On the contrary, scholars like Matthew Lindstrom and Hugh Bartling (2003) have argued that the stereotypical elements of single-family residences on large lots, automobile-centred transportation and little support for public transportation are indeed the actual features of suburbia. Already in the early 1960s, Lewis Mumford pointed out what he regarded as the central contradiction of the suburban model:

> In the mass movement into suburban areas a new kind of community was produced which caricatured both the historic city and the archetypal suburban refuge: a multitude of uniform, unidentifiable houses lined up inflexibly, at uniform roads, in treeless communal waste, inhabited by people of the same class, the same income, the same age-group [...] Thus the ultimate effect of the suburban escape in out time, is, ironically, a low-grade uniform environment from which escape is impossible. (Mumford 1961: 286)

In any case, this type of critique, amply shared among urban scholars in the 1960s and 1970s (among which, high-profile theorists such as Jane Jacobs and Richard Sennett), has been far from stopping the spread of the model on the ground. Among the reasons for the prolonged and intense growth of sprawl, factors such as cheap land, lower taxes, better car access and the myth of living in contact with rural settings are usually listed (Ingersoll 2006). If I have quoted Mumford extensively, it is not to engage the vexed questions about American suburban sprawl, but because I would like to test in my case study two of the overall features that the author used to attribute to suburban environment, namely the fact of being 'low-graded' and 'uniform'. In particular, I aim to test it not according to my own aesthetic values, but according to the perception of the inhabitants of the suburbs surrounding the city of Trento. I am likewise going to check whether other characters that in the Anglo-American literature are commonly associated with sprawl, such as the dominance of consumer identity, normalization, anti-urbanity, civic disengagement and self-segregation among the inhabitants, are present or not in Alpine suburbanization and, if so, to what extent.

As said above, the city of Trento is located in the Italian north-eastern sector of the Alps, along the Adige valley approximately between Verona and Bolzano/Bozen (Figure 9.1). Following the typology proposed by Perlik *et al.* (2001), Trento is part of a functional urban area which can be characterized as an 'Alpine agglomeration'. It is both a regional capital which functions as a political centre for its territorial unit and a small-to-medium-size city inserted into several European urban networks. As such, as Perlink *et al.* (2001: 248) argue, it has the 'capacity and responsibility to influence development strategies for the Alpine arc'. The Adige valley is indeed increasingly turning into an urban strip that stretches well into the heart of the Alps as a functional extension of the Po megalopolis, although a modernized agricultural system still occupies large portions of plain areas. If we look more closely at the features of an Alpine city such as Trento (Figure 9.2), some morphological elements stand out. Architecture historian and theorist Renato Bocchi (1989, 2006a, 2006b) has described the city of Trento as a 'polycentric city', an 'archipelago-city' and a 'landscape-city'. By these terms, Bocchi means that the city is formed by a small historic nucleus located in the middle of the Adige valley, drawn upon the classic quadrilateral Roman *castrum*, and later expanded with a Gothic neighbourhood.

The city is surrounded by an agglomeration of small historic villages scattered on the hills around the city at various distances from the city centre, which form a sort of archipelago around the city. These smaller neighbourhoods, usually to be found along ancient communication roads, are called 'sobborghi' (literally, suburbs) of the city and, all together, nowadays host a significant portion of its inhabitants, ranging from about 500 to 5,000 inhabitants each. The closest ones have actually become part of the city itself yet, according to Bocchi, it is still possible to identify their difference from the city. Most notably, the nature of these peri-urban villages is originally and topologically non-urban. Despite their closeness to the city, these suburbs are both structurally and culturally built as Alpine rural villages. Indeed, they look like small, tightly built conglomerates, typically with large houses for lodging extended peasant families with many children. These houses, in many cases physically contiguous to each other, are not originally arranged into flats (although, of course, many of them have been converted into flats), but have large interiors for a range of winter activities, like woodsheds and haystacks. The suburb has usually an irregular main square with a church and shared washing fountain. Several important remnants of common land uses are still in place since the Middle Age (e.g. the institute of the '*regulae*',

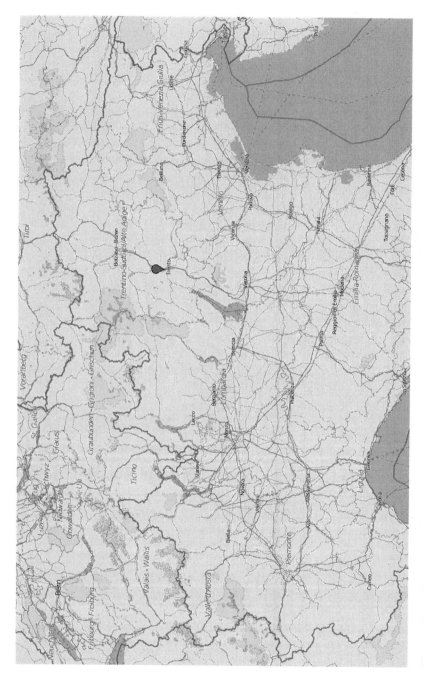

Figure 9.1   Location of the city of Trento in the Alps (map from openstreetmap).

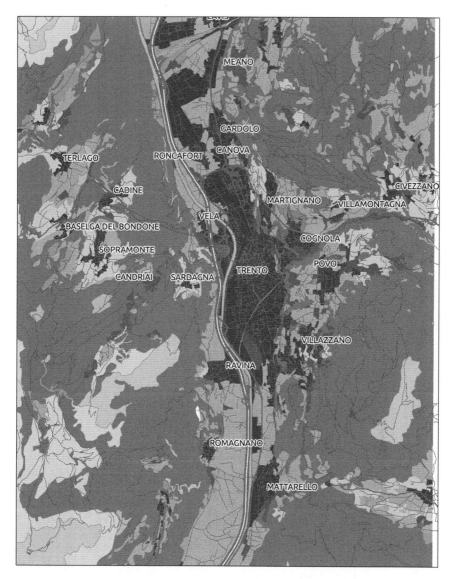

Figure 9.2   Trento and its suburbs (map from openstreetmap).

which regulates the civic commons of water, wood and pasture) (Figure 9.3). Ancient land uses also include the traditional Germanic settlement of the *masi* (*Hofen*) houses, i.e. sparse large colonic houses, sort of independent agriculture-based units. Finally, in some suburbs it is also possible to find ancient noble villas for the summer residence of aristocratic families and the upper clergy (Figure 9.4).

Figure 9.3   The historic suburb of Cadine (photo by Andrea Mubi Brighenti).

Figure 9.4   The historic suburb of Oltrecastello (photo by Andrea Mubi Brighenti).

The research

In my research on the patterns of Alpine suburbanization, I aim to inquire into the experience and the social imagination attached to living in one such suburb. This is an ongoing project which is linked to my major thread of research on public space and its current transformations. I am particularly interested in capturing what is between the 'publicness' of public space – 'what is precisely public in public space?' – and urban life and culture (Brighenti 2010), and I have chosen as my fieldwork a sort of counter-intuitive example, a place where, at first sight, one would never look for public space. In the years 2009–11 I have mapped the suburbs around the city of Trento. Subsequently, I have selected ten of them and have elaborated a comparative observational grid to be filled in. In the grid, I have collected some essential statistical and geographic information as well as more extensive descriptive and visual data related to the suburb. My concern was to record a number of features which could help to make sense – or raise questions – about social life in the suburb, but also about its visible boundaries, its major flows, its core and degree of 'centredness' vs. 'spreadedness', its inner cleavages, quarters, house styles, mobility aspects and so on. After such a preliminary mapping, a first round of about 40 semi-structured interviews were carried out with the help of the students of the Faculty of Sociology at the University of Trento. Inhabitants and local informants were interviewed about their experience of the neighbourhood, their settlement story, their perception of past and ongoing transformations, positive and negative aspects of the suburb where they live vis-à-vis others and, finally, its main problems and potentialities.

Overall, the progressive urbanization of the territory has pushed, to various degrees, towards the transformation of the historic villages surrounding the city into an urban periphery (the same phenomenon has been captured but conceptualized differently by Zaninotto et al. 2008). However, this process is not taking place without resistances and is not without its inner contradictions. For instance, the master narrative of 'community building' has been and still is propounded by the local public administration, local politicians and local media, although of course the process of suburbanization has deeply affected the nature of the local community and the social spaces necessary for the flourishing of the communitarian dimension. Since the late 1980s, the suburbs surrounding the city have experienced a demographic boom, with steady increases in the number of residents ranging from 200% to 400%. The old villages, which were previously poor agricultural and highly localized communities, have turned into relatively wealthy but increasingly residential areas. In fact, most newer inhabitants are commuters who heavily depend on private cars for transport, while the 'historic' inhabitants – in most cases settled in the neighbourhood since before the end of the 1980s – are in significant part an older population that includes retired people and, in many cases, their children's families.

Thus, the impressive demographic increase of population in the suburbs in the last 20 years has not been matched by a corresponding growth of public services, in particular as concerns commercial, cultural and infrastructural services. Commercial services, including for instance food stores and shops, have indeed declined, especially in the suburbs that are closest to the city. The reason is clearly that for small stores it is hard to face competition from large stores in the city, in terms of both prices and, perhaps even more crucially, opening hours. This detail is also revealing of another peculiar trait of urban rhythm analysis. In peri-urban villages circadian rhythms are still somehow tied to traditional rural life. Commercial activities begin very early in the morning – at about 7.00 a.m. – and close accordingly much earlier than in the city. They also include a lunch break between noon and 3 p.m. Now, this circadian rhythm is clearly unfit for commuters who leave at 7.30 a.m. for the city and get back at 6.30 p.m., which is precisely the time when commercial activities in the suburb close. Cultural and organized recreation services, on their part, were only rarely present in old villages and did not develop in the meanwhile. For instance, small town theatres hardly survived because the cost to maintain similar structures has become much higher in the meanwhile. The only surviving public structures in place are, in some cases, so-called 'multi-functional' halls, which are used for all sorts of meetings and administrative services. Similar remarks apply to public transport, which has remained underdeveloped as the all-too-obvious counterpart of the hyper-development of private-car-based transport. Overall, these conditions have determined a trend towards centralization of services in the city and mono-functional (residential) land use in the suburb. In turn, this fact has led to a perceived lack of identity of the suburb, and a recurrent fear expressed by several interviewees is that of living in a 'dormitory neighbourhood'.

Inhabitants old and new

There is of course a significant difference between older and newer inhabitants (distinction based on the length of the residence period). Savage et al. (2005: 29) have argued that 'we do indeed need to fundamentally break from any lingering conceptions of local social relations as defined by the activities, values and cultures of those "born and bred" in an area'. Yet, while the born-and-bred attribute is certainly an ideological construction, in my research a tension between inhabitants of longer and shorter residence seems to be undeniable, especially in terms of representation of suburban life and interpretation of local experience. It is difficult to quantify the period of residence one needs to qualify as an old inhabitant: in many cases, it is a matter of a lifetime or even entire generations; in some other case it is a matter of 20 years, or even less (but perhaps having married someone from a local family). Yet, while most interviewees reject the idea that there is an issue of lack of 'social integration' or 'social cohesion' in the suburb, significant differences between older and newer inhabitants appear. In particular, newcomers are often charged by the old-timers of being 'anonymous', i.e. unknown people, as these interviews make clear:

I also want to underline that for some recently settled families, for many of them, Montevaccino represents if not a *pied-à-terre*, a dormitory neighbourhood, in the sense that they leave in the morning and get back in the evening, I mean. These families could certainly live ... even though they have chosen to live in Montevaccino, with all that comes with it, they could have lived everywhere else. (GF, 53, Montevaccino)

The youngsters who hang around in the main square are born and bred here in Meano. Then I know there are other 20-something boys who live in the new houses and meet in some other places, I don't know much about that. Even if – unfortunately I mean – there's only one bar here in Meano, it's very rare to see around those guys from Meano2 [the residential expansion zone] [...] Meano is a village where everybody knows each other, and I'm talking about the main square. I don't consider Meano2 that much, yeah, it's still part of Meano but ... The historic centre is the place where they all know each other, but if you consider Meano2, it's the place where each minds his own business [...] most of the people are just there for sleeping so I doubt very much that they even know each other. (GL, 34, Meano)

In most cases there is a lack of interaction between older and newer inhabitants in the suburbs. Interestingly, anonymity is a trait associated to the 'public realm' of urban life in open spaces. Thus, a sort of implicit accusation made by older inhabitants is that newer inhabitants, by their very presence, are urbanizing the suburb. While the situation is one of physical proximity – given the generally very small size of these suburbs – there is a perception of social distance, in particular between those living in the historic centre of the suburb and those who live in 'blocks'. Now, these latter seem to be of two different types: on the one hand, there are popular lodgements built in the 1980s in many instances by the public administration (Figure 9.5), on the other hand there are newer small condominiums and row-houses built in large part since the 1990s by private developers (Figure 9.6), the last wave of which is represented by the 'climate house' type. Furthermore, during the 1990s and the last decade, some older inhabitants have also restored their central houses, usually splitting them into more manageable flats (usually destined for their children's families), while others have built two-family houses (more rarely, single-family) on some allotments of their originally agrarian property land (Figure 9.7).

Needless to say, complaints about larger blocks being built in the area are at least in part paradoxical, or ideological, given that in most cases the latter have been built on fields sold by local residents to developers. Nonetheless, it is interesting to observe on the ground the spatial quality of such a cleavage. In different suburbs, the dislocation of the centre and residential expansion zones looks different: in some cases there is a clearly split situation, in which the newest part of the suburbs is spatially far from the historic nucleus (such as for instance in Cadine, Meano and Civezzano), while in other cases the new buildings are quite close to and sometimes even intertwined with the old ones (such as for

Figure 9.5   **Popular lodgements in Roncafort (photo by Andrea Mubi Brighenti).**

Figure 9.6   **Residential expansion in Civezzano (photo by Andrea Mubi Brighenti).**

Figure 9.7   Two-family house in Vela (photo by Andrea Mubi Brighenti).

instance in San Rocco, Villamontagna and Sardagna). An important element to understand such differences is verticality. Alpine suburbs were originally located at the margin of small plains destined for agriculture. The rationale for the location of a suburb was a sort of compromise between a number of environmental factors, including the presence of water streams, safety from landslides and avalanches and quest for sunlight, but also the necessity of leaving the sunniest places to the cultivated fields. Today, verticality has acquired a new meaning, as it may also afford beautiful vistas which are sold as assets by real estate agencies. However, it may also become problematic where it prevents the building of car-accessible asphalted roads. Verticality also turns the suburb into a space that, for an urban pedestrian, is much less walkable than the rest of urban space and can thus (in conjunction to other elements such as the lack of sidewalks) favour the creation of separate areas within the same suburb.

A factor that certainly cannot be charged to newer inhabitants alone is the weakening of traditional socializing institutions of the suburb. The latter classically included the parish (with an oratories hall for the youth) and social clubs such as the Alpine club, the *bocciofila* (bowling club) and the retired people club, as well as sport societies, committees for the organization of traditional *sagre* (celebrations) and the promotion of events and research about local history and memories. Customary seasonal practices also include activities like wood cutting and storing, which are usually carried out not at the community level but among smaller groups of neighbours or close families. These institutions and practices are certainly still significant for a number of inhabitants, who devote a lot of energy to them, but are no longer encompassing of the local community. Younger generations – including the 'born and bred' ones – appear to be generally less available to engage themselves in local associations that are perceived as time-demanding and perhaps, in some cases, also regarded as implicit tools of social control over their activities. In other words, there is a generational issue here, which in most cases does not explode in overt conflict but can nonetheless create invisible tensions. If several older inhabitants seem to be less attracted towards traditional local socializing institutions, in their turn most new inhabitants of the suburb do not usually join them. Some middle class newcomers might join religious institutions and parishes, and they might get to know the community through the activities of their children in the preschool age, but in most cases they are not interested in the traditional activities that are essentially based on working-class culture, with a strong background in popular and peasant mentality. Arguably, several new inhabitants avoid in engaging suburb life too closely because they are wary of the protection of their privacy from local gossip and forms of social control perceived as constraining and oppressive. Often, they also think that old inhabitants are exceedingly traditionalist and not too welcoming. Even apart from newcomers' presence, some old inhabitants, too, feel that they have changed their way of life, to have become 'more bourgeois'.

> Q: As far as you are concerned, what is your relationships with your neighbours? Do neighbours here help each other, I mean … if there's an elderly person, is he helped or… or do you keep the post for your neighbour …
>
> A: Well, let's say that used to happen in the past, right. The true village, the true spirit was this one, right? Now we are more bourgeois even from this point of view [smiles]. So perhaps we help at the oratory or we help the poor who live on the other part of the ocean but then we forget to do something for our neighbour, right. Yeah, this [custom] is lost … Let's hope we can recover that feeling of … 'Cause I remember when I was a kid here, it was all open, right? There were no walls, no fences, everything was open. Instead now we tend to be more … right? To build fences, to fence, and … yes, well from this point of view we have lost [something]. (SG, 46, Oltrecastello)

The outcome of this process is sometimes described by old inhabitants as a 'lack of identity' of the suburb. Besides, such a lack of identity is regarded as going hand in hand with an aesthetic 'uglification' of the suburb itself.

The old inhabitants of the suburbs usually live in old, large family houses. In some cases, their houses are self-built, a not too uncommon practice in Italy from the post-war period until the 1980s. In many cases, these houses have been renovated over the last 10 to 15 years, and their owners are proud of having restored them in order to accommodate their kin families. Typically, they have created space for one or two new apartments within the same building, destined for a recently married or, on the contrary, a single son or daughter. The most wealthy have also had the possibility to build an entirely new house close to their own, usually on the same lot of terrain formerly destined for agriculture. It is interesting to observe how these old inhabitants judge the coherence between the traditional houses of the suburb and the new houses. Such a judgement seems to be based not on matters of style (their own houses built in the 1980s or the new ones built for their children can hardly be said to have anything to do with traditional architecture) but essentially on the basis of dimension. Big buildings that show resemblance with urban blocks are always regarded with suspicion and are variously referred at as *casermoni*, literally 'ugly barrack-like buildings', or *colate di cemento*, 'concrete melts'.

An affective attachment to the suburbs is usually expressed by the old inhabitants. This sense of belonging might in part be explained by early socialization through local associations, such as religious associations, Alpine clubs and committees for the organization of local traditional celebrations (both religious and secular). Other items of affective attachment which are usually mentioned by old inhabitants are the contact with nature, the view of the surrounding mountains and the availability of green lawns, gardens and back-gardens. These are all quoted by the inhabitants to confirm their attachment and prove their true love for their own suburb. Mountain landscape, as known, is importantly linked to the feeling of belonging in the form of nostalgia (the Swiss malady) and the so-called *mal del campanile* (literally, bell tower homesickness). Incidentally, it should also be added that most green areas in the suburb are private. Such a lack of recreational public green areas in the suburbs themselves is only apparently paradoxical: indeed, for traditional Alpine villages, public green areas or playgrounds were of no concern, given that the village was entirely surrounded by woods and green fields. While contemporary urbanites have the problem of how to get in touch with wildlife, old-time mountain villagers had plenty of it around them – actually, in their view, even too much. Where present, public green areas in the suburbs have only been built recently, sometimes obtained through residents' mobilizations that have, not always successfully, also claimed other basic services such as nurseries, post offices and supermarkets.

Elements such as contact with nature, views of the mountains and availability of green lawns and gardens are also important factors that have attracted the new inhabitants towards the suburb (and skilfully used in real estate agencies communication). These newer inhabitants, usually from the middle class and in their thirties, have in some cases long cultivated the dream of a *villa* of their own. They could approximate their dream, or at least move some steps towards it, by buying a flat in a small block or row-house with a small private garden and a panoramic view. Here, the lawn begins to function as a Goffmanian tool for the presentation of the self (Figure 9.8, left): more visible than protected from sight, the small private garden, often enclosed by a low fence with a hedge, heralds a conception and a style of life (as illustrated, for the American case, by Jenkins 1994). Utilitarian factors are more clearly present among these new inhabitants, as their residential choice is a form of what Savage et al. (2005) have called 'elective belonging'. Elective belonging, however, is not simply utilitarian; rather it mixes utilitarian considerations with value-based and affective elements. Perhaps what best captures the dimension of elective belonging is the dimension of the 'project'. Elective belonging distinguishes itself from inherited belonging mainly because it involves some form of conscious project-making. The undertaken project is not necessarily conceived in merely utilitarian terms. To begin with, in Italy the very fact of buying a house signifies a long-term investment in a living project, which inherently entails affective dimensions. And there are a number of significant convergences between the values of the older and the newer inhabitants. Various aspects of life in the suburb appear to constitute a bed of shared values between old and new inhabitants: these include, above all, tranquillity and safety, but also xenophobia and a certain anti-urban attitude. People who live in the suburb explicitly claim the desire to 'live in peace' and attribute all sort of social or material disorder to 'people from the outside'.

The suburban trend, however, should not be understood as homogeneous or even linear. While almost all the interviewees regard their suburb as a 'good place to raise children', there can be a significant diversity between suburbs. In particular, the perception of safety seems to be directly proportional to the distance from the city. In other words, for a number of reasons some suburbs still retain a higher degree of independence from the city, while others have become a mere addition to urban sprawl in peripheral locations. Suburbs can also differ in terms of their traffic problems. In general, Alpine suburbs were not built for car traffic and car parking, and this is also the reason why there tends to be few pedestrian sidewalks in them (which can create dangerous situations for children). Yet, there

Figure 9.8   The old vis à vis the new in Cognola (photo by Andrea Mubi Brighenti).

can be significant differences in terms of the impact of car-based mobility. In some cases, bypasses have been built which have helped to sort local and longer-distance traffic, while in others the historic nucleus has luckily remained at the margin of commuter traffic flow. More generally, as remarked above, some suburbs still preserve a strong village spirit, even when they have become sort of second-rank suburbs or *dépendance*-suburb, heavily dependent upon another, usually larger, suburb for even basic services such as public services and post offices. The fact that the process of suburbanization has not occurred evenly is sometimes even appreciated by residents, as they see a double advantage of being close to the city but at the same time clearly out of it:

> But I have to tell one thing … 'Cause here we are in a centre, a small urban centre that depends on Trento for everything, and we, our luck … we have two … our luck is that we are very close to the city and at the same time out of the city, then … we enjoy all the advantages of being close to the city, because everybody works in the city, everybody, so they all have their job, and we do well … and at the same time when you go back to your privacy, you go to your family and you are out of the city. And were there things in the city that did not work right, here there are none, and thus we are privileged, to my mind, from this point of view, I mean socially, we do well, from that point of view. (PG, 42, Sardagna)

Conclusions: the fringe as an interstice

In this chapter, I have suggested a research approach to the Alpine suburb as a peculiar type of urban interstice rather than a margin or periphery. In a situation of diffused urbanization of territories, borderlands configure themselves more as in-betweens than exteriorities. Such in-betweens are a composition of heterogeneous and sometimes dissonant elements. Visually speaking, for instance, the meeting of the old and the new in the Alpine suburb produces visual clashes (Figure 9.8). To an architect's eye, most of the new buildings in these suburbs look pretty ugly, and certainly the suburbanization process has created major challenges to the territorial identity of these places in terms of landscape quality or, to retrieve a term from Kevin Lynch, legibility.

The Alpine suburb constitutes a sort of urban fringe, a blurred borderland where different territorial components and modalities intermingle. Anglo-American literature on suburbia has highlighted the fact that the suburb itself seems to question the very dichotomy between the urban and the non-urban, given that suburbia and exurbia are located precisely between the city and the countryside (see e.g. Bruegmann 2006). In the case of the Alpine suburb, an additional factor of complexity is represented by the fact that the 'countryside' dimension constitutes the backbone of the original suburb itself. Thus, contemporary Alpine suburbs, whose current shape derives from residential expansion and addition to the historic suburb, present a peculiar mix of traits and ways of life. Suburban life is usually described as dull, yet here we are in fact facing major social transformations. With the transformation of ancient villages into technically and structurally urbanized territories, a degree of anonymity that is typical of urban life ensued. But the overall social organization of local life cannot be said to merely urban. An urbanized territory is not yet a territorial city. On the one hand, newer inhabitants are in fact middle class commuting suburbanites rather than urbanites, and they bring with them a specific version of urban life. On the other hand, older inhabitants have tried to protect a sense of local belonging which is essentially communitarian, grounded in the ideals and values of a peasant society that no longer materially exists but whose imprint is, culturally and socially, anti-urban. Yet these two cultural variants of anti-urbanism are far from coincident.

A number of mediations and controversies have been generated by this complex mix of factors. I would just like to give two small conclusive examples of the curious in-betweenness of suburban life. The first concerns the paradoxical perception of distances. An interviewee has told us that during the weekend he does challenging trekking on the mountains, yet in not much later, during the course of the same interview, when asked about whether he uses public transport or not, he complains that public transport is quite uncomfortable for him given that the bus stop is 800 metres from his place. So, in the same person there seem to coexist two quite different standards of the evaluation of walking distances, one for the weekend (linked to the traditional identity of a good mountaineer) and quite another for the rest of the week (linked to the modernized transport requirements of the urbanite). The second small example illuminates the relations between older and newer inhabitants and concerns snow clearing. After a snowfall, new inhabitants usually only clear their own tract of property. From a modern urban perspective this might be interpreted as fair enough, but it is certainly unfair from the point of view of an Alpine village mentality. Indeed, in a traditional Alpine suburb what really counts is not the distinction between the public and the private, but the dimension of the common. These two dimensions should not be regarded as merely antithetic or tied to a linear evolution from *Gemeinschaft* to *Gesellschaft*; rather, as two fundamental territory-making social resources and two complementary horizons of meaning and action.

The urbanization of territory and the territorialization of the city are, by and large, twin movements. Yet, as the case of Alpine suburbs reveals, they are not coincident. The first movement refers to the spreading of urbanization over larger geographic areas, the crisis of the classical dichotomy between urban and rural areas and the formation of 'urban fields' and large-scale urban regions. In this context, the difference between city and countryside is increasingly reconfigured as a difference between degrees of accessibility to places that are distributed in continuous yet heterogeneous geographies. The movement of urbanization of territory is also crucially related to the fact that urban space is governed and administered (Foucault 2004/1978). To govern a space means precisely to predispose its physical features so as to inscribe into it a series of devices for the government of the population. Contemporary urbanized territory is most notably supported by large networked infrastructures including transportation, telecommunications, energy, water and waste that, as a whole, enable those fundamental interconnections of urban life, but which typically become visible only in moments of failure or collapse (Graham and Marvin 2001). In their daily existence, such infrastructures are based on a complex arrangement and crafty maintenance of their heterogeneous material components. Instead, the movement of territorialization of the city refers to the transformation of those classical values and skills of civility, urbanity and coexistence with diversity that, according to classic authors, define urban life (see e.g. Goffman 1971, Sennett 1978). I speak of transformations since, as remarked by Amin (2008: 5), 'in an age of urban sprawl, multiple usage of public space and proliferation of the sites of political and cultural expression, it seems odd to expect public spaces to fulfil their traditional role as spaces of civic inculcation and political participation'. While to my mind this does not mean, as Amin implies, that the link between public space and politics is irredeemably broken, it does certainly mean that the notions of civility and urbanity are being transformed, and a new culture of publicness suited to the new plural territorializations of the city is to be developed. Yet, how is the new urbanity of the territorial city related to newly emerging forms publicity and commonality? An interstitial territory such as that of the Alpine suburb might represent a case of socio-territorial dynamics that could be studied.

References

Adey, P. 2009. *Mobility*. London: Routledge.

Amin, A. 2008. Collective culture and urban public space. *City*, 12(1), 5–24.

Arnoldi, C. 2010. Inadeguatezze alpine/Alps' unfitness. *lo Squaderno*, 16: 15–22. Available at: www.loquaderno.professionaldreamers.net [Accessed: 1 September 2012]

Bätzing, W. 2002. *I processi di Trasformazioni di Ambiente, Economia, Società e Popolazione Attualmente in Corso nelle Alpi*. Berlin: Bundesministerium für Umwelt, Naturschutz und Reaktorsicherheit.

Bätzing, W. 2005. *Le Alpi*. Torino: Bollati Boringheri.

Beattie, A. 2006. *The Alps: A Cultural History*. Oxford: Oxford University Press.

Beauregard, R.A. 2006. *When America Became Suburban*. Minneapolis, MN: University of Minnesota Press.

Bocchi, R. 1989. *Trento: Interpretazione della Città*. Trento: Saturnia.

Bocchi, R. 2006a. La città-paesaggio, in: V. Bonometto and M. L. Ruggiero (eds) *Finestre sul Paesaggio*. Rome: Gangemi, pp. 12–23.

Bocchi, R. 2006b. *Il Paesaggio come Palinsesto: Progetti per l'Area Fluviale dell'Adige a Trento*. Rovereto: Nicolodi.

Brighenti, A.M. 2010. *The Publicness of Public Space. On the Public Domain*. Monographic issue of *Quaderni del Dipartimento di Sociologia e Ricerca Sociale*, no. 49, March 2010, Università di Trento, 1. Available at: http://www.unitn.it/files/quad49.pdf [Accessed: 1 September 2012].

Bruegmann, R. 2006. *Sprawl: A Compact History*. Chicago, IL: University of Chicago Press.

Camanni, E. 2002. *La Nuova Vita delle Alpi*. Torino: Bollati Boringhieri.

Canzler, W., Kaufmann, V. and Kesselring, S. (eds) 2009. *Tracing Mobilities: Towards a Cosmopolitan Perspective*. Farnham: Ashgate.

Dematteis, G. 1975. Le Città alpine, in: Bruno Parisi (ed.) *Le città alpine. Documenti e Note*. Milan: Vita e pensiero, pp. 5–103.

Dematteis, G. 2009. Polycentric urban regions in the Alpine space. *Urban Research & Practice*, 2(1), 18–35.

Diamantini, C. and Zanon, B. (eds) 1999. *Le Alpi: Immagini e Percorsi di un Territorio in Trasformazione*. Trento: Temi.

Foucault, M. 2004/1978. *Sécurité, Territoire, Population. Cours au Collège de France, 1977–1978*, edited by François Ewald, Alessandro Fontana, Michel Senellart. Paris: Hautes Etudes, Gallimard, Seuil.

Goffman, E. 1971. *Relations in Public: Microstudies of the Public Order*. London: Penguin.

Graham, S. and Marvin, S. 2001. *Splintering Urbanism: Networked Infrastructures, Technological Mobilities and the Urban Condition*. London: Routledge & Kegan Paul.

Jaret, C. *et al.* 2009. The measurement of suburban sprawl: an evaluation. *City & Community*, 8(1), 65–84.

Jenkins, V. S. 1994. *The Lawn: A History of an American Obsession*. Washington, DC: Smithsonian Books.

Ingersoll, R. 2006 *Sprawltown: Looking for the City on its Edges*. Princeton, NJ: Princeton Architectural Press.

Lindstrom, M.J. and Bartling, H. (eds) 2003. *Suburban Sprawl: Culture, Theory, and Politics*. Lanham: Rowman & Littlefield.

Mumford, L. 1961. *The City in History: Its Origins, its Transformations, and its Prospects*. New York: Harcourt Brace & World.

Perlik, M., Messerli, P. and Bätzing W. 2001. Towns in the Alps. *Mountain Research and Development*, 21(3), 243–52.

Savage, M., Bagnall, G. and Longhurst, B. 2005. *Globalization and Belonging*. London: Sage.

Schonthaler, K. and von Andrian-Werburg, S. (eds) 2008. *Indicators on Regional Development in the Alps*. Bolzano: Eurac.

Secchi, B. 2005. *La Città del Ventesimo Secolo*. Rome: Laterza.

Sennett, R. 1978. *The Fall of Public Man*. New York: Vintage.

Turri, E. 2004. *La Megalopoli Padana*. Verona: Marsilio.

Urry, J. 2007. *Mobilities*. Cambridge: Polity Press.

Vitale, P. 2009. Learning to be suburban: the production of community in Westwood Hills, Pennsylvania, 1952–1958. *Journal of Historical Geography* 35: 743–68.

Zaninotto, E., Zanon, B. and Marzan, P. 2008. L'area urbana estesa di Trento: sono necessarie politiche metropolitane?. Public lecture, Palazzo Geremia, Trento, 28 February 2008.

Chapter 10

Active Interstices: Urban Informality, the Tourist Gaze and Metamorphosis in South-East Asia

Ross King and Kim Dovey

Introduction

> Tales of metamorphosis often arise in spaces (temporal, geographical, and mental) that were crossroads, cross-cultural zones, points of interchange on the intricate connective tissue of communications between cultures … in transitional places and at the confluence of traditions and civilizations. (Warner 2004: 17–18)

In the wonderfully encyclopaedic *Fantastic Metamorphoses: Other Worlds*, Marina Warner (2004) speculates on transformations and the underlying energies and processes whereby one motif, representation or idea generates another. She concludes that, on the evidence of history, the transformations that mark great creativity and leaps to new modes of thought and life will most likely occur in those places and times where different cultures collide and all ideas of immutable identity come apart. Metamorphosis, or life-as-change, runs counter to the idea of the unique, singular nature of identity and its defence. It is the vital principle of nature, the dynamic of cultural change, guarantee of personal freedom, the power at the heart of storytelling and creativity (King 2008: 203–4). We search, therefore, for those 'transitional places' or places of becoming (Dovey 2010) where one might detect a new urbanism, politics and aesthetics emerging. Where are the collisions and where are those interstices (rifts, chasms) where one might look for signs of the new?

Ernst Bloch (writing in 1932) coined the term 'nonsynchronism' to identify the phenomenon of living in a range of different times at once and in the same place; where the montage of new and old held potential for the emergence of new hybrid meanings (Bloch 1997) and producing a 'coexistence of realities from different moments of history' (Jameson 1994: 307). Walter Benjamin developed the parallel concept of the dialectic image where one element of an image deconstructs another and both are called into question. Benjamin was interested in the ways the juxtapositions of difference in urban life could reveal something of a larger truth – spatial logic could reveal what a linear logic could not through a 'dialectic of awakening' – for Benjamin dialectic images compel discourse (Buck-Morss 1989: 262). Foucault's theory of heterotopia suggests something similar: 'heterotopia is capable of juxtaposing in a single place several spaces, several sites that are in themselves incompatible' (Foucault 1986: 28). Jan Nederveen Pieterse has more recently drawn attention to the way that globalization produces a proliferation and hybridization of modes of production and organization:

> The notion of articulation of modes of production may be viewed as a principle of hybridisation ... Counterposed to the idea of the dual economy split in traditional/modern and feudal/capitalist sectors, the articulation argument holds that what has been taking place is an interpenetration of modes of production ... Furthermore, not only these modes of organization are important but also the informal spaces that are created in between, in the interstices. Inhabited by diasporas, migrants, exiles, refugees, nomads, these are sites of what Michael Mann (1986) calls 'interstitial emergence' and identifies as important sources of social renewal. (Nederveen Pieterse 1995: 50–51)

De Certeau likewise suggests that as the institutional order of power in space becomes more totalizing it also becomes more available for subversion: 'The surface of this order is everywhere punched and torn open by ellipses, drifts, and leaks of meaning: it is a sieve-order' (de Certeau 1984: 108). Resistance insinuates the very structures of a hegemonic order. It is such interstices – between different modes of production and organization, between different ways of seeing and inhabiting the city – that are the concern of the discussion that follows. We explore these transformations using Bangkok as a case study while insisting, however, that our search is for understanding (theory) that is more widely applicable. The chapter concludes with speculations on the nature of the metamorphoses in attitudes and practices observable in such spaces in the present time.

Interstices, chasms

Our first focus is on Bangkok and on the rift between the formal understanding of the city and an undermining, informal reality. We are, however, looking to the coexistence of such modes of organization and their articulation rather than, simplistically, to 'difference'. This rift is in part represented in the clash between the city of elitist dreaming and the real life of the streets; between the middle classes who view the city from high rise towers and elevated toll roads, and the informal city of hawkers and squatters often hidden beneath the expressways and behind the facades of the formal city (Dovey and King 2011). The formal/informal divide embodies the distinction between those districts, forms and practices within the city that are controlled by the state and the informal settlements and practices that infiltrate. There is also a second tier of intersections that concerns us, in the form of global media and the tourist gaze: both elite dreams and the frequent suppressions that accompany them, as well as the subversions of real life, transform in the withering light of global tourism and mass media.

While the divisions between formal and informal sectors are always blurred and contingent, one way of articulating this condition is through the various relations between the state, the middle classes and the urban poor. To the state, informal settlements and their denizens' presence in the formal city will variously present as visual confrontation (compromising the image of the well-ordered city and the images of state boosterism), a sign of failure (the state's inability to solve 'the problem'), economic subversion (no taxes paid) yet also a low-wage labour force. The poor and the marginal, in turn, may view the state with a mix of indifference, apprehension, fear or hatred over past violence and suppressions. The middle classes tend to bestow invisibility on the poor, the marginalized and their settlements (they are imagined away). Yet this 'unseeing' co-exists with dependence on their cheap labour and an underlying fear of an impending uprising. The poor are also imagined away in another sense since the land occupied by informal settlements is often a golden opportunity for development. The poor and the marginalized, in return, may typically look to the middle class of the formal city with envy, resentment, occasionally obsequious disdain, perhaps the fear of displacement. The gaze between these groups is asymmetric – informal settlements are unseen (and un-entered) by the middle classes yet the poor are often employed in the shopping malls, gated communities and corporate enclaves. The poor see the whole city while the middle classes see just a part; only one half knows how the other half lives and one result is a production of envy without an equivalent production of compassion (Figure 10.1).

These relations are, however, constantly transforming (metamorphosing) through the explosion of new media and the images they transmit and, especially in urban space, through the equally explosive force of the tourist gaze. This gaze

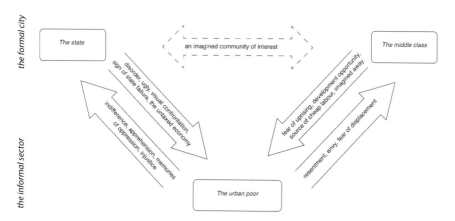

Figure 10.1 **Perceptions, positions linking and de-linking the formal and informal city.**

transforms informal settlements so that they become spaces variously of visual and experiential delight (the aestheticization of poverty) and of global outrage at the condition of the poor; it transforms the everyday life of street hawkers into happy street markets and tourist precincts. All social fractions, however, are confronted by the new form of globalization represented in the tourist onslaught and its disturbing gaze. This gaze disturbs because it insists on seeing what is routinely unseen. The indigenous relations of the state and middle-classes to the poor as outlined above begin to shift, crosscut by altogether new perceptions.

The interstices between worlds

In one sense the metropolis is always interstitial between the global and the indigenous, each variously defined. It is a 'crossroads', in Warner's sense. Nowhere is this clearer than in those cities caught in the grand enterprises of colonial exploitation – Seoul, Shanghai, Jakarta, Calcutta, Manila, Mumbai and their ilk. Bangkok presents the ambiguity of having been at such a crossroads in the colonial age yet caught in the myth of Siam not having been (at least politically) colonized. Siam was itself, in that era, a regional colonizing power, most notably towards the ancient Lanna kingdom to the north, the Lao lands of Isaan in the north east and Malay sultanates in the south. So Bangkok is today interstitial in at least three senses: first, between its ethnic 'others' (Lanna, Lao, Malay, hill tribes, the Burmese diaspora) and the hegemonic urban Thai and Sino-Thai; second, between the persisting remnants of nineteenth- and twentieth-century colonialism and indigenous imaginings of nation and identity; and third, between those same imaginings and the new transnational force of tourism and a borderless, irresistible media.

This third layer of the crossroads is especially problematic because it is both desired and dreaded by hegemonic powers – tourism and media bring vast new opportunities for investment, yet they also open state and society to global scrutiny. They also provide a global audience to the officially hidden, the oppressed and the dissident. Global tourism and media inevitably destabilize. Interstitial Bangkok in the sense described above is macro-scale and, ultimately, abstract. The experience of the city, however, raises instances that are interstitial at a much finer scale, which we reflect upon through the following sequence of cases (Figure 10.2).

Case 1: Protected places

Modern Thailand can be viewed as uneasily wedged between rival polities: a persisting memory of royal absolutism and relict feudalism, the constant threat of military dictatorship and Western-style popular democracy. The initial overthrow of the monarchy in 1932 conferred a form of parliamentary government that was inserted into the Ananta Samakhom Throne Hall, the most emblematic of royal monuments. It was also the most prominently sited of the city's buildings, at the head of Ratchadamnoen Avenue, a grand royal processional way leading from the old palace to the new, and a former king's emulation of modernist imperialist Europe (Figure 10.2). The military (and somewhat fascist) dictatorship that soon displaced the fledgling democracy constructed a signifier of the dream they had destroyed in the form of a Democracy Monument, which interrupts the royal boulevard at its centre. When the dictatorship built the National Assembly as a new parliament house in the early 1970s, it was placed between the throne hall, royal museums and former palaces of Dusit Park and effectively screened by them (Noobanjong 2008).

In present times the Prime Minister is similarly under protection: her office, Government House, is on a side-street off Ratchadamnoen and screened by its trees. Ratchadamnoen, grand avenue of the political, military and royal display, has traditionally been the locus of political protest by the democracy movement led by students and the middle class, with most notable eruptions of violence in 1973, 1976 and 1992 (Dovey 2008: Ch. 7). The next major such events in 2008 were of a different flavour; the middle class crowd donned yellow shirts, the symbolic colour of the King, to show their opposition to the democratically elected Taksin Shinawatra regime. The yellow-shirts, however, were increasingly dogged by others in red shirts, aligned with the rural-poor majority and urban immigrants from the marginalized provinces. In 2009 the red-shirts besieged Ratchadamnoen.

There are protected places where there shall be no protest. The throne hall and other monuments of 'the royal institution' are protected by myth and the transcendence of the King. The National Assembly and Government House are protected by barriers, electronic surveillance, heavily armed police and the proximity of the military – there shall be no popular access to the institutions of democracy. Then there are the temples, the *wat*. These are pre-eminently accessible but there shall be no protest – their carefully constructed image of elevation above the turmoil of politics is to be sustained. This leaves Ratchadamnoen itself as the premier venue of invasion and dissent. There are three foci of dissent on the avenue.

First, in its northern reach near the throne hall, is the Makkawan Rangsan Bridge where the police and military traditionally blockade access to the National Assembly, Government House and nearby ministries. In the 2008 yellow-shirt (elitist) uprising, the defences collapsed and Government House was occupied for 98 days, barring government access to it. A stage was set up for a new form of pageantry – music, rallies, celebrations, anti-government rhetoric from a succession of dignitaries. While certainly reactionary in its intent, the yellow-shirt uprising was unquestionably creative in producing a new form of politics and its imagery.

Second, and most emblematic, is the Democracy Monument which, despite its fascist beginnings, became the focus of the democracy movement and the key site for the vast demonstrations and epochal events in 1973 that ended a military dictatorship. Close by the Democracy Monument on Ratchadamnoen is a highly problematic monument to the 'martyrs' of 1973: deaths are regretted, yet the photographic displays and their rhetorical captions put the blame for such

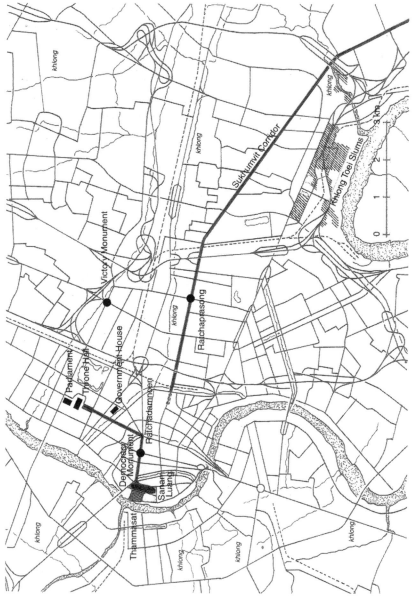

Figure 10.2 Inner Bangkok, indicating sites referred to in the present chapter (map by Ross King).

sadnesses on undemocratic students. Most notably the monument omits any mention of the most outrageous carnage in 1976.

The cynicism of this monument sits in stark contrast with a set of eight other monuments on the campus of nearby Thammasat University (the intellectual home of the democracy movement) that commemorate a diversity of Bangkok's outrages. This campus and the vast adjacent open space of Sanam Luang is the third focus of Ratchadamnoen's landscape of dissent. Sanam Luang is the grand 'royal field' or 'king's ground', site of the most auspicious of royal ceremonies and frequently the assembly point for the rallies that would then proceed along Ratchadamnoen to the Democracy Monument. In 1976, however, it was the venue for the shelling of the adjacent Thammasat University together with the massacre, burning and raping of its students by right-wing and royalist paramilitaries. This is a space haunted by unspoken memories that insert themselves into the conscience of a nation that would expunge such memory.

These stories of protected places and interstitial intrusions, one might argue, are far from unique – one would find similar spaces, memories and repressions in many South-East and East Asian cities – Jakarta, Manila, Seoul, Beijing, Kuala Lumpur (King 2008; Dovey 2008: Ch. 6; Dovey and Permanasari 2010: Ch. 10). The contingencies are always different but the phenomena of protected places, their contestation and proliferating infiltrations are common (Figure 10.3).

Case 2: Khlong

The grand Thanon Ratchadamnoen was one of many roads that were superimposed in the late nineteenth and early twentieth centuries on a city of water – river and *khlong* (canals). Such roads, *thanon*, were initially interstitial in an aquatic metropolis; today the relationship is more likely to be seen as reversed, with the

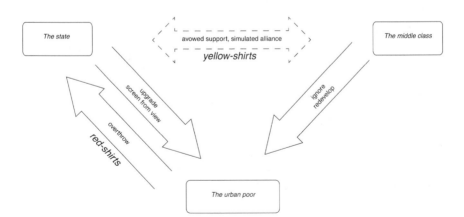

Figure 10.3   Actions and intentions, paralleling the perceptions and positions of Figure 10.1.

still-surviving *khlong* in the marginal, interstitial space of a land-based city. The *khlong* were mostly man-made or at least man-altered in the nineteenth century, often by prisoners-of-war from the Muslim south as semi-slave labour who were then informally permitted to settle along the *khlong* they had been compelled to dig. While such informal settlements have expanded massively through internal migration, their ambiguous land tenure often has a source in sweat equity. These *khlong* now form interstices in the morphology of the city, as do their communities in its social structure (Figure 10.4).

The *khlong*-side communities are among the cities poorest; their houses will commonly be of recycled materials, dilapidated, often on stilts in the water or its marginal marshes. They are for the most part invisible from the roads and repressed from elite imagining. Two processes, however, elevate them to visibility. The first is tourist delight: informed by guides or guidebooks or recounted stories, the tourists have since the 1970s taken boat trips along the *khlong* in search of a mythic 'real Bangkok' of simple lives, photo opportunities and remnant floating markets. The second is an elitist and nostalgic rediscovery of that 'real Bangkok' that extends beyond tourists to encompass the local middle classes: a burgeoning market for 'the real' that manifests in the production of new 'traditional' floating

Figure 10.4   Ban suan rim khlong (*house in orchard along canal*) – the guiding dream of Thai authenticity (photo by Ross King).

markets and *khlong* tours. The *khlong* occupy an imagined interstitial space between modernity and antiquity; a space that is filled by the nostalgic dream of authenticity and an anthropological search for origins.

Case 3: Khlong Toei

Although informal settlements run like sinews through the body of Bangkok, the vast domain of the Khlong Toei slums presents as something especially alien and confronting to any imagining that would pose elitist politics or the contests of Ratchadamnoen as the 'real' Bangkok. There was once a *khlong* called Khlong Toei but the term now describes a district of Bangkok that encompasses its most expensive residential precinct and also its most notorious slums. The former is especially represented in the high-end condominium blocks with grand views into the great expanse of the Khlong Toei slums.

The Khlong Toei district, fronting the Chao Phraya river, became the locale for the relocation of Bangkok's port beginning in 1938 and completed after the Second World War (Figure 10.2). The low-income refugees who built it and others who continue to operate it and its linked industries were, in the Thai manner, permitted to settle on unwanted land behind the port. That land, however, is no longer unwanted: the Port Authority, its legal owner, sees its commercial value in the present metropolis. The slums are mostly unvisited, unseen and undiscussed except when popular media highlight their reported squalor, vice and crimes. Such reports have two, opposed effects: for some middle-class and elite fractions this will build support for Port Authority intentions to forcibly evict the poor from their misery; reformists and their NGO allies see a 'cause'.

As Bangkok's most famous slum, Khlong Toei has engendered a whole sub-culture of reformers and activists along with an industry of 'slum improvement' and welfare-focused slum tourism (Dovey and King 2012). There are innovations in forms of tenure, in new systems of micro-finance, new approaches to education, community health and health care. Tenure is an especially difficult issue: the public-sector National Housing Authority (NHA), long engaged in upgrading in this community, has directly leased 61 per cent of the slum land from the Port Authority. The other 39 per cent were cleared for Port Authority use although the squatters still occasionally re-appropriate it and the authorities again attempt clearance (Figure 10.5).

While the forms of tenure now observable in Khlong Toei are all interstitial between legal and illegal, such interstices arise at multiple levels. In October 2008 the Port Authority contracted Legal Professional Co. to clear and develop the area of the Khlong Toei wet market. There were several months of bitter conflict and standoffs, rent increases to force the vendors out, then thugs and hooligans (often employed from another slum) and finally killings. Then, in March 2009, the guarding screen of religion was invoked to protect the market – quite literally interstitial between poor vendors and poor thugs. All these agents – Port Authority, Legal Professional Co., vendors, thugs – were caught in various crevices of a system over which no one had control (Figure 10.6).

Figure 10.5   **Shades of the Khlong Toei slums (photo by Ross King).**

Figure 10.6   **Interstitial spirits 1: An ad hoc shrine at the Khlong Toei wet market to mark the murders and to intervene between poor vendors and poor (but employed) thugs (photo by Ross King).**

These practices of slum resistance – the reformist 'industry', new tenure experiments, innovations in micro-finance, education, community health, health care – also need to be seen in the context of elite programs and ideologies. First is King Bhumibol's 'sufficiency economy' philosophy: we should all desire no more than is sufficient for a fulfilling, simple life, returning to an older, more sustaining, less ruinous economy. The king's ideas emerged gradually from the rural assistance projects that he began sponsoring in the late 1950s to counter the rural assistance focus of the insurgent Communist Party of Thailand. From 1988, however, this burgeoned into a programme of rhetoric that served to gloss over the worst effects of neo-liberal economic policy. A second elitist movement was the OTOP (*One Tambon* [village or district] *One Product*) programme of the populist Thaksin Shinawatra regime (2001–6) to give 'development' money to rural communities in return for electoral support. Such elite programs also intersect with broadly based ideas and ideologies such as the 'Buddhist economics' or 'Dhammic socialism' of Buddhadasa Bikkhu (1906–93) that date from the overthrow of the absolutist monarchy in the 1930s. All three of these movements (sufficiency economy, OTOP, Dhammic socialism) can be seen as innovations arising from radically different perceptions of the gaps (unresolved interstices) between an elitist, capitalist, formal economy and society, and the 'other Thailand' represented in the depressed, more informal sphere of slum and rural poverty. It is the elitist failure to address rural inequality and deprivation that gives increasing light to the urban slums.

Case 4: Thanon Sukhumvit

Thanon Sukhumvit [Sukhumvit Road] is Bangkok's street of riches and poverty, five-star hotels and shophouse slums, up-market malls and street vendors, royals and beggars, both Western and Middle-Eastern tourist focus, business district and heart of the informal, pirate economy (Figures 10.2 and 10.7). Much of its activity is in its *soi*, laneways running off from it at various angles and constituting a vast, labyrinthine district of great complexity. Part of it adjoins the similarly vast Khlong Toei slums to the south and, from its high-rise hotels and condominium blocks, overlooks them. There is also degraded, overcrowded housing throughout Sukhumvit and its *soi*, on the upper floors of shophouse blocks, in remnant *khlong*-side settlements and in the occasional squat. These expressions of Bangkok's under-side supply much of the very low-income labour that props up the Sukhumvit economy; they also supply many of the entrepreneurs for both its informal and underground economies – the vendors, beggars and prostitutes.

The consequence of these intersecting economies is a zone of spectacle and attraction for the city's millions of tourists. Tourism in large measure becomes the consumption of transgressions and, thereby, is itself transgressive against elitist ideology of unified nation, transcendent monarchy and Buddhist piety. Yet tourism is also the economic prop of the nation.

**Figure 10.7   Sukhumvit as interstitial space: intersecting economies, realm
of consumption and spectacle (photo by Ross King).**

Sukhumvit's underclass is the paradigm of the interstitial. To attempt
conversation with the vendors, beggars, prostitutes, pimps, stand-over men, bike
riders, *tuk-tuk* (motorized rickshaw) drivers and the like can be illuminating. In
hundreds of such encounters over a decade, a question of 'Where do you live?' was
mostly answered with 'Sukhumvit' – Bangkok's most upmarket and expensive
locale. So where? The answer is in the interstices of the tourist, expat and royal
realm, in the over-crowded upper levels of dilapidating shophouses, old offices,
buildings awaiting redevelopment, abandoned houses from earlier eras, ruins and
squats. These, rather than Khlong Toei, are the real slums. Another question would
be: where do you eat? Again, *locally*, from the vendors of cooked food on the
sidewalks at night and early morning (when the more up-market vendors of tourist
trinkets have vacated). It is never necessary to ask them where they work, for the
conversation will occur as they work their beat or their spot on the sidewalk. The
vendors, stall-holders and beggars do *not* insert themselves in the protected locales
of case 1, above, except when they join an uprising.

There are yet more layers to Sukhumvit interstitiality. While the prostitutes
may be swift-of-foot and able to vanish into the crevices of the *soi* as the police
descend, illegal vendors and stall-holders are not so mobile. Nor can they easily
avoid either the police or the gangs and their standover thugs collecting 'taxes' to
pay for their protection (Dovey and Polakit 2010; King 2011). Then there are the

tourists: while it is the tourists' spending that enables the panorama of Sukhumvit, they are forever *farang*, foreign, alien. They and the congeries of the expats are, in the final analysis, in the interstices between the elite and the marginalized.

Sukhumvit emerges in the interstices of the most global and the most local; in the interstices of rival yet mutually dependent economies from a hybridized mode of production (Nederveen Pieterse); meshing the flows of desire of the post-modern hyperspace (Jameson) with the struggle for survival of the urban poor. How is this gargantuan transgression and its venality to be reconciled with the benefits it brings to the nation as well as to the urban poor (services, the hawkers, beggars, prostitutes) for whom the elites offer nothing? Sukhumvit is the quintessential heterotopia, in Foucault's terms:

> The space in which we live, which draws us out of ourselves, in which the erosion of our lives, our times and our history occurs, the space that claws and gnaws at us, is, also, in itself, a heterogenous space. In other words, we do not live in a kind of void, inside of which we could place individuals and things ... [but] inside a set of relations that delineates sites which are irreducible to one another and absolutely not superimposable on one another. (Foucault 1986: 23)

Sukhumvit, in other words, is many spaces, many realities. One of the more fascinating of urban places in any city, it has generated a significant literary and cinematic expression (King 2011) and offers insight to a much broader set of urban conditions. In Thailand it tends to compel some redefinition of the nation (possibly even of monarchy and religion).

Case 5: Ratchaprasong

Sukhumvit is the west-to-east armature along which Bangkok expanded in the nineteenth and twentieth centuries. Close to the historic heart of Rattanakosin, the foundational point of the city in 1782, it has a variety of names, most notably Thanon Rama I and Thanon Phloenchit, although it is all the same road. The point where these two exchange names is the Ratchaprasong intersection, a major node framed with the city's most upmarket shopping malls and plazas, greatest concentration of five-star hotels, embassies and the emblematic Erawan shrine. Here the elevated railway (completed in 2006) that now covers most of the boulevard for most of its length in the city, peels off into a branch line with a spaghetti junction of flyovers and pedestrian conduits (Figure 10.9). For those who can afford it, the new railway provides fast access up and down the length of Sukhumvit as it also produces a new range of views into and across the city and its *soi*. At *Ratchaprasong* the aerial infrastructure places the public space of the intersection (normally choked with traffic) in the full glare of the global gaze.

In April and May 2010, this intersection became interstitial in an entirely new way. Before this time demonstrations by both yellow-shirts (urban elite) and red-shirts (mostly aligned with the rural poor) had focused on the more symbolically potent sites along Ratchadamoen Avenue as outlined in Case 1. In September 2006 a yellow-shirt-endorsed military coup ousted the democratically elected, allegedly corrupt and red-shirt supported Thaksin Shinawatra government. A further election reinstated majority rule, which led in turn to further yellow-shirt uprisings in 2008 with the occupation of Bangkok airport, closing down the tourist industry until a judicial coup initiated a yellow-shirt-supported government. 2009 saw red-shirt counter-rallies of increasing size and vehemence, peaking in March to May 2010. This insurgency was notable initially for its mobility. The rural poor not only had access to the city but to motor scooters and mobile phones that led to an ever-moving spectacle of red crowds that were able to move not only up and down Ratchadamnoen but also across the city, around the Victory Monument, the television headquarters and commercial districts. At the height of the uprising the spatial focus was moved from Ratchdamnoen to Ratchaprasong, where the red-shirts captured and held the intersection and surrounding streets, closing it to traffic for some five weeks in April–May 2010.

Ratchaprasong was an astute choice of location. While the symbolism of the Democracy Monument, the king's ground (Sanam Luang), and Prime Minister's office had long lent potency to various movements for change, Ratchprasong reflected a different strategy that focused on flows more than static symbols. They had learnt from the yellow-shirts' success in closing down the airports but they now seemed to use rather than exclude the tourists. The intersection is the primary entrance to the Sukhumvit district whether by car or public transport; to control it was to control those flows and indeed to capture the attention of global tourism and mass media. In the middle of the intersection the red-shirts set up a provisional stage surmounted with a banner in English saying 'Welcome to Thailand – We just want Democracy' (Figure 10.8). The first part of this slogan echoed a tourism marketing slogan repeated on billboards all over Thailand. The second part piggybacks off the first as a direct address to the *farang* (foreigner): 'Please come, and support democracy'; perhaps 'Welcome to the real Thailand'. The exposure of the demonstrators to global media became (for a time) a form of safety zone, a buffer against the state's attempts to remove or harm them. When government media portrayed the redshirts as 'terrorists' to pave the way for violent eviction, a banner appeared on the stage and in Western media proclaiming 'Peaceful protesters, not terrorists.'

While the occupation of Ratchaprasong opened a window to the glare of mass media, it substantially closed the flows of capital in Bangkok – middle-class shopping, business and entertainment became largely paralysed. On 19 May the army counter-attacked, casualties were heavy and the city centre was torched – most notably the adjacent Central World Plaza shopping mall – tarnishing the symbols of prosperity, globalization and modernity (Figure 10.9).

The colour-coding (yellow, red) is a superficial expression of a series of deep divides in Thai society: within the capitalist market they reflect opposed media empires; socially they reflect the urban elite versus rural poor; ethnically the Thai versus Isaan-Lao; and for some military/monarchy versus democracy, also army

Figure 10.8   Ratchaprasong in April 2010: Uprising as grand theatre in the interstices between revolution and Rock concert (photo from flickr.com).

Figure 10.9   Interstitial spirits 2: The Erewan shrine at the torched Ratchaprasong intersection (photo by Ross King).

versus police. Between these it is difficult to identify any interstitial zone yet there are interstitial classes. The first is also colour-coded: yellow and red give orange, the colour of the jackets worn by the army of motorcycle taxi riders (Figure 10.10). They are at the bottom of the transportation hierarchy yet, without them, the city could not function. As they wait on street corners, weave through the traffic, *soi*, alleys and communities, they gather information that is then passed on variously to police and gangsters. Both police and *agents provocateurs* will know of the assembling mob. Yet the orange-jacket taxi-riders are typically ex-rural, refugees from the poor countryside; they are thereby also the reporters of events in the city back to the rural villages and red-shirt cadres; they are the essential intelligence service of the radical rural poor. They are interstitial in their colour coding, as a class, as a sub-economy, and in their communicative function.

The second interstitial figure is also orange, in this case the beautiful blazing saffron of the Buddhist monks who emerge every morning in almost every community in Thailand to engage in the exchange of offerings and merit with rich and poor alike. The monks serve as reminders of the immanent sanctity (and

Figure 10.10   Interstitial colour: Orange-shirt motor-cycle taxi riders awaiting clients, under the sign of middle class imaginings (photo by Kim Dovey).

therefore equality) of all life and of the ideals of Dharmic socialism. Yet one does not see saffron mixed with the red or the yellow; the *wat* compounds in which they live have been largely spared the politics and the violence.

The final interstitial figure is the foreigner, the tourist, *farang*, the distanced observer – us. Most would gaze upon this uprising from the high-rise hotels, offices or trains like de Certeau's (1984) distanced observer. Yet down in the street, as well as on the banners, the foreigner is welcome. The most furious of dissenters will make space for the outside observer who may then transmit their grievance to a global audience and polity. The foreigner, who appears so totally global, occupies a crucial interstice between local and global, while the rural poor, who appear so local, have learned well to use the city and its interstices for their representational and spatial tactics. In the chasm represented by the burnt-out shells of Ratchaprasong, a new consciousness at many levels and perhaps a new Thailand is emerging. This is the sort of evolution – metamorphosis – that Warner's argument could refer to. Certainly a new politics emerges, mediated by new classes (like the orange-shirts, always interstitial) and new technology (the mobile phone, Facebook, the internet blog).

Finally...

We return to Warner's concern with metamorphoses, of which she suggests four modes – mutating, hatching, splitting and doubling (this last really a manifestation of splitting). We have already described aspects of Bangkok in terms of the mutation of different modes of organization and production. Warner illustrates hatching with Leda's seduction by Zeus in the form of a swan, from whose egg (in one version of the legend) is hatched Helen of Troy and a never-ending sequence of misfortune. Bangkok's Sukhumvit is a constant display of Siam/Thailand's impregnation from its own erstwhile colonies, now its invaders, and from the neo-colonizing hordes of global tourists and mass media. What is born from such intrusions, suggests Warner, will be surprise (Warner 2004: 18). The fourth of Warner's modes of metamorphosis is doubling – the horror of the *doppelgänger*, the 'double walker'. At one level, this is the experience of being simultaneously in mutually contradicting scales of existence – as being both de Certeau's eagle on high *and* the walker in the streets. The intruding gaze of tourists and media can come to warp the vision of the city's denizen who also begins to see the society distanced, from on high, and thereby to see its inequities, injustices and monstrosities. Yet this indigenous observer is still also the walker, reproducing the world that now horrifies. The self begins to metamorphose, to split apart and double under the alien gaze. This is the same form of metamorphosis that can beset the writer, investigative journalist or artist in the movement towards the avant-garde.

Sukhumvit is not a work of art, let alone avant-garde. Its effect, however, is that of the avant-garde – it outrages and overwhelms; it crosscuts elite and official imaginings of the city. While tourist interpretations of Bangkok are likely to be mistaken, they are also likely to fly in the face of both elitist views of the Nation as harmony and middle-class 'unseeing' of poverty and exploitation. When the television documentary, investigative journalism or tourist happy-snaps go global, there is a challenge to both elitist boosterism and middle-class delusion. The Ratchaprasong events of May 2010 can be viewed as profoundly subversive street theatre in the same sense as Beijing's 'Tiananmen Incident' of June 1989 (Wu 2005). Ratchaprasong, however, is more global than Tiananmen, occurs in a less repressive society and at a later stage in the evolution of global media technologies. Like Tiananmen it engenders a global outrage that inevitably tears at indigenous perceptions and values. The outcome is metamorphosis of ideas and behaviours.

In the end two urban interstices loom large: first, the gaps between economies and ways of life – between formal and informal, between wealth and poverty, between different urban morphologies and modes of production – whether seen from on high or on the street. Second, there are the gaps between what is seen and reported by the society's outsiders – its tourists and media commentators – and, in contrast, the official and elitist imaginings of how the city *should* be. It is in these gaps that one looks for the emergence of new dissent, resistances, aesthetic expressions and, accordingly, creativity.

References

Bloch, E. 1997. Nonsynchronism and the obligation to its dialectics. *New German Critique*, 11, 22–38.

Buck-Morss, S. 1989. *The Dialectics of Seeing: Walter Benjamin and the Arcades Project*. Cambridge, MA: The MIT Press.

de Certeau, M. 1984. *The Practice of Everyday Life*. Berkeley and Los Angeles, CA: University of California Press.

Dovey, K. 2008. *Framing Places* (2nd edn). London: Routledge.

Dovey, K. 2010. *Becoming Places*. London: Routledge.

Dovey, K. and King, R.J. 2011. Forms of informality: morphology and visibility of informal settlements. *Built Environment*, 37(1): 11–29.

Dovey, K. and King, R.J. 2012. Informal urbanism and the taste for slums. *Tourism Geographies*, 14(2): 275–93.

Dovey, K. and Polakit, K. 2010. Urban slippage: smooth and striated streetscapes in Bangkok, in: *Becoming Places*. London: Routledge, pp. 167–84.

Dovey, K. and Permanasari, E. 2010. New orders: Monas and Merdeka Square, in: *Becoming Places*. London: Routledge, pp. 153–65.

Foucault, M. 1986. Of other places. *Diacritics*, 16, 22–27.

Jameson, F. 1994. Foreword, in: Kojin K. (ed.) *Origins of Modern Japanese Literature*. Durham, NC: Duke University Press.

King, R.J. 2008. *Kuala Lumpur and Putrajaya: Negotiating Urban Space in Malaysia*. Singapore: NUS Press.

King, R.J. 2011. *Reading Bangkok*. Singapore: NUS Press.

Mann, M. 1986. *The Sources of Social Power*. Cambridge, UK: Cambridge University Press.

Nederveen Pieterse, J.P. 1995. Globalization as hybridisation, in M. Featherstone, S. Lash and R. Robertson (eds), *Global Modernities*. London: Sage, pp. 45–68.

Noobanjong, K. 2008. The National Assembly: an Ironic Reflection of Thai Democracy. Paper at the 10th International Conference on Thai Studies, Thai Khadi Research Institute, Thammasat University, Bangkok, 9–11 January 2008.

Warner, M. 2004. *Fantastic Metamorphoses, Other Worlds: Ways of Telling the Self*. Oxford: Oxford University Press.

Wu, H. 2005. *Remaking Beijing: Tiananmen Square and the Creation of a Political Space*. London: Reaktion Books.

Index